SEMINAL

SEMINAL

THE ANTHOLOGY OF CANADA'S GAY MALE POETS

edited by

JOHN BARTON and
BILLEH NICKERSON

ARSENAL PULP PRESS
Vancouver

ARSENAL PULP PRESS
Suite 200, 341 Water Street
Vancouver, BC
Canada V6B 1B8
arsenalpulp.com

The publisher gratefully acknowledges the support of the Canada Council for the Arts and the British Columbia Arts Council for its publishing program, and the Government of Canada through the Book Publishing Industry Development Program and the Government of British Columbia through the Book Publishing Tax Credit Program for its publishing activities. Financial support for translations in the book provided by the Canada Council for the Arts and the Department of Canadian Heritage through the Book Publishing Industry Development Program.

Cover art by Attila Richard Lukacs, *Claus on a Sunday Morning*, 1995, oil on canvas, 180 cm x 150 cm
Text design by Shyla Seller

Printed and bound in Canada

Library and Archives Canada Cataloguing in Publication:

Seminal : the anthology of Canada's gay male poets / edited by John Barton and Billeh Nickerson.

Poems.
Includes index.
ISBN 978-1-55152-217-3

1. Canadian poetry (English) 2. Gay men's writings, Canadian. 3. Gay men—Poetry. 4. Canadian poetry (French)—Translations into English.

I. Barton, John, 1957- II. Nickerson, Billeh, 1972-

PS8283.H66S44 2007 C811.08'09206642
C2006-906977-8

Contents

"The homosexual poet," according to Robert K. Martin, "often seeks poetic 'fathers' who in some sense offer a validation of his sexual nature. Whatever he may learn poetically from the great tradition, he cannot fail to notice that this tradition is, at least on the surface, almost exclusively heterosexual."[1] It is out of such a desire for affirmation, for exemplars and mentors, that the impulse to compile *Seminal*, the first historically comprehensive compendium of gay male poetry written by Canadians, first arose. Even today, after the hard-won battles in the political arena to enshrine the equal rights of gay men and lesbians in Canada as legitimate have been won, the desire to make gay experience a more traceable plotline in the "central" Canadian story is difficult to realize. The reader—and writer—of gay poetry in this country still has a hard time finding it easily, as if it were composed just outside the spotlight of mainstream literary success.

In the almost forty years since May 1969, when the Trudeau government decriminalized homosexual acts between consenting adults, one would think that an anthology like *Seminal* would have already been published and dog-eared in the hands of the aspiring and the curious. Most express surprise that no previous compilation is to be superseded by this present effort. Such a long-standing gap in the published record does not fit with Canadians' sense of themselves as well informed and living within an enlightened community of ideas. Yet librarians still do not routinely provide apposite access points in their catalogues; publishers may not always choose to highlight the gay content in a forthcoming book for fear it would compromise sales; and poets themselves may sometimes continue to hesitate in characterizing their work as homoerotic—or themselves as gay—anxious that the appreciation of their accomplishment could potentially be narrowed to this single trait of their humanity or, worse, be dismissed as ghettoized.

In the past, for anyone interested in how a gay tradition in poetry might actually read in Canada, the search for it could

1 Robert K. Martin, *The Homosexual Tradition in American Poetry* (Austin: University of Texas Press, 1979): 148.

yield to feelings of creative frustration, even isolation. *Seminal*, therefore, is an attempt, in Canadian terms and in a single comprehensive volume, to prevent our gay poets of present and future generations from being obliged to approach the literary "past" as something that must be "repeatedly reinvented anew, [as a] tradition [to be] created afresh."[2] Readers and writers may wish to do so nonetheless, but now they have a clearly defined point of previous departure to revisit, revise, or even repudiate.

This first anthology of Canadian gay male poetry takes its place in a line of similar anthologies published elsewhere in the English-speaking world, including Edward Carpenter's *Ioläus* (1902)[3], Patrick Anderson and Alistair Sutherland's *Eros: An Anthology of Friendship* (1961)[4], Ian Young's *The Male Muse* (1973) and *The Son of the Male Muse* (1983)[5], and Stephen Coote's *The Penguin Book of Homosexual Verse* (1983)[6]. Carpenter, Anderson and Sutherland, and Coote all start with ancient times and work their way up. In the case of the first two, they do not focus on poetry exclusively while, in the third instance, Coote also includes work by women. Only living poets appear in Young's anthologies, with mutually exclusive sets of contributors published in each. In 1995, Michael Holmes and Lynne Crosbie, two straight Toronto writers, published the much smaller *Plush*[7], Canada's first contemporary anthology of gay male poetry, featuring

2 Ibid, 161.

3 Edward Carpenter, ed., *Ioläus: An Anthology of Friendship*. The online version found at *www.fordham.edu/halsall/pwh/iolaus.html#pref* is the edition that was published in New York by Mitchell Kennerly in 1917.

4 Patrick Anderson and Alistair Sutherland, *Eros: An Anthology of Friendship* (London: Anthony Blond, 1961).

5 Ian Young, ed., *The Male Muse* (Trumansburg, NY: Crossing Press, 1973). Young tried to interest Canadian publishers in *The Male Muse* without success, so instead went south of the border where it was accepted without reservation by John Gill, publisher of The Crossing Press and also one of the contributors (letter of August 25, 2004, from Young to author). *The Son of the Male Muse* was also published by The Crossing Press in 1983.

6 Stephen Coote, ed., *The Penguin Book of Homosexual Verse* (London: Penguin, 1983).

7 Lynn Crosbie and Michael Holmes, eds., *Plush: Selected Poems of Sky Gilbert, Courtnay McFarlane, Jeffrey Conway, R. M. Vaughan, and David Trinidad* (Toronto: Coach House Press, 1995).

three Canadian and two American poets. Five years later, Timothy Liu published *Word of Mouth*[8], collecting into a single volume fifty-eight American poets born in the twentieth century (he did not have to deal with Whitman or Crane, as a consequence), an anthology he affirms in the introduction was conceived in light of the many gay male poetry anthologies that had already been published in the United States; Liu's efforts to map American gay male poetry have served as a model for *Seminal*.

Unsurprisingly, few Canadians appear in any of the anthologies of international scope. In either of the *Male Muse* anthologies, Young includes only two Canadian poets of note, Edward A. Lacey and bill bissett, besides himself. Edward A. Lacey does appear in Coote's Penguin anthology, though he seems to have been a last-minute addition, along with a handful of other contemporary poets who are tacked on at the end and not interfiled by date of birth among the majority of the contributors. Coote also leaves out Patrick Anderson, an important figure in the Montreal poetry community of the 1940s, a fellow Briton who returned to England in the 1950s and who died in 1979, four years before the anthology was published—or at least Anderson is left out by name, for his poem, "Spiv Song," is attributed to Royston Ellis. Anderson happened to have represented himself with the same poem in his earlier *Eros* (Coote must have been conversant with this trailblazing anthology, one would think, and should have caught his mistake).

Just how much the approach to gay writing has and has not changed over the course of the twentieth century is revealed by what each editor has to say about how and what they chose. In 1902, Carpenter reflects that while *Ioläus* "is only incomplete, and a small contribution, at best, towards a large subject,"[9] he feels he has succeeded in making visible what was previously hidden, noting that "I have been much struck by the remarkable manner in which the customs of various races and times illustrate each other, and the way in which they point to a solid and enduring body of human

8 Timothy Liu, ed., *Word of Mouth: An Anthology of Gay American Poetry* (Jersey City: Talisman House, 2000).

9 Carpenter, *www.fordham.edu/halsall/pwh/iolaus.html#pref.*

sentiment on the subject."[10] Almost sixty years later, after acknowledging that the contents of *Eros* has "teased [him since] adolescence" and has revealed itself to be "less of the smell of sulphur than [he] had imagined," Anderson describes his subject as "any friendship between men strong enough to deserve one of the more serious senses of the word 'love'" and goes on to say—remember that he was writing at the height of the Cold War between the release of the Wolfenden Report in 1957 and the decriminalization of homosexuality in the United Kingdom in 1967[11]—that "this limiting extremism is far from most people's taste. Against the background of our society, whether conceived in terms of Christian ethics or of the 'natural' self-realization implicit in scientific humanism, to accept it for oneself is pretty obviously to invite moral and psychological disaster."[12] Young in contrast claims *The Male Muse* is "not an anthology of 'gay poets' (a difficult and useless category), but rather a collection of poems by contemporary writers on themes relating to male homosexuality, gay love, romantic friendships, what Walt Whitman called 'the dear love of comrades, the attraction of friend to friend.'" He further contextualizes his work by maintaining that "until 1972, the project [of anthology-making] seemed impossible to carry out ... because the aura of taboo was still strong enough to prevent all but a few writers from contributing. But quite suddenly ... the growing impetus of the homophile/gay liberation movement began to be felt by the rest of society—both gay and straight—and 'Gay Pride' became not just a slogan but a reality."[13] A decade later, Coote articulates his own rationale for his Penguin anthology, contending that "a gay poem is one that either deals with explicitly gay matters or describes an intense and loving relationship between two people of the same sex."[14] For Crosbie and Holmes, compiling *Plush* still another decade on, their "conviction grew that the poems—

10 Carpenter *www.fordham.edu/halsall/pwh/iolaus.html#pref.*

11 For a good synopsis of the Wolfenden Report, which influenced social change on both sides of the Atlantic, see Hugh David's *On Queer Street: A Social History of British Homosexuality, 1895–1995* (London: HarperCollins, 1997).

12 Anderson and Sutherland, 8–9.

13 Young, *The Male Muse*, 7.

14 Coote, 48–49.

words and work all too often neglected by the mainstream—spoke to one another and to a much wider audience than any notion of an anthology of gay poets could possibly suggest"[15] while, for Liu, his millennial *Word of Mouth* was "a gathering of poets whose poems represent a plurality of forms, poems that may or may not directly traffic in 'gay experience,'" acknowledging that he "still question[s] the notion of gay sensibility."[16]

As a consequence, it is very difficult not to be affected by, respond to, or work against the assumptions of anyone previously, or even currently, working in the area or not to be influenced by the attitudes of the poets under consideration. The fifty-seven writers in *Seminal* were born between 1878 and 1981 and represent over a century of writing. They each reflect the beliefs and aesthetic concerns of their own time and, depending on when they were born, have been more or less open about their erotic lives in and outside of their work. It seems less interesting nowadays to consider what legitimately constitutes a gay poem or whether someone is a "gay poet" versus a "poet who happens to be gay." The time to feel diminished or emboldened by labels—or to feel one should trumpet, duck, whistle around, or deny them (strategies that all imply hubris, anxiety, or discomfort)—should be long over. Any of the poets in *Seminal* could as validly fit into an anthology organized around an entirely different point of commonality, for all poets are both one and many, but at the same time, the placement of universal truth and universal experience above all else risks homogenization through a denial of specificity. A simple recognition of fact—that a poet is homosexual / gay / queer / same-sex / bi / transgender / poly-amorous or not—should be sufficient and demands a reading of his work (and what it took him to write it) that goes as far as possible into its depths in order to see what it reveals about *his* human condition—and about his sense of the human condition *itself*.

What the human condition really is persists as yet another conundrum, and appropriately enough, like so many things

15 Crosbie and Holmes, 8.

16 Liu, xv, xviii.

pertaining to gay experience, *Seminal* begins on a speculative note, a gaydar moment, if you like. The earliest poems are by Émile Nelligan, the second poet by chronological arrangement, and date from the late 1890s. Born in 1879, Nelligan was at the beginning of what should have been a long and celebrated career when, after a mental collapse, he was committed to an asylum in 1899 until his death in 1941. Robert K. Martin suggests that his "incarceration is widely taken to indicate his homosexuality and he can still function as an icon of the gay man in Quebec, destroyed by his culture and his assimilation into English."[17] Whether or not Martin's supposition is accurate and whether or not every cause needs a martyr to whatever rallying cry—culture, sexuality—as a kind of tragic inspiration, when it comes to Canadian gay male poetry, this is where *Seminal* draws the line in time's very unsettled sands. Frank Oliver Call, another Quebec-based poet born one year before Nelligan, is in comparison forgotten, though he is credited with being among the first poets in Canada to have experimented, however tentatively, with modernism.[18] Call's pamphlet with Ryerson, *Sonnets for Youth* (1944), could be considered the first collection of homoerotic verse published in Canada, however coded and oblique it happens to be in its references.[19]

The poets born in the two decades after Nelligan's confinement could not be forthright about their sexuality in their work for obvious reasons. John Glassco, notorious for *Memoirs of Montparnasse* (1973), a "nonfiction" account of his years in Paris now more often characterized as fictional revisionism, even as a kind of in-joke send-up of the reader in its twisting of the author's personal gay history[20], did not start

---

17 Robert K. Martin, "Gay Literature" in *The Oxford Companion to Canadian Literature*, 2nd edition. Eugene Benson and William Toye, general editors. (Toronto: Oxford University Press, 1997): 453.

18 Louis Dudek and Michael Gnarowski, eds., "The Precursers: 1910–1925," *The Making of Modern Poetry in Canada* (Toronto: Ryerson, 1967): 3 and Ken Norris, *The Little Magazine in Canada 1925–1980* (Toronto: ECW Press, 1984): 10–11.

19 Letter of August 11, 2004, from Ian Young to the author.

20 See Richard Dellamora's "Queering Modernism: A Canadian in Paris," *Essays in Canadian Writing* 60 (1996): 265–273 and Andrew Lesk's "Having a Gay Old Time in Paris: John Glassco's Not-So-Queer Adventures" in *In a Queer Country: Gay and Lesbian Studies in the Canadian Context*, Terry Goldie, ed. (Vancouver: Arsenal Pulp, 2001): 175–187.

publishing poetry in book form until later in life (interestingly, he did not include "Noyade 1942," a poem dating from 1958, in his Governor General's Award-winning *Selected Poems* of 1971). The fact that he had two marriages in the last half of his life after an earlier fifteen-year live-in relationship of some description with a man, and also had a reputation as something of a squire and gentleman farmer active in horse-racing circles in Quebec's Eastern Townships, may have influenced how he negotiated the writing and publication of his work. Douglas LePan "came out" as a gay poet memorably at the age of seventy-six, when he published *Far Voyages* in 1990, a passionate extended elegy for a recently deceased male lover many years his junior (though anyone who carefully reads the new autobiographical poems in the earlier *Weathering It*[21]—LePan's new and collected poems published in 1987—can see how he was consciously working up to his great moment of openness). Brion Gysin, raised in Edmonton in the 1920s by his Canadian-born mother after his British-Swiss father died on the battlefield during World War I, was perhaps an exception. He pursued a more open homosexual lifestyle in the Isherwoodian sense from young adulthood onwards. However, except for a stint in the Canadian Army on the home front during the World War II, he cut his links with Canada and instead moved, as a poet, artist, and novelist, in the circles of Paul Bowles, William Burroughs, Gregory Corso, and Harold Norse in London, New York, Paris, and Tangiers. Still, his experiments with form brought him to the heart of the innovations in sound poetry and performance at a world level, which in turn informed so much of what came to pass of a similar nature here.

The sexuality of a gay poet was seldom, if ever, impugned publicly in Canada until the poetry of Patrick Anderson was reviewed by John Sutherland in 1943. While the import of Sutherland's remarks are still raised in the debate over the origins of Canadian modernism, little is ever made of them beyond their characterization as part of the persistent "disagreements" between *Preview*, the little mimeographed

21 Douglas LePan, *Weathering It: Complete Poems, 1948–1987* (Toronto: McClelland & Stewart, 1987).

magazine that Anderson edited, and Sutherland's equally modest *First Statement*. While it is true that queer scholars have recently "reread" Sutherland's "outing" of Anderson[22], I suspect that a deeper understanding of what transpired between these two men could go a long way to explaining why Canadian gay male poets have had to work in isolation, with barely a sense of community or wider recognition, in the decades since, even the decades after Stonewall.

In "The Writing of Patrick Anderson,"[23] Sutherland asserts that something is not quite right in Anderson's poem "Montreal" commenting that

> Now I am willing to take Anderson at his word that the boy [in the poem] is "a substitute for poetry." As I interpret it, in his case the boy adds an impetus to poetic creation, and is even the source of his present poetry. At the same time, while I have no desire to make an exposé of Anderson's personal life, I surmise that the distinction between the "frightened boy" and "the hero who sings of joy" could be traced back to some period in the writer's childhood, when there occurred a sexual experience involving two boys, one of whom was frightened and the other demonstrated his joy. Whether or not this deduction is completely correct, I do know that something of the kind occurred in Anderson's childhood. The point that I wish to make is that, in the lines quoted from "Montreal," some sexual experience of a kind not quite normal has been twisted and forced into its present shape in the poem, where it wears the false aspect of some universal fact, or has to be

22 See the following chapters and articles: "Critical Homophobia and Canadian Canon-Formation, 1943–1967: The 'Haunted Journeys' of Patrick Anderson and Scott Symons" in Peter Dickinson, *Here is Queer: Nationalisms, Sexualities, and the Literatures of Canada* (Toronto: University of Toronto Press, 1997): 69–100; Justin D. Edwards, "Engendering Modern Canadian Poetry: *Preview*, *First Statement* and the Disclosure of Patrick Anderson's Homosexuality," *Essays on Canadian Writing* 62 (1997): 65–84; Robert K. Martin, "Sex and Politics in Wartime Canada: The Attack on Patrick Anderson," *Essays on Canadian Writing* 44 (1991): 10–25.

23 John Sutherland, "The Writing of Patrick Anderson," *First Statement* 1.19 (1943): 3–6.

> accepted as a general mood in which people today participate. Surely, these lines alone would signify the falsity of the poet's medium and his habitual distortion of content. His message is not wrong in itself, but his method of arriving at it, and his manner of stating it, make his poem appear like a wholesale falsification.

We can only imagine the impact such a review would have had on any poet. Anderson was then married and taught school-age boys during a time when homosexual crimes were punished with prison sentences. Though the circulation of *First Statement* was miniscule, Anderson threatened to sue. To placate him as well as to protect his own reputation, Sutherland printed a brief retraction in a subsequent issue.[24] Though the "crisis" passed, it was very likely not forgotten, especially by Anderson who was then no doubt aware of his own homoerotic desires[25] and may have felt that Sutherland, in his blundering and bombastic way, had intuited something essential.

This apparent defamation has to be read in context of the larger ongoing disagreements and rivalries between *Preview* and *First Statement*—and especially in context of how they have been conceptualized and distorted by later critics[26]—in order to understand how it might have affected the gay poets to come. Quite simply put, the poets of *Preview*—P. K. Page, A. M. Klein, and F. R. Scott, being the best remembered today—were perceived as older, upper-class, cosmopolitan, artificial, and too influenced by the "foreign" or "imported" British modernism of T. S. Eliot (formerly an American), W. H. Auden (a Briton then living in the United States), and Dylan Thomas (a Welshman). The poets of *First Statement*—Irving Layton, Louis Dudek, Raymond Souster—were considered to be young, native, and natural, connected to the robust (albeit American) modernism of Ezra Pound and

24 John Sutherland, "Retraction," *First Statement* I.20 (1943), cover.

25 See p. 91 in Patricia Whitney's "First Person Feminine: Margaret Day Surrey" in *Canadian Poetry* 31 (1992): 86–91.

26 For an excellent overview of the battles between *Preview* and *First Statement*, see Brian Trehearne's "Critical Episodes in Montreal Poetry in the 1940s," *Canadian Poetry* 41 (1997): 21–52.

William Carlos Williams. A. J. M. Smith inadvertently first coined and enshrined the distinction between "cosmopolitan" and "native" in *Book of Canadian Poetry* (1943)[27], with the poets of each "tradition" grouped together. Because many of the *First Statement* poets were left out entirely, unlike those of *Preview*, this canonizing anthology provoked immediate anger (the small world of poetry does like its dust-ups).

It is not hard to see how the terms "cosmopolitan" and "artificial" could become further tainted with queer inflections, particularly when "native" became allied with "masculine." Sutherland further stirred the pot in 1947, when he harshly reviewed Robert Finch's Governor General's Award-winning book, *Poems* (1946)[28] in *Northern Review*, the successor to both *First Statement* and *Preview*, when the two editorial boards merged. Sutherland refers to Finch as a "dandified versifier."[29] An unsigned editorial in the next issue gave notice that several board members (or what amounted to all remaining members formerly associated with *Preview*) had resigned en masse over "a difference of opinion about editorial policy, particularly concerning criticism and reviews."[30] Thirty-five years later, in a review of Finch's *Variations and Theme* (1980), Susan Gingell-Beckman noted that "Ever since John Sutherland's virulent attack on the bestowing of the Governor General's Award on Finch's *Poems*, Finch's critical reputation has dwindled to the point where he has been excluded from virtually all the contemporary major anthologies of Canadian poetry...."[31]

In the criticism that started to appear in the 1950s and

---

27 A. J. M. Smith, *The Book of Canadian Poetry* (Toronto: W. J. Gage, 1943).

28 John Sutherland, Review of Poems by Robert Finch, *Northern Review* I.6 (1947): 38–40. It is interesting to note that Louis Dudek and Michael Gnarowski reprint this review in *The Making of Modern Poetry in Canada: Essential Articles on Contemporary Canadian Poetry in English* (Toronto: Ryerson, 1967) but not Sutherland's attack on Patrick Anderson of three years before.

29 For an in-depth discussion of how Finch's poetry fits into the aesthetic tradition, see Brian Trahearne's article "Finch's Early Poetry and the Dandy Manner" in *Canadian Poetry* 18 (1986): 11–34.

30 Editors of *Northern Review*, Notices of Resignation, *Northern Review*, II.1 (1947): 40. Reprinted in *The Making of Modern Poetry in Canada*.

31 Susan Gingell-Beckman "Against an Anabasis of Grace: A Retrospective Review of the Poems of Robert Finch," *Essays on Canadian Writing* 23 (1982): 157–62.

1960s and became the texts to which later critics would in turn invariably refer, the opposition of "cosmopolitan" and "native," with its echo of "artificial" and "masculine," attained the status of received wisdom. The poets associated with *First Statement* wrote the story of Canadian modernism in part because key *Preview* poets had left the country by the early 1950s—Page as the wife of a Canadian ambassador and Anderson to England, where he continued to teach and wrote travel books. He did not get a chance to address the distortions of his legacy until the 1970s, when he renewed his tie to Canada and also again began to write poetry. Yet, by then, the position advanced by the *First Statement* diaspora had inveigled itself firmly into the chronology of Canadian poetry rehearsed almost to this day. The very heterosexual dramatic personae of poets like Irving Layton, arguably the preeminent poet of the 1950s and early 1960s, and the critical assessments of Louis Dudek and those who trained under him, raked the stage sharply in their favour, a stage upon which they have had enormous, long-lasting, and influential careers. When considering the straight male poets who have held sway in Canada for the last sixty years and while acknowledging the growing diversity of their aesthetics, it is striking how much of a boy's club Canadian poetry has remained (just ask the girls). Their articulations of self recall the goings-on of a club or a locker room, a locker room from which, ironically if typically, many straight male poets also have felt excluded. Even in today's climate, which is nuanced by multiple perspectives and subject positions, it feels inevitable that a Gen-X frat pack will assert itself, assume the mantle of their elders, and attempt to hold sway.

Wanting to be on an equal footing in society, to "belong," to be one of the boys, has proved complicated for many gay poets, who may well write from a slightly different point of reference, but with the same sense of engagement as all poets do. In 1944, American poet Robert Duncan, then a young man in his mid-twenties, published his essay, "The Homosexual in Society,"[32] in which he declares his homosexuality, and goes

32 Robert Duncan, "The Homosexual in Society," *Politics* 1 (August 1944); it is included in his *Selected Prose* (New York: New Directions): 38–50.

into detail about the predicament in which he finds himself as a poet who wants to be honest:

> In the face of the hostility of society which I risk in making even the acknowledgement explicit in this statement, in the face of the "crime" of my own feelings, in the past I publicized those feelings as private and made no stand for their recognition, but tried to sell them as disguised, for instance, as conflicts arising from mystical sources.

While Duncan comes across as unwilling to identify himself too closely with "the homosexual cult," he does make a case "for a group whose only salvation is in the struggle of all humanity for freedom and individual integrity," making a plea for homosexual themes to be written and read as human themes, not written and consequently corrupted (which he defines as "the rehearsal of unfeeling") for a coterie of sympathetic readers, but for the most widespread audience. However Duncan's public declaration of sexual orientation might now be read (in 1959 he characterized it as more of a "confession"), it is impossible to image that Patrick Anderson could have met his accuser's allegations in a like statement in Canada the year before. Nor is it imaginable that any Canadian publisher or poet could have won a case like the obscenity trial that City Lights Books and Allen Ginsberg fought successfully over *Howl*.

Instead, in 1965, Edward A. Lacey privately published *The Forms of Loss*. In 1963, Lacey, who would spend most of his adult life in the Third World teaching English and working as a translator, had been teaching for a year at the University of Alberta in Edmonton when he became reacquainted with Dennis Lee, whom he had known as a student at the University of Toronto (Lacey studied languages with Robert Finch at University College). Lee encouraged him in his project to compile a first book of poems, and two years later, with Margaret Atwood and Dennis Lee's financial help[33], the

33 In an email to me, Ian Young indicates that both Atwood and Lee underwrote the cost of publishing *The Forms of Loss*, not just Lee, as Fraser Sutherland

book was printed.[34] This slim volume of twenty-six poems is considered to be the first openly gay poetry published in book form in Canada.[35]

While the importance of Lacey's book cannot be overestimated, he was not the lone Canadian to write on homoerotic themes in 1965. The consideration of *The Forms of Loss* as our first openly gay book of poetry must first be tempered with the recognition that, in the same year, Jean Basile's *Journal poétique*, published by Les Editions du Jour, featured several homoerotic poems. Phyllis Webb's landmark *Naked Poems*[36] also appeared that year; it is considered to be "an early example of Canadian literature with lesbian content."[37] Webb may not have been as open in her book as Lacey—she "reveals that the object of her love is a woman while deflecting attention from this fact by avoiding pronouns and using codes ... she withholds as much she tells"[38]—but the book attracted immediate interest and is still remembered because of its formal finesse and because it was written by an already admired poet.

John Herbert was also then refining his play, *Fortune and Men's Eyes,*[39] which examines the violence and homosexuality at a reformatory. After rejections elsewhere, Herbert submitted it to the Stratford Festival, which accepted it for the 1965 Young Actors Workshop. Yet because of the content, "the Stratford Board of Directors forbade the single planned public performance, and it was performed privately for the Stratford actors."[40] It eventually premiered in New York in 1967 (one year before *The Boys in the Band*), running to acclaim for nearly a year, followed by a tour to Chicago and

---

indicates in his introduction to Lacey's *Collected Poems*.

34 Coincidentally, *The Forms of Loss* did not include "Quintallas," which dates back to the 1950s and was, according to Sutherland, Lacey's first openly gay poem.

35 Fraser Sutherland, "Introduction," The *Collected Poems and Translations of Edward A. Lacey* (Toronto: Colombo & Company, 2000) vi–vii.

36 Phyllis Webb, *Naked Poems* (Vancouver: Periwinkle Press, 1965).

37 Catherine Lake and Nairne Holtz, eds., *No Margins: Writing Canadian Fiction in Lesbian* (Toronto: Insomniac Press, 2006) 310.

38 Ibid.

39 John Herbert, *Fortune and Men's Eyes* (New York: Grove Press, 1967).

40 See entry on *Fortune and Men's Eyes* in *The Canadian Theatre Encyclopedia* (Athabasca, AB: Athabasca University) at *www.canadiantheatre.com*.

San Francisco, new productions in Toronto, Montreal, and Los Angeles, and a return engagement in New York under the aegis of Sal Mineo. It is also the most widely published and most anthologized play by a Canadian.

Daryl Hine, a Vancouver-born poet on faculty at the University of Chicago who would later hold the position of editor at *Poetry* from 1968 to 1978, had already published four books (the first two in Canada, the third in England, and the fourth in America). From the beginning, his work was homoerotically allusive,[41] with openly gay poems like "The Visit" published in *Minutes* (1968). From 1965 onwards, he published almost exclusively with Atheneum, one of the most respected literary houses in the United States, and built an enviable reputation as part of America's literary establishment. In contrast, Scott Symons' novel, *Place d'Armes*,[42] was published by McClelland & Stewart in 1967 to almost universally bad notices that seemed motivated by an intolerance that was "as much a political response as it was a reaction against Symons' exploration of homosexuality."[43] Not only did the book foment critical outrage, it emboldened the parents of Symons' underage lover to have authorities chase after the couple all the way to Mexico.[44] Symons has enjoyed an outlaw or antiestablishmentarian reputation ever since, though, in 2005, the *Literary Review of Canada* placed his novel among the 100 most important books written by Canadians.

Lacey may not have fared as well in reputation as Webb, Herbert, Hine, or even Symons, but he was very much part of a trend towards more openly gay writing by Canadians. Out of the social and political changes wrought by the 1960s, a more confident gay male poetry emerged. Dennis Lee, Lacey's benefactor, read Ian Young's work in *Acta Victoriana*, the Victoria College literary journal at the University of

---

41 In an email to me, Hine described some of the poems he published as early as 1955 (in *Five Poems*) as "explicit," an opinion he says was shared by others.

42 Scott Symons, *Combat Journal for Place d'Armes* (Toronto: McClelland & Stewart, 1967).

43 Peter Buitenhuis, from his introduction to the paperback edition of Symons' book published by McClelland & Stewart in 1968.

44 *Place d'Armes* went on to win the Beta Sigma Phi Best First Canadian Novel Award for that year.

Toronto, and, in 1967, featured several of Young's poems in the anthology, *T.O. Poetry Now*, which he published through his new press, House of Anansi. In 1969, Anansi released Young's *Year of the Quiet Sun*,[45] making it the first book of openly gay male poetry to have appeared under the imprint of a recognizable English–Canadian publisher. Lee's support of Young (and Lacey) could be said to be the planting of a seed from which many roots spread—disoriented, far-ranging roots whose awareness of one another seldom intertwined, but from which, however distantly, so much else that has grown up since may choose to trace its origins.

By the early 1970s, the poets born between 1939 and 1950—whom I consider to be the Stonewall generation, for they were the first to benefit as young men from the liberalizations by then well underway in Canada, Britain, and the United States—were able to write more directly about their erotic lives, should they choose to, without real fear of legal consequence. Along with a proliferation of gay liberation groups on and off university campuses and the founding of community-based gay newsletters, newspapers, and magazines, the most famous of which is Toronto's *The Body Politic*, attempts were made to establish gay-centered literary presses. In 1970, Young founded Catalyst, which he describes as the first gay press anywhere in the world, and published thirty gay and lesbian titles in diverse genres before ceasing operations in 1979, including Edward A. Lacey's *Later* (he also distributed Lacey's self-published *Path of Snow*) and his own book, *Common-or-Garden Gods*.[46] A more modest attempt at gay publishing was made by Doug Wilson when he founded Stubblejumper Press in Saskatoon in 1977, publishing only a handful of titles, with his own single book of poems as its first. bill bisssett's legendary blewointmentpress, established in Vancouver in the 1960s, was not exclusively gay in its mandate, but bissett did publish several gay poets, including himself and Bertrand Lachance. From the first, gay publishing has only ever been an ephemeral grassroots activity in Canada, with no viable and independent, solely gay literary press or

45 In 1968, Anansi had published an edition of Allen Ginsberg's *Airplane Dreams*.

46 Ian Young, "Memoirs of a Catalyst," unpublished memoir, dated April 2003.

magazine of any consequence able to survive for long (though after bissett sold blewointment, its new owners rechristened the press Nightwood Editions, now an imprint of Harbour Publishing and the home of Andy Quan's and Norm Sacuta's first books of poetry, which appeared in 2001). Also, since the mid-1970s, several other mainstream literary presses have laudably fostered the careers of many gay male poets, most notably Anansi, Arsenal Pulp, Coach House, Écrits des Forges, ECW, Guernica, Les Herbes Rouges, New Star, Noroît, Polestar, Talonbooks, and TSAR.

bill bissett, as an icon of the 1960s and 1970s counterculture, is as beloved today as he was reviled by members of the House of Commons who denounced him as much for the "extremity" of his work as its manner, which did not conform to their limited understanding of literary forms. bissett is almost a "trickster" figure, due in part to his memorable sound-poetry performances complete with rattles and to early poems like "eet me alive" or "a warm place to shit," that manifest an ecstatic awareness of the body. A colleague of bpNichol, who published his first book, bissett expresses his dissidence—a dissidence that cannot be defined as queer—through a highly personalized, decades-consistent, morphologically, and orthographically aberrant approach to the transcription of text to the page and through his virtuosic concrete poetry. His work demands that the reader ascribe to the principles under which it has been written, a demand that is in no way aggressive, for once the challenge of breaking his "code" has been met, his world of subtle insights, candour, and fine simplicities opens beautifully.

Immediately before and after 1970, Robin Blaser, Stan Persky (both in 1966), and George Stanley (in 1971) arrived from San Francisco. Protégés of Jack Spicer and Robert Duncan and, except for Persky, older than the gay-liberation-inspired poets of Stonewall, they brought with them a core of aesthetic principles that have had an enormous impact on the writing of the West Coast. Blaser in particular, with his cosmic sense of language and the public interconnectedness of texts, traditions, philosophies, and politics, is today a poet of international standing perhaps better recognized outside the country than within. Blaser and Stanley retained their links with the writing communities they were attached to in the United States and continued to publish there, perhaps initially to the detriment of their Canadian reputations, where their "foreign" books and pamphlets would not necessarily have been available. Stanley, however, did issue several books of new and previously published poetry with New Star, Oolichan, and Talonbooks, and in the 1980s, Blaser began to publish regularly with Talonbooks and Coach House. Persky only published one book of poems, but has made his reputation on such pioneering works of creative nonfiction as *Buddy's: Meditations on Desire*.

Blaser has described himself as "cosmopolitan," a loaded concept that is recognizable from Anderson's experiences as difficult for Canadians to metabolize.[47] In 2000, when asked if he felt that he had a queer poetics, Blaser replied, "No, I would not. I am queer and I concern myself with a poetics, and queer would not describe everything I attempt in my poetics. I'm hoping that the world of queer poetics is included and that gay people will be interested in what I am doing, because they are very much a part of my community."[48] Known for his great "Image-Nation" poems as well for the ongoing project, *The Holy Forest,* that contains them, Blaser voices an eloquent queer poetics in "In Remembrance of Matthew Shepard."

It is an understatement to say that gay writing in Canada, like everywhere else, was profoundly changed by AIDS in the 1980s. Michael Lynch, Michael Estok, and Ian Stephens all succumbed to the disease, leaving behind moving records of its effects in their collections of poetry, *These Waves of Dying Friends* (1989), *A Plague Year Journal* (1989), and *Diary of a Trademark* (1994) respectively, the first two being posthumous. Doug Wilson also died from AIDS-related complications, but lived long enough to complete the last novel by his lover, Peter McGehee, who predeceased him. Estok's *A Plague Year Journal* is a particularly remarkable document for the bite of its anger and passionate, even vehement, use of language, almost as if,

47 R. W. Gray, "'...we have to think in communities now...': An Interview with Robin Blaser," *Arc* 44 (2000): 34.

48 Ibid.

ironically, the experience of the disease itself matured him as a writer.

AIDS, of course, became one of the great themes of the age, with its "treatment" poetically evolving almost as rapidly as medical understanding. Even a cursory perusal of the books by any of the contemporaneous poets in this anthology will locate individual poems that respond to the social and physical challenges that it has posed for gay men, excellent examples being Gregory Scofield's *Native Canadiana* (particularly his poem, "Queenie"), André Roy's *On sait que cela a été écrit avant et après la grande maladie*, or Richard Teleky's allegorical "The Hermit's Kiss." Sadly and strangely, with the turn of the millennium, it appears that, for some, the urgency to address AIDS has fallen off. Is it because of its transformation from an automatic "death sentence" into something "chronic" and "treatable"? Or because of its widening sweep into straight communities in the Western democracies and through the Third Word—almost as if it were no longer "ours"? Or maybe gay male poets have exhausted it as a theme or have simply become exhausted? Still, AIDS has had a profound effect on the psyche of any "active" poet. Self-consciousness must be at play during the composition of an erotic love poem since we have all had to become, even in the performance of the most casual acts of love, more self-aware. As Robin Blaser says, "Any poem is close to the body."[49]

The number of gay male poets writing in Canada has continued to grow, with nearly half of the poets in *Seminal* publishing their first book that contains (openly) gay-themed poems since the late 1980s. In her foreword to the 1991 issue of *The Church-Wellesley Review*, Jane Rule begins "In the olden days, we had few choices of tone, either the tragic self-pity of Radclyffe Hall in *The Well of Loneliness* or the flippant disguise of Oscar Wilde and Noël Coward. Now, as is evident in this second literary supplement to *XTRA*, we have claimed the full range of attitudes toward our experience." After summarizing the strengths of the writing to be found within the supplement, Rule cautions readers and writers alike that

49 Ibid, 28.

"content still too often overpowers form because we are new at being able to speak the range of our experiences, and urgency overcomes us. Critical of styles used to disguise, we must not make the mistake of discarding eloquence now that it can serve the truth." [50] While Rule was no doubt responding to the grassroots or amateur ambitions of many of the featured authors, her call to action has certainly been answered in the collections of poetry published by writers as diverse in style, attitude, and background as David Bateman, Todd Bruce, Clint Burnham, Brian Day, Gilles Devault, Dennis Denisoff, Sky Gilbert, Blaine Marchand, Daniel David Moses, Jim Nason, Billeh Nickerson, Ian Iqbal Rashid, Brian Rigg, Stephen Schecter, and R. M. Vaughn. They have broadened and enriched Canada's gay men's poetry, bringing into play issues of race, ethnicity, and post-colonialism that have leavened the narcissism, stridency, and technical infelicity of some of their peers, lessers, and forgettable antecedents.

Jean-Paul Daoust's remarkable *Les cendres bleues*, which won the Governor General's Award for Poetry in French in 1990 (Nicole Brossard was on the jury), is one of the period's masterworks. Narrated by a middle-aged man who exposes, mourns, and celebrates the adult lover of his preteens—the lover who initiated him to the joy and complexity of physical and emotional intimacy, the lover who commits suicide (subverting the paradigm that it is only the recipients of 'abuse' who are the victims)—this book-length poem is audacious as well in its technique. Structured as a single unpunctuated sentence, it proceeds for over fifty pages without pause or stanza break, relying only on line breaks to calibrate the unfolding of its bold and compelling story. Walter Borden's verse play, *Tightrope Time: Ain't Nuthin' More Than Some Itty Bitty Madness Between Twilight & Dawn*, a one-man show performed by the author that George Elliott Clarke has described as "a contemporary Africadian drama,"[51] is equally important. Though not primarily gay in focus, it

50 *The Church–Wellseley Review* was a literary annual published in the late 1980s and early 1990s as a supplement to the Pride issue of *XTRA!*, Toronto's bimonthly gay and lesbian newspaper.

51 George Elliott Clarke, "Must All Blackness Be American? Locating Canada in Borden's 'Tightrope Time,' or Nationalizing Gilroy's *The Black Atlantic*" in *Odyssey's Home* (Toronto: University of Toronto Press, 2002): 74.

features a "*bizarrerie*" of twelve characters who in cabaret-style monologues articulate a Canadian perspective on black experience distinct from its American counterpart and "rescue[s] the devalued black body" and, through Ethiopia, a drag queen, and Chuck, a rent boy, "redeems that of the homosexual."[52]

A new generation of gay male poets—poets born in the 1970s and 1980s and who are publishing their first books today—is beginning to make its presence felt. They express a more fluid sexual orientation than the one voiced by the poets of Stonewall and AIDS, a sexuality that may often be secondary to other preoccupations. Without deflecting the marginalization or anger that are among their elders' traditional themes, they take their sexuality in stride and do not automatically let it trouble the surface of their poems or draw attention to itself. Seldom do they attempt to state a case for tolerance or solicit empathy for themselves as gay men, but when they are motivated to address issues of sexuality, as does Michael V. Smith in "Salvation," they often do so in order to shed light on a transgressive complexity which might have daunted past generations of poets, or in order to connect their sexuality to issues like masculinity, as Michael Knox does in his book, *Play Out the Match*. These poets do not inhabit a "subculture," do not see themselves as outside the "canonical" traditions of poetry, and do not perceive their stories as excluded from it or something to slip in subversively because in broad strokes, if not in the details, they feel more confident that these stories are now recognized as part of an inclusive human narrative.

These poets are perhaps the natural inheritors of Robin Blaser, if not in style or ability (for how they mature as poets is yet to be seen), then in an emphasis on a queer poetics felt as a *part* of a larger poetics that embraces the plenitude of experience in the public realm. The stridencies of the past forty years may not necessarily interest them, but their sense of themselves is not in any way a reversion back to the straight-acting and polarizing rubric of not being a "gay poet" but being a poet "who happens to be gay." Rather,

52 Ibid, 79.

their attitude is one of synthesis, a confidence that moves beyond identity politics because identity itself is no longer questionable, but a fact to be parsed and questioned. Compare Sean Horlor's "In Praise of Beauty" or "For St. Jude, or What Gets Him Where He Is" to Blaser's "In Remembrance of Matthew Shepard." All three see experience on a higher metaphysical plane that neither denies its grittiness nor excludes queerness.

Seminal, with its self-confident, even arrogant, subtitle, "*the* anthology," is a representation of the gay male poets writing in this country past and present as well as a sampling of the poetry written by its fifty-seven contributors. Billeh Nickerson and I have attempted to broaden its scope by locating and including poets writing from other subjectivities besides our own—black, aboriginal, Jewish, South Asian, Chinese, Québécois—those poets whose points of reference are different from the blandishing defaults of "English" and "white" culture. We hope our efforts provide the basis for a more nuanced understanding of what it has meant to write "queer" poetry in Canada for just over one hundred years.

Of course, there are inevitable omissions. Several poets declined our invitation (or declined on behalf of the deceased whose estates they happen to represent) because they felt discomfort at being included in an anthology circumscribed by the word "gay," believing this criterion "narrowed" possible readings of their work—a fear that in its diversity *Seminal* entirely refutes—thereby de-universalizing and devaluing it in some diminishing way. More worrying are those writers whom we might have left out simply because we could not find them. We did not widely circulate a call for submissions (concerned that only those poets who did not heed Jane Rule's call for technical rigour would respond and overwhelm us) and instead solicited recommendations from as many quarters as possible. Still, who knows what questions we failed to ask, what leads we did not pursue diligently enough? That a poet might not have been found after such an exhaustive search as ours suggests Canada may still have a long way to go as an inclusive literary culture.

During the assembly of any anthology like *Seminal*,

the question of greatness inevitably comes up—raised immediately after the question as to why such an anthology is needed at all (a question usually raised by straight middle-aged men who hate to be excluded from any club that's going, even if they do truly grasp what the method of initiation is) has been ignored as defying credulity. Who is Canada's great gay male poet? Is there more than one? Why haven't we produced a Walt Whitman? Where is our Hart Crane? Our W. H. Auden, our Robert Duncan, our John Ashbery? Why do we not see one or more among us, or is it only that we don't know where to look? Each of *Seminal*'s readers will decide on his (or *her*) own, but I hope critical judgement will not be clouded by typically Canadian myopias not too different from the ones I raised when discussing the long shadow that I believe the fate of Patrick Anderson's work has cast over Canadian gay male poetry in general.

As Canadians, we have a hard time keeping track of our expatriates while at the same time appreciating the "strangers" among us, and English Canadians have a particularly hard time developing an awareness of anything written or experienced in the "other" official language. Would not permanent expatriate Edward A. Lacey (whose published works have never moved beyond a basement-press milieu) or Illinois-resident Daryl Hine (whose *Recollected Poems* will be published in 2007 by Fitzhenry & Whiteside, making his work available in a Canadian edition for the first time since his *Selected Poems* of 1980) or Idaho-born Robin Blaser (whose revised and expanded collected poems, *The Holy Forest*, was published by the University of California Press in 2006) or Jean-Paul Daoust (who has published two limited *Selected Poems* in English translation with Guernica in 1991 and 1999) all be worthy of consideration as equals among Canada's other canonical figures? To be fair, Blaser is revered in many quarters and Gary Geddes did represent his work in *15 Canadian Poets X Three*,[53] but when an anthology of contemporary Canadian poetry was recently published in the United States, its Canadian-born editor admitted that the name of no living Canadian gay male poet came to mind when

53 Gary Geddes, ed. *15 Canadian Poets X 3* (Don Mills, ON: Oxford University Press, 2001).

drawing together its contents.

However, the merits of gay male poetry and its potential to grasp Parnassus have been placed into perspective for me by John D'Emilio in an article recently published by *The Gay and Lesbian Review*. This respected University of Illinois historian makes the following salient observation:

> *Since the early 1960s, the lives of many, many heterosexuals have become much like the imagined lives of homosexuals*. Being heterosexual no longer means settling as a young adult into a lifelong coupled relationship sanctioned by the state and characterized by the presence of children and sharply gendered spousal roles. Instead, there may be a number of intimate relationships over the course of a lifetime. A marriage certificate may or may not accompany these relationships. Males and females alike expect to earn their way. Children figure less importantly in the lifespan of adults, and some heterosexuals, for the first time in history, choose not to have children at all. [The italics are D'Emilio's.][54]

Who knew that the Joneses were trying to keep up with us and not the other way around? Though D'Emilio happens to be talking about social change in context with the Gordian knot that same-sex marriage has sadly proven itself to be in the United States—a knot that certain conservatives[55] in our own country have attempted to retie without any judicial or legislative success—he affirms and reminds us that the social standing we have built for ourselves is the definitive "new normal" (to appropriate—and hopefully debase—another politically loaded term).

---

54 John D'Emilio, "The Marriage Fight is Setting Us Back," *Gay and Lesbian Review* 13 (November–December 2006) 10–11.

55 The social conservatives have their apologists in surprising quarters. Even respected McGill University ethicist Margaret Somerville, while first arguing discrimination based on sexual orientation is morally repugnant, attempts to develop a convincing argument against same-sex marriage in the 2006 Massey Lectures (see *The Ethical Imagination* [Toronto: House of Anansi, 2006]: 101–104).

In decades past, we have viewed, even valorized ourselves as aberrant and have been treated as such. We have decried and praised ourselves for our innate and accursed "otherness." Though some in the queer community truly do mourn the loss of our fabled outlaw status in exchange for the attainment of our rights (as if we should have our cake and still be able to eat it, too, on the sly), this new normal we have called into being opens up our possibilities considerably today—especially if we continue to *drag* the rest of society forward with us.

For the gay male poet, the range, parameters, and depth of potential themes at last are limitless. Still, simply to imagine that the societal changes improving our queer lives might have been triggered more by heterosexuals following our subliminal cues and less by our persistent demand for an equal (poetic) voice could turn any understanding of a century's progress on its pink-lined ear.

Who knew our poets had been queering the world so beautifully and productively all along?

John Barton
Victoria, BC
December 2006

Acknowledgements

The compilation of an anthology—above all one that is the first of its kind and draws upon the work of so many writers, especially writers who are often either culturally obscure or forgotten, or who may have chosen or been forced to write elliptically from a historically marginalized perspective—depends on the generous support, interest, and cooperation of so many more stakeholders than its editors.

First, thanks must go to the contributors as well as to the families and executors of those contributors who are no longer with us. Their interest, excitement, and faith in this project have truly been gratifying. Much of the work gathered here is also still under copyright to over twenty publishers. Thanks go to these presses for allowing us to reprint their authors' work.

For advice about and assistance in determining who to include, we would like to thank D. M. R. Bentley, University of Western Ontario; Dennis Denisoff, Ryerson University; Peter Dickinson, Simon Fraser University; Terry Goldie, York University; Brett Josef Grubisic, University of British Columbia; David Jarraway, University of Ottawa; Thomas Lacroix for recommending Brion Gysin; Andrew Lesk, University of Toronto; Gerald Lynch, University of Ottawa; Christian Mondor, the Canada Council for the Arts; the staff of Special Collections, University of Victoria; Tracy Ware, Queen's University; and Bruce Whiteman, University of California, Los Angeles. We would especially like to thank Don McLeod and the other volunteers at the Canadian Lesbian and Gay Archives, Toronto, for their invaluable help during the initial stages of this project.

Our thanks are also due to Jonathan Kaplansky for his English translations of the poems by Québécois contributors that were commissioned for this anthology. We acknowledge the support of the Canada Council for the Arts through its Book Publishing Support program, which awarded a translation grant to this project.

Many friends and colleagues helped us track down the whereabouts of some contributors, provided useful insights into the life and writing of a specific contributor, or were our eyes, hands, and feet in far-off places. We would like to thank Mary Louise Adams, Queen's University; Henry Beissel; Kate

Braid; Nicole Brossard; Ronnie R. Brown; David Brundage, Athabasca University; Jeffrey Canton; David Estok; Endre Farkas; Clarise Foster, *Contemporary Verse 2*; Sky Gilbert; Glad Day Bookshop, Toronto; Karen Haughian, Signature Editions; Michael Holmes, ECW Press; Ed Jackson; Jody James, Storytellers School of Toronto; Evan Jones; Mary Beth Knechtel; Don LePan; Kitty Lewis, Brick Books; Little Sister's Book & Art Emporium, Vancouver; Tanis MacDonald, Wilfrid Laurier University; Robert K. Martin, Université de Montréal; Lianne Moyes, Université de Montréal; David Rimmer, After Stonewall Books, Ottawa; André Roy; Martha Sharpe, formerly of House of Anansi Press; Luc Simard, Library and Archives Canada; Gord Shillingford, The Muses' Company/ J. Gordon Shillingford Publishing; Sandy Shreve; Richard Teleky; Randall Ware, Library and Archives Canada; and Dan Yashinsky, Toronto Arts Council.

For their help in creating an audience and context for this anthology, thanks go to Janne Cleveland, Gary Sealey, Jo Van Every, Tuan Vu, and the other members of The Lambda Foundation, organizers of Wilde About Sappho, a nationally significant gay and lesbian writers' festival held annually in Ottawa and other cities. One Foundation member, Jodie Medd, merits especial thanks. Equal thanks are also due to sheri-d wilson and the Calgary International Spoken Word Festival. We also thank Blaine Kyllo for his early support of this project.

We acknowledge the support of the Association of Writers and Writing Programs (AWP), which made it possible for us to present our early findings in "Seminal: The Voice of Canada's Gay Male Poets," a panel we convened at its 2005 annual conference in Vancouver. We also thank Miss Cookie LaWhore for being our moderator.

A publisher's commitment to a project of this nature is crucial. At Arsenal Pulp Press, we thank Brian Lam, Robert Ballantyne, Shyla Seller, and Janice Beley. We are also grateful to Attila Richard Lukacs for permitting us to feature one of his paintings on the cover and to Jayson Junge for his capable cover design.

John Barton and Billeh Nickerson

I would like to thank George Elliott Clarke, who was a key resource in the necessary widening of the breadth of this anthology. His expertise about black writing in Canada enriched our choices. He is a busy man, so I value his real interest and prompt replies to my letters and emails. For advice about Québécois gay writing, I am indebted to Jean-Paul Daoust, who suggested many poets and provided essential contact information. I also appreciate the insights that Ian Young provided into the community of gay writers active in Ontario and Quebec in the 1970s and 1980s, into the history of Catalyst Press, and into the activism he was engaged in during the post-Stonewall years in Canada and abroad. I must especially thank Jason Weiss, New York, for his fine-tuning of the details reported here about the life and unique accomplishments of Brion Gysin.

On a more personal level, I thank my friends who were always available to listen to me ramble on about the joys and challenges of anthology-making: Rhonda Batchelor, Holly Pattison, and the other members of *The Malahat Review* team; Alison Beaumont, Brenda Brooks, Bruce Chambers, Lorna Crozier, David Day, Chris Fox, Gordon Fulton, Mark Gallop, Robert Gore, Neile Graham, James Gurley, Jonathan Kaplansky (who transformed my emails to francophone contributors into a French cogent and unjarring in its grammar), Anita Lahey, Tanis MacDonald, Blaine Marchand, Erín Mouré, Bill Ralston, Harold Rhenisch, David Rimmer, Philip Robert, Doug Schmidt, Michael V. Smith, Lynne Van Luven, and David Young. Above all, I am indebted to David Katz, who listened to me more than anybody else.

Finally, I thank Billeh Nickerson for inviting me to join him in this very seminal project.

John Barton

I would like to thank bill bissett for his recollections on blewointmentpress and the gay writing communities of the 1960s and 1970s; Wayde Compton; Lynn Crosbie; Lorna Crozier and the Department of Writing, University of Victoria; Ron Dutton, Vancouver Public Library, for his assistance with both library holdings and his extensive personal collection; *Event*; *Geist*; Ryan Knighton; Patrick Lane; Meredith Quartermain; the staff at the UBC Library Archives; and Sarah Warren, Talonbooks.

I would also like to thank the following friends and supporters: Elizabeth Bachinsky, Matt Davy, Genni Gunn, Sean Horlor, Kwantlen University College, Alma Lee, Jamie Poll (whose bed allowed me to attend many Victoria meetings), Michael V. Smith, Hal Wake, and sheri-d wilson (who lobbied valiantly for inclusion).

And finally, a special thank you to John Barton, the senior editor of this project, for his expertise. This anthology would not have been possible without his tireless support and extensive scholarship.

Billeh Nickerson

Note on the Text

The poets are arranged by year of birth. The majority of poems for each contributor are placed in chronological order according to the date of their first appearance in book form; this date is indicated after the last line of each poem.

For previously uncollected work, the year of publication is noted for any poem that appeared only in magazines, newspapers, or online; for any poem appearing for the first time in print in this anthology, the year of composition is indicated. In the rare occasion that a poem was published posthumously, the date of composition is indicated (if known), followed by the date of first publication—either in a magazine or book form—in parentheses. In the case of a work in translation, the date of the French original's publication in book form is indicated, not the date that its English translation first appeared in print.

Also, occasional variations and inconsistencies in spelling and punctuation have been preserved when no sources exist to verify an author's original intentions.

SEMINAL

Frank Oliver Call, 1878–1956

To a Greek Statue

Beautiful, statue of Parian marble,
Dreaming alone in the northern sunlight,
Ivory-tinted, your slender arms beckon;
I follow, I follow.

Slender and white is your beautiful body,
Gleaming against the grey walls that surround you;
Like hyacinth-flowers beneath the snow sleeping
Is the dream you emprison;—

A dream of beauty that lingers forever,
A dream of the amethyst sky of midnight,
A dream of the jacinth blue of still waters,
Reflecting white temples.

Your white arms beckon, I follow, I follow,
My dream goes forth with your dream to wander;
You lead me into a moonlit garden
Beside the Aegean.

White in the moonlight gleams the temple
Cutting the purple sky with its pediment;
Diamonds and sapphires fall from the fountain;
Black are the cypress trees.

The gods are asleep in the silent temple;
Only the lapping of waves on the sea-sand
Mingles its drowsy rhythmical beating
With the bells of the fountain.

Soft lie the panther-skins on the cool grasses,
Not in vain are your white arms lifted;
And my dream of beauty and your dream eternal
Embrace in the moonlight.

1920

The Hill-Top

Across blue hills white wisps of cloud are scudding;
Our path has led us to a rocky crest
Through fields where autumn crocuses are budding
Beneath the sun, fast bending to the west.
We left behind the thronged and dusty highway
Where all day long the tired footsteps beat,
And climbed together up a lonely byway
Where stones were rough, but where the flowers were sweet.

Too soon my path may lead me to the valley
While you still linger on the sunlit height,
But all their strength my faltering feet will rally,
And all my spirit rise above the night,
If I, in memory, still may touch your lips,
Or feel across the dark your finger-tips.

1924

White Hyacinth

We put the dog-eared lesson-book away,
Pondering the classic story. Pale and dead
Before our eyes young Hyacinthus lay
Upon the Spartan shore. From stains of red
Beside the blue Aegean, star on star,
White hyacinths sprang up to greet the dawn,
Each leaf a cry of pain, re-echoing far
A voice that mourned for beauty past and gone.
You paused a moment as you left the room,
Bending a slender form above a bowl
Of white and blue where hyacinths were abloom.
Once more the far Aegean seemed to roll
On flower-clad shores, but brought no cry of pain,
For Hyacinthus breathed in life again.

1944

Émile Nelligan, 1879–1941

Almost a Shepherd

The breezes are murmuring like litanies
And the flute fades out in soft aphonies.

The great steers are back. They moo in the stable
And the piping hot soup gladdens the table.

Pray, O Pan! Let us now go to bed, my lamb,
May our pickaxe-weary arms at last grow calm.

To silk horizons moonlight ripples and sways:
O Slumber! Give me your kiss of many joys.

All is shut. Night. Silence ... a dog yelps out back.
I bed down. But in my soul a dream has struck.

Yes, it is delightful, this: to be so free
Living almost as a shepherd. A memory

Thrills in me. Back there, in childhood, my life flowed
Like that, pure and enraptured, far from the crowd!

1904 *Translated by Fred Cogswell*

Song of Wine

Fresh in joy's live light all things coincide,
This fine May eve! Like living hopes that once
Were in my heart, the choiring birds announce
Their prelude to my window open wide.

O fine May eve! O happy eve of May!
A distant organ beats out frigid chords;
And long shafts of sun, like crimson swords,
Cut to the heart of the scent of dying day.

How gay, how glad am I! Pour out, pour out
Once more the wine into the chiming glass
That I may lose the pain of days which pass
In scorn for all the wicked human rout.

How glad am I! My wine and art be blest!
I, too, have dreamed of making poetry
That lives, of poems which sound the exequy
For autumn winds that pass in far-off mist.

The bitter laugh of rage is now good form,
And I, a poet, must eat scorn for food.
I have a heart but am not understood
Except in moonlight and in great nights of storm.

Woman! I drink to you who mock the path
Where the rose-dream calls with arms flung wide;
I drink, too, to you, men with brows of pride,
Who first refuse my hand then scorn my life!

When the starry sky becomes one glorious roof,
And when a hymn resounds for golden Spring,
I do not weep for all the day's calm going,
Who wary grope within my own black youth.

How glad am I, May eve, all eves above.
Not drunk but desperately glad am I!...
Has living grown at last to be a joy?
Has my heart, too, been healed of my sick love?

The clocks have struck and the wind smells of night....
Now the wine gurgles as I pour it out.
So glad am I that as I laugh and shout
I fear I shall break down and sob outright.

1904 *Translated by Fred Cogswell*

The Spectre

Through all my winter eves he sat
In my chair of green velvet
        Near to the hearth;
Smoking my pipe of thin-glazed earth,
He sat, a spectre tall in height,
Under the dying coals of light
Behind my screen's funereal blight.

He has haunted, like a pale ghost,
My dark hovel, and his accursed soliloquys
Have filled it with strange maladies.
Speak freely, spectre, your name indite
That is bound to wrench my heart outright
Behind my screen's funereal blight.

When I asked his name, the skeleton
Bellowed like a mighty cannon
        And bit the blue
Veins of his lips almost in two.
With his face inclined, he stood upright
And his wild howl had force to smite
Behind my screen's funereal blight.

"In your awful nights you call me
The spectre of your ennui,
        O brother mine.
To my sad breast your breast consign
That I may press it with my might
And triumph at the hour, right
Behind my screen's funereal blight."

By fiery eye and madness stung,
He gnashed his teeth and then unslung
        A sash from his throat.
With bony fingers, like harpstrings mute,
Thin saffron-yellow in the light,
He hooked my heart in his grim bite
Behind the screen's funereal blight.

1952 *Translated by Fred Cogswell*

Robert Finch, 1900–1995

Egg and Dart

This never-ended searching for the eyes
Wherein the unasked question's answer lies;
This beating, beating, beating of the heart
Because a contour seems to fit the part;
The long, drear moment of the look that spoils
The little bud of hope; the word that soils
The pact immaculate, so newly born;
The noisy silence of the old self-scorn;
These, and the sudden leaving in the lurch;
Then the droll recommencement of the search.

1936

From a Hammock

Policeman of contentment, stay
The official process of dismay,

Arrest each ambush thought has laid,
Nip it in bud, clip it in blade,

Escort these eyes to walk the wood
Of sloth, the labyrinth of mood,

Through a green algebra to brims
Of water where reflection swims,

To where, its spring ordeal sustained,
The willow mourns the trophy gained,

While poplar pedestals, that fling
Askew to stretch this cloud of string,

Topple the cloud of cloud they bear
To cushions for the patient stare

That holds both vision and the viewed
Fixt, in a soundless solitude

Whose brilliant exile, for the heart,
Is, and makes, a work of art.

1936

The Livery

Insolent youth that walks superb
In shorts and singlets, pumps and tails,
Letting no accident disturb
A camouflage of triple scales,

Swinging a racket or a book
Like gods that need no other sceptres,
Freezing your elders by a look
To prisoners of indifferent captors,

Lolling in cars while Time careers
Down the redoubtable avenue,
Or hair astream stripping the gears
To overtake and pass him too,

How timidly you win the race
And how demurely take the prize,
With wondering mind, expressive face,
Tentative hand, and lowered eyes,

As pins and ribbons, ties and shirts,
In shades less arrogant than they
Like your bright panoply of arts
Fade to the livery of grey.

1946

Scroll-section

you who practise the four elegant occupations
tea music calligraphy and checkers
follow me over the snow in search of plum blossom.

Leave kingdom breakers
to juggle nations,
and care's broad
cloud
to the white hare that with mortar and pestle
sits in the moon by the cassia tree,
leave your lacquer trestle
of puppets, your aviary
of pets in petrified wood,
your malachite lion with its ball of brocade,
your clique to scribble the past
on dust,
and with no inlaid saddle,
no jewelled bridle,
follow me over the snow in search of plum blossom.

The leaping salmon rainbows the cataracts,
the dragon in chase of a pearl skips space
and the phoenix, alighting, first selects a place
to arrange its tail. Emulate in a degree these agreeable acts.

Silent though peach and plum
a path is trod to them.
Every rustic talent
till seen is silent.
Even the hollow bamboo
has leaves that droop.

Come back over the snow,
set up
wrist-rests, paint in ink
mountains trees creepers clouds
gorges rivers cascades
the brink

of wind, monasteries in mist,
beauties that have no best,
that through your purpose a longing be learned, earned
the seal of your mind borrowed and not returned.

1946

The Painters

A man's life is his portrait. Not till death
He sees his portrait mirrored in the past
With the first brush-stroke vivid as the last
And finally varnished with his dying breath.

He is far from knowing he paints his portrait,
Barely flatters himself, and, though he should,
The impartial portrait never flatters, good,
Bad, indifferent, it renders trait for trait.

He paints it in with act and thought and word
And paints it out with word and thought and act,
Fooling himself but not the painted fact
Where every overt and covert stroke is scored.

The many paint their lives as they have spent them.
The few spend them as they would wish to paint them.

1948

The Moth

No two days in a forest are the same.
This morning the grey beeches wait beside us
On a brown tapestry; no path to guide us,
No leaf that signals, as when last we came;
Only the grey beeches column a grey room
Whose brown aisles emptied of the gold of Midas
Betray us now where no one could have spied us.

Yet not a thing moves in the grey-brown dream

Except there, very quietly, as though
Its transit were the soul of brown and grey,
Grey and brown as the stillness it steals through,
A moth plays truant from the tapestry,
Then, lost in undiscernible inaction,
Leaves the whole wood astir with recollection.

1961

Real and Remembered

Which, the real or the remembered, I asked,
Is better? Unhesitatingly you replied:
Neither, both are different, descried
Differently.—Is not each the other but masked?

—No more one than the boat and the dock it leaves,
No more one than flight and a dream of winging,
No more one than song and a song for singing,
No more one than the loom and the web it weaves.

Real is a memory that has not set sail,
Real is a phoenix this side the singe of change,
Real is a song, familiarly strange,
Real is a web before the loom is still.

Remembered is a boat in a shoreless ocean,
Remembered is wings that carry the way they came,
Remembered is a song no voice can frame,
Remembered is a less a kerchief than its motion.

I said: These sayings are easy to listen to
Not only because they are yours; this must be added,
Real and remembered are best when undivided
As now when they have us both to fasten to.

1961

Midsummer

Six o'clock. The sun clambers out of the sea,
Drying himself on shimmering cloths of mist,
Treading the green rollers from crest to crest
Until he steps on the beach, gilding its grey,
Laughing the ladders' ghostly acrobatics
Into a game that angles play for gold,
Rippling the parallel bars to unparalleled
Silver departures for higher mathematics,
Filling the air with the sparkle of the lark,
Drenching hydrangeas rose and buddleias mauve,
Shining each foxglove with a shining glove,
Turning everything light, even the dark,
Lifting everything up, stature and creature,
Making everything sing, even this watcher.

1966

Summation

Assessing characters it is preferred
To sum them up in an embracing word,
A global term fixing a changing shape
As cameras immortalize a snap.
Yet every man being clever and obtuse,
Learned and ignorant, rigorous and loose,
Snobbish and humble, tearful and courageous,
Is not a single adjective outrageous?
One thing predominant? It dominates
The inconsistencies that mould its traits.
How can one modifier radiate this:
The artist posing as a prophet; bliss
Mistaking superstition to be science;
Thinking certification of reliance
On facts lies in one's own belief in them?
What word can be reduced to a sole theme?
'He is modest,' you say, or 'average' or 'proud,'
but at each word he melts into a crowd.

1981

Gone

You are gone from the garden where Hercules strangles
The snake that would strangle the strength which creates,
You are gone from the lure of the alleys at angles,
The beds where the flowers hold coloured debates.

You are gone from the vista that eats the horizon,
From the arches of triumph that triumph each end,
You are gone from the circles of statues that rise on
The velvety sward like thoughts a knife penned.

You are gone from the pool with the sky-reaching fountain,
From the boats that come back to the hand they have left,
You are gone from the foursome of rivers aslant in
A rush or a reed or a marble shell raft.

The view from the terrace sees others, not you,
The armschairs of iron are filled but your form
Never rocks them, the tap of a truculent shoe
Is prelude no more to your transient storm.

The horses of wood ride the merry-go-round
And the donkeys go round with as merry a crew
And still from the Judy-and-Punch tent a sound
Calls out for the comment that made them all new.

1981

Rue de Richelieu, rue des Petits-Champs

Rochester's *Sodom* in the National Library
Must be applied for formally by letter
Stating one's status and one's subject matter,
Scholars may wait for weeks with no reply.

Around the corner in the Sexashop
Rochester's *Sodom* is waiting to be had,
And many another *Sodom* quite as sad

With covers meant to make the eye go pop,
No letter need be written to obtain
What anyone can buy for ready money,
The dealer is a drone who combs his honey
From distillations of the special bane

Every *Sodom* secretes, ancient or recent,
Adjacent, unadjacent, derelict or decent.

1984

The Shirt

I own a shirt of stuff that will not tear,
A perfect fit, suitable for all moods
And weathers, rare protective goods
That insulates from any atmosphere
Of hate or hopelessness or brutish force,
Its every seam, set by conviction's trend
Guides my erratic urges till they end
By modelling what they threaten to disperse.
At this shirt's fashion, fashion cannot cavil,
No laundry ruins what is self-renewing,
Fresher each day than even day can be,
No rift occurs that calls for subtle sewing,
No mishap mars what death shall not unravel
And, best, this shirt is worn invisibly.

1984

John Glassco, 1909–1981

Stud Groom

Your boy's-ambition was to be a Horseman,
Some day to hear tell or overhear your name
Linked with that word. This was the foreseen
Reward for the five years in the dealer's stable,
For strewing your childhood nightly under his horses' feet
And bearing it out at sun-up on a shovel,

When you met all claims with waiver and deferment,
And learned the habit of not coming to grips
With any unhaltered thing that's not dependent
On a boy's will like a pious man on God's,
Till language lapsed back into clucks and chirps,
Hisses and heeyahs, steady-babes, be-goods.

And now it has all come true! and the mountains spill
Your world of cousins, a chorus of witnesses:
Lost Nation, Bolton Centre and Pigeon Hill
Acclaim you who combine, deny and defer
With straps and stalls the heats and rampancies
And the act that's blessed with a bucket of cold water.

Well, there is the World, in the attitude of approval,
Hands in its pockets, hat over its eyes,
Igorant, cunning, suave and noncommittal,
The ape of knowledge.... Say, through what injustice
Has it gained the bounty, by what crazy process
Those eyes fell heir to your vision of success?

For the goal has changed—It's rather to have made
Of the welcoming music of nickers and whinnies
At feeding time, the brightness of an eye
Fixed on a bucket, the fine restraint of a hoof
Raised and held in a poised meaningless menace,
To have made, of these, assurances of love,

And of the denial of all loving contact
When the ears flatten, the eye rolls white,
The whirring alarm that keeps the dream intact
For poet and pervert too, whose spasm or nightmare
Makes, with the same clean decision of a bite,
Divorce between possession and desire.

For 'one woman leads to another, like one war
Leads to another,' and the fever has no end
Till passion turns—from the bright or bloody star,
Form the bitter triumph over a stranger's body,
To something between a deity and a friend,
To a service halting between cult and hobby,

And nothing is left for the family or the nation
But a genial curse, and silence. It may be
You are the type of figures long out of fashion,
The Unknown Soldier and the Forgotten Man,
Whom the rest might envy, now, their anonymity
And the fact they were at least left alone;

And who might have said, like you, to a pair
Of nags looking over a sagging roadside fence,
Good Morning, girls! O greeting washed in air,
O simple insistence to affirm the Horse,
While the Loans and bomb-loads are hitting new highs
And youth is deducted at the source.

For 'Horseman, what of the future?' is a question
Without a meaning: there is always another race,
Another show, the unquenchable expectation
Of ribbons, the easy applause like a summer storm,
And the thrill, like love, of being in first place
For an instant that lasts forever, and does no harm

Except to the altar-fated passion it robs,
The children it cheats of their uniforms and wars,
And the fathomless future of the underdog

It negates—shrugs off like the fate of a foundered mare—
As it sparks the impenetrable lives, like yours
Whose year revolves around the county fair.

1958

Noyade 1942

The taxi headlights sweep the palings
And the horn summons you. Goodbye.
Reassumed-gaiters-and-battledress
Clumps down the steps. The car door slams.
—See how the pattern of paired lives
Has turned in the end to a series of partings!

Well you are gone and there's only God
The last discovery—for either one:
Tonight in your seat that screams through darkness
And here, in the bed too wide, too empty,
Another assault of bleeding hands
On the citadel of His-will-be-done....

But tomorrow, when the daylight hurts
And penetrates, when the khaki mud
Poured round you in the recurrent hour of waking
Dries, cakes, hardens into stone, until
The stone grows inward and you become
A monument with a dwindling core of blood,

And far away here, when the daylit frame
Of room and field wavers for eyes
That find you and feel you not at all,
And the heart made to tremble at shadows
Weaves round itself a solitude
Vaster than space, to suffocate its cries—

What wonder then that love and faith
Turn coward ere these days are ended?

The drowning stony lover grasp
At straws of pleasure, the weak faithful
Prove constant only to despair?
So reveries flower in fierce air

Where the pure and tender thoughts—that take
Too many tears to keep alive—
Are stifled, and see: the age's will is done!
A little sacrilege and murder
Wreaked on the private effigies
Of bodies joined and put asunder.

O love that thinks it could always
Suffer all things, live on the crust
Of letters and orgiastic leaves!
Too soon the pointed bones appear
Of your beginning and your end
In this long summer of malison and lust.

1958

Villanelle

My love and yours must be enjoyed alone:
My sleeping sister and internal twin,
I know your body better than my own.

Only the natural conscience of the bone
Protests the sadness of the dream wherein
My love and yours must be enjoyed alone;

But the body has reasons to the soul unknown:
The soul of another is dark, said Augustine;
I know your body better than my own.

You that know everything that can be known,
Tell me through what punishment of what sin
My love and yours must be enjoyed alone?

Why have the darkness and the distance grown,
Why do we fear to let the stranger in?
—I know your body better than my own,

I know the lamp is out, the bird has flown.
To find that end where other loves begin
My love and yours must be enjoyed alone:
I know your body better than my own.

1958

Fly in Autumn

Here he is, the loathsome one
Pushing from a crack in the window,
Fat with unseasonable seed, making his way
Towards the light of the dying year,

Washing his hands wearily, bemused
By the fictive summer of the house,
Driven from sleep by his god,
Feeling for his destiny.

Where are his parents, those spry lechers
Of a summer of roses and wine?
Papery corpses crumbling. Their bloated child
Stalks the failing sun.

Beelzebub, Prince of this World,
Is this not your servant in whom you were well pleased,
Now beloved of none, and sick?
Worthless one, Prince of this World....

Maggot, call on a greater god today:
Mercy, mercy, avert your lethal finger!
Let me but live to suffer the frost,
The slower death accessible to all.

1964

Brummell at Calais

A foolish useless man who had done nothing
All his life long but keep himself clean,
Locked in the glittering armour of a pose
Made up of impudence, chastity and reserve—
How does his memory still survive his world?

The portraits show us only a tilted nose,
Lips full blown, a cravat and curly wig,
And a pair of posturing eyes,
Infinitely vulnerable, deeply innocent,
Their malice harmless as a child's:

And he has returned to childhood now, his stature
That of the Butterfly whose *Funeral*
He sang (his only song) for one of his
Dear duchesses, Frances or Georgiana,
In the intolerable metre of Tom Moore—

To a childhood of sweet biscuits and curaçao;
Hair-oil and tweezers make him forget his debts,
The angle of his hat remains the same,
His little boots pick their way over the cobblestones,
But where is he going as well as going mad?

Nowhere: his glory is already upon him,
The fading Regency man who will leave behind
More than the ankle-buttoning pantaloon!
For see, even now in the long implacable twilight,
The triumph of his veritable art,

An art of being, nothing but being, the grace
Of perfect self-assertion based on nothing,
As in our vanity's cause against the void
He strikes his elegant blow, the solemn report of those
Who have done nothing and will never die.

1964

Douglas LePan, 1914–1998

Coureurs de bois

Thinking of you, I think of the *coureurs de bois*,
Swarthy men grown almost to savage size
Who put their brown wrists through the arras of the woods
And were lost—sometimes for months. Word would come back:
One had been seen in Crêve-coeur, deserted and starving,
One at Sault Sainte Marie shouldering the rapids.
Giant-like, their labours stalked the streets of Quebec
Though they themselves had dwindled in distance: names only;
Rumours; quicksilvery spies into nature's secrets;
Rivers that seldom ran in the sun. Their resource
Would sparkle and then flow back under clouds of hemlock.

So you should have travelled with them. Or with La Salle.
He could feed his heart with the heart of a continent,
Insatiate, how noble a wounded animal,
Who sought for his wounds the balsam of adventure,
The sap from some deep, secret tree. But now
That the forests are cut down, the rivers charted,
Where can you turn, where can you travel? Unless
Through the desperate wilderness behind your eyes,
So full of falls and glooms and desolations,
Disasters I have glimpsed but few would dream of,
You seek new Easts. The coats of difficult honour,
Bright with brocaded birds and curious flowers,
Stowed so long with vile packs of pemmican,
Futile, weighing you down on slippery portages,
Would flutter at last in the courts of a clement country,
Where the air is silken, the manners easy,
Under a guiltless and reconciling sun.

You hesitate. The trees are entangled with menace.
The voyage is perilous into the dark interior.
But then your hands go to the thwarts. You smile. And so
I watch you vanish in a wood of heroes,
Wild Hamlet with the features of Horatio.

1948

A Man of Honour

When he awakened to himself, it was
Perpetual day. He must go on beneath
The midnight sun that hung its icy laws
Rebukingly about him, purging his breath.
Sharp lookout must be kept. No slackened pause
To sleep, no night to sip one drop of death.

Silently as an Arctic convey steers
He must be stern and lonely, from the raked wings
Of his patrolling vices hide his fears.
At action stations always. One false move brings
A pack of submarines, one whimper tears
The tissued pallor where salvation sings.

Round many a crackling North Cape must he pass
Estranged from land, long centuries move
Snow-blinded, bewildered by the hectic compass,
Till at the valid pole at last arrive
His bearded honour frozen green as grass
And ashen eyes the sun burnt out, alive.

1953

The Green Man

Leaves twist out of his mouth, of his eyes, of his ears,
twine down over his thighs, spring out of his heels,
as he runs through the woods as a deer or an outlaw, or curled
up in moss and bracken, light speckling him feckless,
he watches the other animals, himself hidden
like an animal, although so strangely human
that if you surprise him you might think yourself looking
into the eyes of the mad but all-wise Merlin.

Boreal forest his most natural habitat
from the edge of our cities up to the tree-line
where at summer's end in the spongy Mackenzie Delta

he glides through pale yellowing poplars before the snow flies
or at Northwest River slips out of the spruce to play
with the huskies, chained on the shingle. His territory
spreads far and wide beneath the Bear. Morose
and frolic and savage his sports where the forests are.

But I have glimpsed him almost everywhere.
In pool-rooms and bargain-basements. In the glance of the dark
prisoner in the dock, not knowing how to plead,
passionate the criss-cross light that sifts through leaves.
In pale changing-rooms at the atomic energy plant
the young technician is changed into a sylvan man,
shadowed with mystery, and suffering from the sap
like a young green tree, quick thrall of earth and frenzy.

And quick he runs through my dreams, so quick and grieving,
to banish grey calculations of tomorrow,
to banish old gods with gay assurance,
impatient of bounds and all mere definition,
but sometimes himself a god, now minor, marginal,
now reigning sovereign over an empty tomb,
the incised leaves on his flesh now wounds, now blood,
now flame. The forest reeks now with vermilion.

There is a shade that glides beneath the skyscrapers
and makes those papery steeples soar and tremble
like poplars in the breeze, a green man's shade
who came before Champlain, green traveller, trader,
debauchee, wearing around his neck
gull's feathers and four new sweetwater seas,
interpreting the woods to Europe and Europe to
the woods—till finally he was cooked and eaten.

His taciturnities were our title-deeds,
his heart divided food that our hearts have fed on,
so many morsels from that seething pot,
some for the merchant princes in their lofty
boardrooms (a long long way from poor Étienne Brulé!),
but more for more ravenous hunters through other wastes,
lost, lost, and wild in utter inner dark

where the hunters and the circling hunted are the same.
And so I circle on the green man's tracks,
allured, bewildered by the bright green shoots
and headsman's axe he holds, those baffling icons
(for all the subtle theories that I half believe in)
that lead me on and down. But past all doubt
there thrives an underworld where life and death
are woven. And it is bright and dark and savage,
as speckled and as rippling as a snakeskin.

Outlaw or god this cunning harlequin?
I feel him darkening my glittering veins,
he kennels in my loins, knows every crevice
of my half-breed heart, and yet eludes me still,
though rumours reach me of him fugitive,
laughing and drinking behind an empty warehouse,
disguised in rags, and tossing empty bottles
to splash and sparkle on the cindery railway-siding.

Scion of the undergrowth and underworld
but a prince of darkness in all daylight polity.
I could lead you on a perfect summer afternoon
into a clearing where the trees are still and lucid
and have you stare and listen till a rustle comes
of a serpent moving underneath the columns.
Light slows. Leaves tremble—with Marsyas's blood as much
as Apollo's brightness. Now break a branch, it bleeds.

Some nights and seasons are his own, and sacred.
Then dreams flow into the woods, woods flow
into dreams, the whole pent city dreaming of a carnal
wood, confluence that empties into the streets
with a scurry of leaves and carnival drums and flutes,
and torches that set fire to the leaves and the city, a blaze
of harlequin crimson, skyward, as quick he still winds
among the masquers mocking, a green man with green wounds.

1982

Astrolabe

Now it seems almost as easy as breathing
this commerce of bodies and souls, unlicensed.
There was a moment, though, when it cost almost
everything—the explorer, tense, frightened, resolute,
with his cargo of musket, memories, diaries,
astrolabe, committing himself to the tender
skin of a birch-bark canoe, and a new continent,
and a new world, where anything might happen,
anything, not knowing that the thin skin of birch
might hold the weight of a lyric future
as well as the weight of suffering Europe on its ribs.
They grew to each other, though, slim lyric sweetness
and grim tension of the malcontent, till they
worked out new terms of trade, the musket
melting beside the pile of beaver pelts
till it rose again as a rod of almost god-like strength
and sweetness, and the pile of musky pelts flowered into
an ineffably golden fleece. At last the moment came when
he searched no longer for the stars, throwing away
his astrolabe to rust beneath a pine-tree,
and moved at last at ease in a world he never dreamed,
this new world, ours, where savagery and sweetness melts as one.

1982

A Nightpiece, of London in the Blackout

A wash of greatcoats circling about the foot of Eros
dethroned. Of nameless and almost faceless figures in the dusk,
drawn from a dozen countries, but all homeless, solitary,
adrift, uneasily on leave for a few brief hours or days
from history and its iron formations—or else deserters from them.
And a sombre sky, that's careless of the heart's elections
but carelessly forgiving of every anonymous encounter,
a sky quivering to a subtext hidden beneath the greatcoats,
tissues and textures throbbing with their own imperatives

(which might be gross or pure, promiscuous or crazed with love,
or both), with a thousand different objects and inflections,
that yet transmit a single impulse to the indulgent air,
a deep pulse of loneliness and outright lust and longing—
to share their nakedness with someone. Now! Tonight!

1987

A Head Found at Beneventum

Begin with the likeness of a young man's head on a coin,
as if he were perhaps the Antinous beloved by Hadrian,
and let that grow into a bronze head, more strongly and subtly
modelled, the eyes deep set and heavy lidded, looking
a little like the bronze head found at Beneventum
and now in the Louvre. And then bring all that to life
in the figure of a young American with the gentlest eyes
in all the world, a fine oarsman, but deep into Proust,
Joyce and Mann, always *disponible*, always open
to what the world had to offer, but always reserved,
always sure—a little too sure—of his own innocence.
The hooks went in very quietly. As no doubt they did
when Hadrian lost his heart and head to Antinous.

1987

Walking a Tightrope

The delicate wavering line between fantasy and fact,
a line that has to be redrawn almost every time
that the house-lights go down and the scene is made
to glow from within the phosphor of kindled passion.

What is needed as kindling is fantasizing that may have
been smouldering for days, and may persist till the final act,
or perhaps well beyond. The trick is to let it ignite
and illumine, without ever letting it burn the house down.

It's as though the boundary between two sovereign states
had to be redrawn at every encounter. Or, better still, as though
that line between settlement and wilderness were endlessly shifting,
with now the palefaces, and now the redskins, advancing.

It's a little the same, but not quite, as the strict dramatic
tension between illusion and reality, between Theseus' world
and Oberon's and Titania's, between the world of the lawgiver
and their wildwood realm of illusion and metamorphosis,

where what you imagine, what you desire, can happen,
does happen, but also where a clumsy artisan can be tricked
into absurdity, as he rehearses his interlude—a performance
of one mimesis in the arms of another, mirror echoing mirror.

To come nearer home, I think of Blondin crossing the Falls,
his tightrope swaying in the wind, a long pole steadying him;
and of his audience (who now are part of the performance);
young gentlemen of delicate sensibility in wide-awake hats

(I wonder what their fantasies are?); and the young ladies with them
in Paisley shawls; and then behind them a scuffle of rubes
and suckers, with hucksters of cheap souvenirs and candy-floss
to add a rank demotic flavour to the thin mist from the Falls,

all watching Blondin, with his powerful thighs, as he glides
out, along the rope as if he were a dancer in ballet slippers
and then runs to do a dancer's leap over the Gorge, till one
viewer after another asks in astonishment, "What is real?"

Well, what is? What is real in the shadowy engagement,
not only between two agonists, but between their fantasies
and their physical entanglement, where the inner stage is a bed
now fresh as green balsam tips, now soaking in sweat?

You are, for one thing. What gives coherence to the action
is you at its centre, deft, skillful, affectionate, a creature
of fantasies (like me!), but able to make our different fantasies
so clasp and intertwine that they bind us closer together.

Gross as they may be, or of gossamer fineness, the stuff
of our dreams, you're never afraid of them. You play to them
like a snake-charmer, handling them proudly in their speckled
sinuous glory as though they too were sent by a god.

You know all about the ballets and masques at court,
masques interspersed with antimasques with ballets of courtiers
followed by ballets of beasts, at the pleasure of princes.
But you never forget that what matters most is the moment

when the mist of our fantasies (which are easier to manage
here where the actors are their own directors, and where roles
can be tossed back and forth freely) is suddenly burned off
in the great lion glare of naked carnality, and when

your eyes (like mine!) are drilled right down to the soul,
the sovereign self is surrendered, and each offers the other
not only strength, secrecy, repose, but whatever it knows
of godhead, that godhead that burns in your thighs like a bush.

1990

On a Path Behind the Hotel

He has picked himself up again and again
after being knocked down more times than
he cares to remember. And now here he is
idling along the pathway behind the hotel
high above the lift-locks that lead to the canal.
It's summer, and he's wearing a torn straw-hat,
and carrying a fishing-rod as if he'd just
climbed up after trying his luck in the river.

But nothing is simple behind those candid eyes.
Does it show? he is wondering. His questions are legion.
Is it a blessing of sorts or will it spoil everything?
How large is the band of those who are like him?
Have there been times and places where things
were different? He doesn't know how to answer.

Or to define what it is that separates the courage
he needs from the cowardice with which he's been branded.

He is waiting for someone. But who? That too
is concealed from him. It might be a sadist
or brother, a pilgrim or dissolute wanderer,
a face now muffled in weeping or clouded in beauty.
If only there were a voice from a cloud to tell him
that Aeschylus, who was proud to have fought at Marathon
(so proud that he had it carved on his tombstone),
had no doubt that Achilles and Patroclus were lovers.

2004 (c. 1995)

Willow Trees, By Killarney Channel

Green willow leaves reach sinuously down like fingers
to fashion a green silk pavilion for lovers to sport in

as, earlier, catkins had silkily burdened the branches
with a soft flicker and flowering, burgeoning downwards

like light through a window on lovers undressing, speckling
their hummocks and hollows of nakedness, stippling them

as they advance, retreat, now shyly, now boldly, but never
with shame, or with anything other than compassionate lust,

till, overhead, what is created is a heavenly canopy,
something that is common and royal, sacred but natural.

There is room here for amorous couplings. And for the thin
wing-beats of butterflies, airy, ethereal, ephemeral,

within a green pleasance bathed in a tented transparency,
where sun mottled with shade calls out to androgynous angels.

But this is a trope that can move either forward or back
(and either languidly or strenuously from one side to another).

Your fingers as they search down the curves of my thighs, make
me remember green willow leaves and the light falling through them.

Your tongue as it ripples from side to side makes me think
of the sough of willow branches as they sigh in the wind,

of their taut springiness, of the strength of their pliancy,
of their relaxed stalwartness seemingly made for serious play.

It's from play of that kind that our union is formed, white-hot
and sacred between us, to burn at the core of our world,

while far at its outskirts torchlight carries the flame
through dark nerves and sinews, extending the bonfire light

till the flame dies down. And then blue skies. And a sea-blue calm
that now washes everywhere, to mirror the sky-blue of heaven.

2004 (c. 1995)

Patrick Anderson, 1915–1979

Edward Drew

Edward Drew was innocent
As soft and pink as a roll of lint,
    He never explored tunnels
    Or dirtied his grey flannels.

On his twenty-first birthday he was given
A parcel of snow, undriven,
    A bunch of crocuses and violets
    And some Abdullah cigarettes.

He never married. He never squandered
His strength. He never blundered;
    But with mild eyes, mild as a cow's,
    Stared at medical drawings, and wondered.

1942

Montreal

Under my head domed like a theatre
I walked by houses spilling their look and their dark
between great trees on the boulevards of summer,
and on my stage the frightened boy uttered his tedious soliloquy
while my other hero sang of joy like a tenor:
then from the bogus façade of my middle class face
my talent-scout glance was impresario
of children playing in alleys I could not follow
for puberty sprouted between: of men and women
seen in my magic mirror and the glass of class.
I belonged to the theatre, I knew, and also this:
that love and fear were equally booked at my house.

Thus I passed lovers in the boom of love
who drew two curtains across the window of sorrow:
one told me much was changed and many were gone

and life was raw and rude to pouring boys—
another said, Look! I looked, and saw the city
guarded by planes which in true flight's perversion
curse from the praying blue, their height a dart.
I saw the mothers' sons in a rage of Asia
move the jungle salient without the tourist's usual smile
to crouch by a palm in a dream of technicolour
with the newsreel and the movie at last made one.
Then I came to the abstract place: a red brick wall
guillotined with shadow a square of added dust—
O the human clasp had shrunk from its finger-nails,
the head was drowned below antennae-aerials!
Suddenly a radio blared like a paper flower
in a bowl of brass. Against one wall I saw,
almost invisible, the sandy soldier
through whose wounded face a stone face was trying to form.

I climbed the mountain into that Sunday air
to which rising slowly from aquarium slum
on Sundays only the double people come—
I saw the terraces of class run down to our nationhood
by river and railway: the broad street of the Jews
lay open between the twisted fascist alleys
and the holy rolling negroes rolled in unholy smoke
beyond the tracks: I saw quarter and counter quarter
in block and check—O French and English
Jew and not Jew, artist and public,
child, parent, rich, poor, where the bully of stone
whacked in the cringing wood. Yes there I stood
where sunlight taught in the tree, hearing the immense cultural silence
float up through the birds singing like English Verse:
and tasting a bird's voice in its wooden spoon
I heard the silence about pain, the ambiguous human silence,
while Jerusalem rang in the green—silence so great
one could hear the nightingale and then Keats' cough in answer.

Then thought I of a different silence, wired for sound,
for artists' variations on the workers' steady chorus,
when the heart adjusts the lovers show listening love,
and the trumpets are long cars in the people's armies.

1942

Rink

Here I am drifting, darkness in my heels,
while out of little winds they crouch and prey,
handling their sticks across these frozen zones
where I am gliding, twilight in my skates

on tallow ice and murky shallowness—
and they are furious, candles in their heels,
braggart and target from the lovely circles
they build and kill across their yellow zones

spurting a dirty powder from their skates—
how distant like a dying of the day
that saffron placard of Sweet Caporals
blurs in the rafters of this gloomy barn

where yellow echoes break from schoolboys' yells—
I whistle like a bird to mark half time—
the kids stretch out and freeze their sweaty curls
but one goes skidding with the female goal.

Rubbery puck is whipped against the boards:
begin again, again. My whistle pares
the twilight with the muscle of a bird—
the afternoon, the game, the cold seems endless.

And I am master adult and alone,
inexpert, tragic and responsible,
make a mystique of motion like a swan
or lose myself in loving the description,

in which some meaning meets me on these zones,
where they sweep by with murder in their heels,
skating on history and on young men
towards the female goal and all the girls.

1945

Drinker

Loping and sloped with heat, face thatched and red,
hating his engine boots spraying mechanical pebbles
he slowly comes through the white blocked light to the fountain:
his shirt clinging about him wet and rose
hangs heavily in front with his chest's sour bracket.

He crouches then: he turns with a serious hand
the little wheel: hangs, freckles over the jet
rising in a crush of water towards his burning mouth:
his eyes are wide and grave, his act seems private,
and as his hand spreads on the green stained stone
his massive working throat is a column of pure love.

He tastes with the iron pipe the very roots of water
spreading under the ground, which in multitudinous dirt
and infinite threaded dark are purified—
he draws the long stalk of water up between his lips
and in his sandy mouth there bursts its melting flower.

1945

Armaments Worker

Mechanic drunk with grease wearing your work
standing amongst machines in the shaking factory
turning the valve drawing the lever over your breast
lying in the noonhour flat on your back at rest—

and quietly on concrete amongst great machines
forging the weapons to reclaim a landscape,
whose green again will be a people's corn
when guns uncover evening—

work here in cities only half awake,
quicken the anger and increase the pace,
look hard as comrade in your human strength
and soft as love on iron and its peace.

1946

Boy in a Russian Blouse

First, twelve year old with the mouse fringe, you wear that blouse
slippery with boyhood and a cold grace
which looser than your body and wrinkling with light
reminds me of the neutral texture of water
and is neither male nor female, neither a shirt nor a dress.

Its ruffles, Timofyey, about you though stricter at your waist
with almost breasts maybe or a panic shiver
but for the rest you have how strangely the big boots
that leather you under with a heavy walk—
though even these have high heels and sharp toes for the dancer.

And when you stamp on the floor it is not only your eyes
under the fringe, or the green blouse so careless
simple subtle with light that I notice,
but how you shoot out and strut your legs,
how you stand and are strapping, like an acrobat.

Why does the icy silence that folds your torso
go with the making bold of the legs, the crude
hand snap? And why, Timofyey,
are you so manic like this and so much a bride
so awkwardly human, O brutal and half-a-girl?

1946

The Candles: Dorchester Street

Because it was so hot you took off your shirt
but no one notices how the light came alive:
no one talking in the small room,
by the window, of this and that,
the war, the summer and the great heat
noticed how, with your blue shirt tossed aside,
you became a lamp. Except for the soft
and crazy moths who flew around you
and touched the flames of your skin in their play,

dizzying themselves about
your angular shoulders and deep heart
while in your casual drift you brushed them away.

I tell you I have noticed
the same thing happen when I write
late, on these sultry summer nights.
It seems my paper becomes their candle
on which a poem hardly makes a shadow;
they flock to it with gentle vehemence
and land upon it, as a thing of light.

1953

Spiv Song

Where are you going, my spiv, my wide boy
down what grey streets will you shake your hair,
what gutters shall know the flap of your trousers
and your loud checked coat, O my young despair?

Have you been in a blind pig over whiskey
where bedbugs spot the discoloured walls,
did you play barbotte and lose all your money
or backroom billiards with yellowed balls?

It's midnight now and the sky is dusty,
the police are going their rounds in the square,
the coffee is cold and the chromium greasy
and the last bus leaves, O my young despair.

Don't you just hate our personal questions
with your "Take me easy and leave me light,"
with your meeting your friends in every direction
—and sucking in private the thumb of guilt.

There are plenty of friends, my man, my monster,
for a Ganymede kid and a Houseman lad
and plenty more you would hate to discover
what you do for a living, my spiv, my id.

And isn't it awkward, their smiles so friendly,
their voices so bright as they ask where you work:
a job in a store, or driving a taxi,
or baseball still in the sunlit park?

O why do you sit in the nightclub so sulky,
why so dramatic breaking the glass:
you've heard again that your mother is dying?
You think that you've caught a social disease?

Your looks are black, my spiv, my wide boy,
will you jump from the bridge to the end of the world
and break on the ice, my pleasure, my puppy,
your forehead so hot and your kisses so cold?

What desperate plan is this job that you talk of—
we'll read tomorrow what happens tonight...?
and where are you off to, my son, my shadow,
with the bill unpaid, as the door swings shut?

1953

Y.M.C.A. Montreal

The swimming-bath smells of
chemicals
its surface balances
in a chequered network of light
yellowgreen jellies
bouncing and slopping up against the tiles

and the locker-room too is tiled and
clinical

where folding and hanging up the coarse collapsed
shapes of themselves,
trembling not shivering, much slighter in white

underwear the boys undress. Naked their bodies

sweat shadows of flesh
as flesh, disguised in itself

        I see
their skins misty and tremulous
like substances long packed
away in the dark
danked yellows, tied up creased pinks.

Too many absent-minded inches to touch
in more evasions than following
hand-spans
or the fingers' calculus
can warm from abstraction
"Boys put that sort of thing right out of their minds"
they loom up taller than the longest stroke.

Even our literature cannot embrace
and comfort them
we have few poems for naked sixteen-year-old boys

falling headlong through the doorways of themselves
hanging back loitering
on a luminous threshold
or like runners breasting the rope winning and
                                        fainting

in their cold scorn I know they are puritans
I know they keep bleak
the lyrical theories sketched by their long bones

or big realistic feet. They have to
run throw themselves away
dive and be hidden again
in the big pool in water and horseplay

where even their magnified voices
in which a hero might be trying to speak
are muffled by echoes.

1976

Advice to Visitors

What I suggest is you are first
taken round the garden to be divorced
from your motorist's arrogance, your self-indulgence
in the loose mysticism of a dreamed distance,
experiencing with the speed's passion
the hills to be moulded, the villages overtaken,
trees pouring towards you, barred and dark, a farm
adored and discarded, swinging away from your horn
until it is only the weather-filled sky you have raced
when you stop for a map and it strips the entire East.

I should prefer you to shorten your stride
and keep your face quiet as a door and wait inside
its formal shining; or move no faster
than in a gallery between Old Master and Old Master
overwhelming your shadowy image; or sensing danger
imagine a landmine in every bed and border
where the splash of dew-rolling leaves discloses
bees at their fiery work and other fuses
while the paths too have ankle-snatching snares
being difficult to find, overgrown with flowers
(the lilies lurching out on their brittle stems,
the disorderly catmint, the honeysuckle's whims)
so that you are soon forced to learn
distance had better be measured between fern and fern,
damsons allowed their cave, an entirely new view
be five yards of bumpy grass behind the bamboo,
for everything is small, with the smallness growing,
and most planned, designed and, through that, overflowing.
Four bits of lawn, three terraces—who passes
the huge domed veronica and the moss roses
as though his one idea was to outflank
all this for the orchard and the septic tank,
let that wobbling concrete lid confound his greed,
or a bombardment of broom pod and euphorbia seed.

The point is to call in your vision
to a composed place; you may call it the prison

that art makes with its balancing and shaping
except that the prisoners are all everywhere escaping
into the eternity of their summer gesture.

Only then, having learned good manners, you may enter
the house. It is very small. Its walls are thin
lath and plaster which gleams, flakes in the west rain,
its joints woodwormed, its tiles cracked and mossed,
its windows leaky. It is so easily crossed
from front door to back or side to side
the insensitive scarcely know they have been inside
a house, let alone a life. As for atmosphere
it has none: no period charm. It is simply there
rigid and plain like the box that children draw
to stand for home on sheets of cartridge paper
with two windows below and three above. Its stance
is that of a theorem, it has to prove its existence
and is far too preoccupied to be more than plan
or Platonic echo. The most it can do is pure line
just holding against decay, putting first things first.
I stood in Euclid, it seemed, and outstared the waste
my first weeks here as I mixed the paint and paste
for terracotta walls and bull's-blood doors
while it rumbled my alien footsteps under its floors.
I'd have liked more mystery but it cleared the ground
for my own ideas to play with gold and be grand:
my rickety antiques to unsheathe their light,
my carvings clinch, my books rise winter-bright,
Italy on one wall, elsewhere a glance
from classic Greece to classic-loving France,
as bibelots theatrically displayed
both crowded space and had it amplified.
Not less now would I ask you to observe
the pictured porcelain, the swirl and curve
of reliquary bust or Chinese dragon
than when within some corner of the garden
you watched a plant continually renew
its thrust and poise as gently it outgrew
your faltering glance till time burned off like dew.

Finally I suggest that *gemütlich* stamps and shouts
be countermanded—and please do not throw your coats
just anywhere that occurs to you or dribble
your bags and baskets as though this were a youth hostel
or a site for a picnic. Lighting your cigarettes
and stretching your legs, remember to pay your respects
to my shadowy self who on an objective plinth
of books and pictures revolves the mind's labyrinth
and might, if encouraged enough, actually dare
to believe he existed too. I think three or four
is the maximum number. I have to study each guest,
awarding marks for looks, scholarship, taste,
sweetness of manner (this lonely lust takes fright
at the merciless clarity of a tête-à-tête,
aesthetic disaster, roses turning to ash).
Or two? A pair on the conversational leash
run smoother, mutually confirm attention
to the confession mixed up with the lesson
I'm liable to give; they can't afford
like groups to look away in bits and be bored.
But of course ultimately one still thinks of one,
the fabulous stranger, adept at communion,
easiest to show around, scaled to a space
so small its surest freedom's an embrace,
who might glance, then know, and talking less and less
look through the silence to the second face.

1977

Brion Gysin, 1916–1986

from **I Am That I Am**

I AM THAT I AM
AM I THAT I AM
I THAT AM I AM
THAT I AM I AM
AM THAT I I AM
THAT AM I I AM
I AM I THAT AM
AM I I THAT AM
I I AM THAT AM
AM I I THAT AM
I AM I THAT AM
I THAT I AM AM
THAT I I AM AM
I I THAT AM AM
I AM AM THAT I
AM I AM THAT I
I AM AM THAT I
AM I AM THAT I
AM AM I THAT I
AM AM I THAT I
I THAT AM AM I
THAT I AM AM I
I AM THAT AM I
AM I THAT AM I
THAT AM I AM I

I I THAT AM AM
THAT I I AM AM
I THAT I AM AM
AM THAT I I AM
THAT AM I I AM
AM I THAT I AM
I AM THAT I AM
THAT I AM I AM
I THAT AM I AM
I AM THAT AM I
I THAT AM AM I
THAT I AM AM I
AM THAT I AM I
THAT AM I AM I
AM AM I I THAT
I AM AM I THAT
AM I AM I THAT
I THAT I AM AM
THAT I I AM AM
I I THAT AM AM
I I THAT AM AM
THAT I I AM AM
I THAT I AM AM
I THAT AM I AM
THAT I AM I AM

1959

Minutes to Go

the hallucinated have come to tell you that yr utilities
are being shut off   dreams monitored   thought directed
sex is shutting down everywhere   you are being sent

all words are taped   agents everywhere
marking down the live ones   to exterminate

they are turning out the lights

no   they are not evil   not the devil   but men
on a mission   with a spot of work to do

this   dear friends   they intend to do on you

you have been offered a choice   between liberty and
freedom   and   No!   you cannot have both

the next step   is everyone into space   but it has been
a long dull wait   since the last tower of babel
that first derisive visit of the   paraclete

let's not hear that noise again   and again

that may well be   the last word   anywhere

this is not the beginning   in the beginning was the word
the word has been in for a too   long time
just in the word and   the word in you

we are out
you are in

we have come to let you out

here and now we will show you   what you can do
with and to
the word

the words
any word
all the words

Pick a book   any book   cut it up
cut it up
prose
poems
newspapers
magazines
the bible
the koran
the book of moroni
la-tzu
confucius
the bhagavad gita
anything
letters
business correspondence
ads
all the words

slice down the middle   dice into sections
according to taste
chop in some bible   pour on some Madison Avenue
prose
shuffle like cards   toss like confetti
taste it like piping hot   alphabet soup

pass yr friends' letters   yr office carbons
through any such sieve   as you may find or invent

you will soon see   just what they really are
saying   this is the terminal method for
finding the truth

piece together a masterpiece   a week
use better materials   more highly charged words

there is no longer a need   to drum up a season of
geniuses   be your own agent   until we deliver
the machine   in commercially reasonable quantities

we wish to announce   that while we esteem
this to be truly   the American Way
we have no commitments   with any government
groups

the writing machine   is for everybody
do it yourself   until the machine comes
here is the system   according to us

1960

from **The Poem of Poems**

whither has my beloved gone?
We shall not dwell forever in these golden sands
where we must seek him
although our undivided loves are one
One
Into his garden, to the beds of spices and pale embers
under the ashes
I am my beloved's honey colour
colour of immortal things
the whole grassy earth have I seen gentle beneath the shears
Gentle beneath the shears of last winter's storms
revolt
my love away
terrible let the fields march forth under the scheme of
the harvest sky
Take thine eyes from me they have overcome me
Thy hair is a flock of goats that appear kissing
with golden faces the meadows green
sheep go up from the washing sewn with pale mauve scars
alchemy
and there is not one barren among them
Roses have thorns and silver fountains in the smoke of dreams

thy locks
There are four score queens in the pale eastern sky
straining moon and sun
My dove, the shadow of a great bird falls on my face
He is the only one of his mother
He is the choice one
The dicer, the knuckle bone player the juggler the poet
The daughters saw him and were on his tracks
Yea the queens and the concubines and the man with the falcon
The man with the flute. The man with bees
Look forth in a morning fair as the moon clear as the sun
and terrible as an army
I have halted my horse by the tree of the doves
I went down into a garden of nut trees
and I whistled a note so sweet in the valley
Mine eye and heart are at immortal war
pomegranates budded
or ever I was aware of my soul made me like the chariots
beneath the dove mourning trees
Return   Return   that we may look upon thee
Peace to the dying who have not seen this day
How to divide the conquest of thy sight O prince's daughter
the joints of thy thighs are like jewels
the work of the hands of a cunning workman
thy navel is like a round freshly cracked stone
that wanteth not liquor
or raspberries or the maggots of the palm tree
a heap of wheat with lumps of fossil gum
thy breast like a conch to the ear that are twins
thy neck is as a tower, a sugar loaf
a closet never pierced with crystal eyes
thine head upon thee and the hairs of thine head like purple
the key is held in the gallery
How fair and how pleasant art thou O love
like the fine bread of barley and sesame
is thy stature like to a palm tree
thy breasts like clusters of money changers
I said, I have no precious time for the white worms in the
soil, the bowels thereof
Now also are budding populations under the sheds in front

of the frying vats
and the smell of thy nose like apples
So am I as the rich whose blessed key
like the best wine for my beloved
then bring him to his sweet up locked treasure
the lips of those whom he will not every hour survey
are my beloved's and his desire is towards me
Nor marble nor the gilded monuments of princes
Let us go forth into the fields
Let us lodge in the villages
Sweet love renew thy force in the vineyards
Let us see if the vine flourisheth
Whether the tender grap is here
Like as the waves make toward the pebbled shore will I
lave thee with my loves
so do our minutes hasten to their end
The gates are hung about with all manner of pleasant fruits
New and old which I have laid up for thee, O my beloved
each changing place with that which goes before

1961

Robin Blaser, 1925–

The Borrower

the one loved is
holding a moth
thin, metallic dark
model with a triangular
crest

what's out and secret
spills
the wind dries
moves on

                the interior
of his body
                  red water
with white threads
                              the bone
a ghost of his thigh
                                  pale
blue gut holding the shit

highway

1964

Image Nation 3 (substance

what if the body goes   the sense
of the word which draws amor
in a body his arrows leafless, shining
steel   his meaning in that meeting of
hands, tastes, bitter
filling fountain   if that language goes
whose power drank from the body, gave
the body, gave amor a skin,

an act, the worshipped height higher
than what is left
another amor inescapable pouring, holding
that shape here together   all ways,

born through all the elements, the night
singing sparrows are arrows   I define
the dark correct   allowing that I to appear
naked, an unyielding form of I   acting apart,
but it is Naught   the other is that   unlearned,
this fear and charm of words   O shepherd, his way apart,
flower and youth   *with an arrow offshot*

1964

The Cry of Merlin

out of the blue that moves the curtain
out of the stone that smooths the body

statuesque   that spiritual thing   inside   outside
on and on   over us   out of us   to be

joined sundered the active image
of a man who stepped out   from a cracked egg

the room is unmoved   the lamps burn
only for themselves   the story

seems the whole business the out the taken
the lifted   the lost in the shape

or unfolding   as in the exact moment
the rose opens   for which there is no word

shedding   by a *strange sweetness*

the friends built a city, enormous images
and high thought,   and shed it

like clothing on the floor beside the bed
all these Pacific Slope men came to the sea

as if they just got here by stagecoach
or revved-up Model A with a rumble seat

and made out in the brown grass
which caught in their hair and sweaters,

the tell-tale—the cock swelling
in the mouth fills the throat

the lips tight with the strangeness
the mouths, so far apart, meet

in the air   the space between love's
substance and him   is here recorded

he leans over the loved body
to kiss the belly   blue veins
at the surface   lead the life
he wished to enter   a ghost
river   true and false   as a map
made up to change the boundary

the domestic glares   a circle
that holds within its prickteasers
mindfuckers, and the beloved,
a mix like a movie on television
or two radios, one upstairs and one down,
sending parts and flowers
in another body

here he was caught   the room unmoved
with the lamps out   I think he heard
the tick of the leaves of the plants
drawing together   and the clock
he sticks a triple branch of daphne
into the head of the lady in the shape
of a blue bottle   by the light

of the street-lamps, she shone
and loved lovely,   when she said,
'This is the first time you've given me power in the house.'

1968

Image-Nation 9 (half and half

there are shining masters
when I tell you what they
look like   some of it is
nearly false   their blue hair

but they are not ourselves   they
are equivalents   of action   they
compose forms,   which we hear

sound within a context
as if that action we are
images of   used us
the body becomes an instrument

sometimes the harp pierces the body
and a man only hangs on the strings

I hear the airborne-fire, the dead rebels'
second speech, which follows their live words,
and the rice, and the motorcycles

but public life has fallen asleep
like a secret name   the wrong-reader
will say he has pity for others
where the thought is born in *hatred*
of pity, which is *only feeling*   the action
we are only images of   hates pity
and its *reduction of horror to sentiment*

wordlessness   no thing is so simply
personal   I put my hand out to catch

beauty in the act of   I know no beauty
which is not permanent   not invoked
in splendour   the words are meaningless
until they emerge in the action   they are

images of

I was once a youth,   and I was
a maiden,   a bush, a bird, a fish
with scales that gleam in the ocean

they come from the dark   under
many names   the blue   wind
they are not ourselves,   not even
the moon drawn down   into our
breasts   that we may strike others
with eros   the

body gleamed so   wind
master   *a bone, a ball, a top*
an apple, a mirror, a skein of wool

wind — words   wind — hair   we

have dismembered the earth   and
are born lifeless on the moon   mouths
to the wind

unthought *the many mountains, the many*
cities,   the many houses

I was once   another man's heart
an eagle, a wolf   cloud, smoke,
splash
            psychron   (cloud, refreshing
anapsychsai   (to be refreshed from evil

we have eaten ourselves   luxurious and
careless   I must bathe at the
gates of the city   I must tell you

they have been blue in the heart,
in the wind
I have opened my mouth

they have come from the black-fire
we have stiffened
the terror of earth, as if terror were the only unearthly
thing in our hearts
we have given her *rivers*
of our own salt earth then remains uncanny,
sublime water is fear's movement grief cries
in the air like birds fire is hidden in the imageless
self
the blue hair *the face of gold the clothes*
like snow the blood
is light

zero

enacts it

Jack Clarke's 'we are under image'
rythmos (form's movement) to walk into 'the
primordial always exists' face to face always outside
ourselves the astonishment is
that *it is kosmos*
playing out with one man entheos
they are
the *flowing boundary* taking birth *taking leave*
at the point of the heart a continual
division of halves

for Dennis Wheeler

1974

Image-Nation 14 (the face

O golden flower

the guest of the window   the air
fills with motorcycles   echo and shadows

the *backward-flowing*   astonishment

the wings

the multi-coloured play, as if the years
were one destiny and eros

as if the moth-heart stayed at the real
door-way

the ghost-heart   it is the kind of

daemon he is to become that
governs   entangles   at the edge

of his words,   the laughter

that would bring the world
back
            into the square inch

in the field of the square inch of the
house of the square foot
the house of the square foot is the
face
the field of the square foot is the
face alive
in the middle of the square inch
the SPLENDOUR   moves

a footstep   in the furnace

the traffic hits the house
with its winds   and the house
turns a little as if walking
away to join a movement

or is the house still and a
gigantic footstep creaks on
the narrow blue front-steps

form is alive   it begins as
the *light-flower*

like dry wood
like cooled ashes

where the work begins again
in *the white snow*

the horizon of every form where
he journeys
                    the blue-heart of the centre
of the flower
                         turning like a sun-flower

the mirror in the garden doubles
the garden
                  there and not there
we had stolen the mirror from
the wrecked house next door
over the fence near the willow,
across the heather, the talisman
rose, and the wild-flowers under
the blue back-steps

in the white-heart

O

1974

The Pause

out and wondrous, there, where
I found them someone wanders,
pauses 'O, it was you, was it!'

who was it said, 'only the belovèd answers,'
that gardens close and walls limit
because they are paradise and untrue

the wall around heaven is untrue, stings
in all the political ferment where I
found it, topsy-turvy, raggedy-ann of

that deadly plaything, thought, the leading
edge of the process, why will you
try to find yourself finite and sure,

the pleasure-dome, and then excuse
its irrealism by futurity, this
desire-to-live does not stop there

you've got a share of it, only the dis-
missed quality is the momentary
now I see 'you,' now I don't

that is the pleasure of the kingdom, old
vocabulary—replaced by the dictatorship
of a sameness

the big, white ball of thought
with its patent leather evening shoes, tap-
dancers that don't need polish until they've

worn-out like you, I found
them, a radiance, without cause,
like trees, long-life and short-life,

'nothing remains constant,' I tried
with my love to stop them, to fuck

them, but they are the transformation

of everything, rising into other
things   and 'things' are a desire
big as you are

do you know that Copernicus attacked
and Darwin attacked and Freud attacked
our self-love

the transcendent value of the future
mystification, the death of so many,
things do appear in their own terms, changing

I found them in a mist and a glade,
and a stone, and a shattered wind-
shield, driven to the wreckage of one sweet thought

1988

Romance

the opposite of meaning is not
meaninglessness, what do these big
words mean in the panic, well,
panic means heart   before we had
formed this, it was Pan, my dear,
and tufts of plants   before we had
planned or kissed it, before
we had dreamed the leaves and
historical consequences, before the
painted ocean and storms, before
the water everywhere, drunken and
sunned, stopped us, before the
rock of our spirit, before doorsteps
and fountains and fragments, before
cats and dogs and cities, the
endless footsteps, before sweetness
and mountains, before paradise

and walled gardens, before
streets and manufacture, cars
and desire, after stars and
constellations are probable, we
found it

1988

In Remembrance of Matthew Shepard

How sad I am. How sad
this violation of the existential
given and Matthew's song—
another debt of this indecent
century—what is to be said
about this *hideous traffic*
in religion that has taught
blasphemy for centuries
against Jews, blacks, aboriginals,
women, Gypsies, and homosexuals
everywhere. "They" put on Jesus-shoes.
He never wore them.
"Their" *sacrifices to hate and hell.*
There is no more to be said
about God, except the *infinite exposure*
of our finitude that "they" have taught.
Love arrives as a promise.
Every particular love is Love,
dear Matthew. How love shatters
when they stopped your song—
the shatters in which we trust.
Yes, the philosopher said: *The glorious body*
cannot but be the mortal body itself.
What changes are not the things but their limits.
It is as if there hovered over them something
like a halo, a glory. Dear Matthew.

1999

David Watmough, 1926–

Berlin in 1982

A special bar, all glass and glitz, right of the Kurfurstendam,
The breezy ethos that of split Berlins (and the right side of The Wall)
The laughter and the larking of young men roughly the same age.
Uniformly handsome, middle class and camp, as I recall.

A gay bar, then, and frenetic—nothing unusual about that.
Until one's roving glance no longer hungrily on track,
Compassion moved between the stools as hope turned into dread.
For they weren't arms held up to buy—but fleshly fins instead.

Thalidomide, malforming drug, behind these substitutes for hands.
Intended first to shoehorn birth, and safeguard sexual pangs.
It brought a harvest of misshapen forms to many lands.
An irony, this Berlin crop, bought with a German pharmaceutical brand.

More than ironic, though, among the merry cripples in the bar I saw,
Their laughter and their beauty as they sucked their drinks through straw.

2003

John Grube, 1930–

Forgiveness, a Meditation

Trying to put yourself together
you reach back in time, to the
Grade Eight graduation when
someone yelled 'faggot' at you

onstage. You calmly continued,
red-faced. To the fight with the
schoolyard bully. Blood-stained
but getting upright slowly again.

To the Christian camp that was
supposed to make you like girls.
To your religious grandmother
locked tight into the Apocalypse.

You reach back to your years
on the street, bringing pleasure to
older men, never surrendering
to its seductive culture of easy

money, drugs, shame. Proud of
your own therapeutic work, a
little self-centred, you agreed to
visit your folks and family again.

Your uncle and father went with
you to see your grandmother,
suddenly your dad told her that
you were a male prostitute, and

laughed, your own dad shaming
you again in public, hoping to
drive a wedge between you and
your apocalyptic grandmother.

As she cleared the table, she said
when she was young, men took her
out to dinner, to dance, paid for it.
Was that so different? Her words

offered support and true Christian
understanding. The word ‘forgive’
came into your vocabulary for the
first time. Grandmothers still rule.

2000

Jean Basile, 1932–1992

Give Only What We Can

Who was the master who was the student

From the start our lessons
flowed from our fingers, a natural river

You owe me all I learnt from you

Ambiguity

Deceptive deceiving
I see suddenly appear
helmeted booted
looking proud
by your side like Minerva's
this man young and white
that we call war
quick he travels the road
separating us
we were fused to one another
emerging from you
I can feel him enter me
resurfacing later
fortified by my side
nourished by my heat

A lie

Winged despair lifting me

This little death I feel
each time I see you
laughable
and more fatal still
and more explicit than theirs

Without reason

And I, resting in your head
like a gothic Lazarus
in his coffin of lace

Or else

1965 *Translated by Jonathan Kaplansky*

A Rather Sentimental Excursion

Careful not to disturb the surrounding silence
cautiously I explore the avenues
where I pass
wandering like white shadows
reversed negatives of a fabulous film
the army of those I loved

of those I will perhaps love

Very difficult to recognize them

They all have the same faces

Their hands touching me as they pass
are like the summer dampness
when night falls near a lake

Myself a black ghost
and more silent than they are
moved yet troubled

I surprise myself hoping
that one of them will explode
like a firecracker
that this jarring noise will bring me back to life
and that their flight
will be a kind of chaos at which I would smile
if I could

1965 *Translated by Jonathan Kaplansky*

George Stanley, 1934–

Achilles Poem

for Armando

I thought of Achilles,
trying to get at the blood, where it is all
shadow. The life

Odysseus, to whom Death is another place,
like Phaeacia, not letting
too many of them come close at once

trying to get at the blood
The arteries and veins

the jut of the chin and the fire of eyes
beyond the trench,
wanting.

On the hill, at
11 o'clock, the Searchlight Market closed.
No more ice cream from Swensen's, no more
chilled wine.

Where the "E" car ran, oh
fifteen years ago, when I was a kid,
turned left at Larkin and right again at
Vallejo, to miss the hill. Where Fran lives now.
It seems strange
a streetcar ever ran there,
iron-grey, maroon trim, one door in the middle

I told you all this when I said
it was something else that made me
freeze with terror of the dark,
not the loss
you knew. You said, "Of course."
The hill
tilts me, nightly.

Stars I can see from Union & Leavenworth
high in the sky. They make me think—
It's later than I think. But when I get to Columbus,
they aren't risen yet, they're sunk behind
Telegraph Hill, it's only 12:30.

Cut the throat of the lamb, it flows in the trench. "Baa,"
lambie-pie.

                    The streetcar, in an early dream,
a "K" or "L," in the tunnel
turned off suddenly to the left
or right on a new route,
emerged into an underground cavern,
a new world! where it streaked
past lights, and trees—like a model train layout.
This place of dim expectancy
brightened gradually. It wasn't the sun

it was Dawn in the world where I sleep.
But I woke as a child and I wake as a man
to a familiar-ness.
A room.

Oct. 18. I want all my love healed.
I want this in! The heartache stilled

(Later) The day. When it seems all these sorts
aren't being played out, sliding downhill.

Oct. 20. I brood over giving, receiving
imagined slights.
Bill says, "Don't call up on the telephone
      and apologize—live with it."
I wonder how these lines will be read

A moth flying around the lamp
that shines through its grey wings

Oct. 21. The full moon rose
with the clearest face I've ever seen.

            I had had all those thoughts about Death,
suffered from them, told them to you
in the bar that night, Love
and my sense of humour
you said were evolutionary. Then grew proud of them
(on the hill, in the other direction—no longer needing
to act out of reasons or power or fame. Love
be my Master (Richard Burton as Anthony) Incident
And
woke up again.

                        and the bower-bird
builds,
in Australia,
plants
          stems
in the ground

around a tree
          that keep on growing
and arch, to form his roof.
and a lawn,
tuft by tuft,
          where we look to find something
          when it is no longer lost
As I said, I
                        saw the moon

(Later) The days are still,
autumn grey, with heat of breath
A sighing, in and out

Oct. 28. Waking up this morning, I thought
It wouldn't be so bad to die, drowsily,
at the end of life. Last night I saw
ivy, rain-spattered, in the alley outside the Spaghetti Factory,
the big white veins standing out.

Manger says you can tell a man's age
even if his face is smooth as a boy's
by his veins. On the backs of his hands
and wrists.

Nov. 6. We know the body is immortal, but the spirit dies.

Nov. 8. Withdrawing from the feast, Achilles doesn't see
Patroclus crawling out of his little hole.

Robin wrote: "It won't be complete darkness because there
isn't any. One thing will stop and that's this
overweening pride in the peacock flesh."

Ajax stands stock still,
won't answer Odysseus' relentless questioning.

rain on Filbert St., on the steps
leading down into the stars.   The

Joy of each thing to be utter,
not frittered away in its connection to other parts

Monday no more than Tuesday,
dying-day, lying-day,
this day in the rain.

A poem like a hunk of conglomerate.

Can we and it live in this year?
but in the stream-bed, untimately dislodgeable.
The streams of Time, like one of the freshets on the Sierra,
a trickle in summer, but now, November, with the rains starting,
swelling, foaming over the little dams

Patroclus in Paul's painting
lunges forward, like he does in the Sixteenth book of the Iliad,

It is existence in reverse, Beauty and Youth

returning, refreshening the Source. It
takes place in absolute quiet, and Hector
and even Apollo seem like cops next to him.

Here in the stream-bed.

1968

After Verlaine
(Vers pour être calomnié)

for Scott

At 4 A.M. I saw you sleeping
Your naked body in the narrow bed
And I saw—looking for the meaning—
I saw how hopeless all is here on earth.

Life itself is such a fragile process
The mind a flower that is falling apart—
Oh, when I think so I think I am going crazy!
Sleep on, I—Fear keeps me awake, thinking

Passionate sadness to love you—you can do nothing—
You will go breathing then as you breathe now
Oh look closed that death will then set so

Oh mouth, smiling in dreams, next to mine
I hear eternal unloving laughter—
Wake, and tell me there is another life!

1974

The Stick

My father stole my cock from me.
He did it with a look.
He tried to put it back

many, many times.
His eyes almost teared.
He said to me, "There were things
I could have done better."

The night he died
I said "Good night,"
& he smiled sweetly.
Such little things:

a look, a word, a smile.
And all this while
I have used this stick,
this weapon,
to replace the loss.

Now I know it is not
a sexual organ,
and I lay it down.

1974

Prince Rupert Blues

O Eros, have you finally escaped
me, so that neither in the streets
or the pubs will your prowling, animalistic power,
manifesting itself through the slow smiles,

graceful-awkward demeanor & straightforward talk
of the young guys who are your embodiments,
locate me gladly, on this earth
as if at home, as in a place

where my nature is permitted,
not divided from my behaviour
by abstract precepts & propositions?

Return to me in the night, be
purest sensation, a one night
stand, i won't try to understand.

after Paul Goodman

1983

Naked in New York

Ralph Macchio kissing Eric Stolz on the lips, impulsively,
on the screen at the Hollywood. In the audience loud gasps,
as-if-sickened groans. These goofs must have known
their arrant discourtesy—o not to us,

but to *them*, the two giant heads soft as flags
or luminous clouds above us negotiating
a moment of intimacy—Macchio ruddy-cheeked,
        high on his cupid daring,
Stolz (the beloved) cool, 'vanilla pudding' (Spicer)—

two Harvard boys at an arty New York party,
the straight one mildly pissed at being hit on—wanted,
but gratified by the compliment paid to his beauty
(not cataloguing the gay one's pain at his coolness),

but the guys in the seats, beneath them, the offended,
not wanted—outside this story—outside *Hollywood*—
this Harvard boy, really the actor Eric Stolz,
rich, young, handsome, wanted,
& they not.

A boy being kissed by another boy could tip over the applecart,
all the shiny red apples in the stacks, pyramids, buffed up for sale,
that were once in the dark of the barrel, homophobia high school,
hoping none of us was rotten, no bad apple, no queer,
certain we were all unwanted, none wanted by any of the others—
tipped over, apples rolling, bumping, bouncing in the street, in the

mud,
bruises, kisses (like pool balls), bites,
desire all over the place.

2000

Sex at 62

for R.

His head bent toward me, he demanded,
'Lots of kissing, when I make love'—I could
let my mouth be devoured, I could be held—
back & forth rocking, from being held—
& his arms, his hands, all over my body,
admiring its smoothness, I said, no, yours
is smoother, mine is horny, scaly as a
reptile—it was in these moments of talk,
a gift, a joke, the rocking stopped—
we were falling (through the bed
it seemed, the drugs were wearing off),
into some kind of knowledge, unspoken,
this physical syntax—

I knew him, then all through the morning
as we sucked & kissed & caressed
that it was him, got ahead of
this jerky demanding need to *do*
sex, when it was him there was no choice,
only a face, his rough chin, tousled hair—
then we sat in the Naam eating cereal,
his face & neck white, & the black overcoat.

The fear & the demand, to *make* love,
are still here, but the mythology is gone—
the fear & the demand weaker, & desire
weaker—but that it is him, that is
stronger, that the night lit up from inside

the cab when my arm turned not-
unwilling face to me & the body answered—

he was (is) connected to the night, the city—

The cock is a torch, a light,
that lights up the body & our bodies light up
the night—
                    I can see the end
through him as I kiss him goodbye
at the bus stop, but the face & the words
& that it is him, that shines—

What else—oh that he was Stephen & I
Leopold & the hours were also rooms—
the bar & the taxi on Hastings & the bedroom—
lighted—moving (losing it, touching,
knowing, losing it

towards the mouth, mouth on mouth,
        the mouth warm wet,
dark red the lips around, the dots
of beard, the eyes that would suddenly
open to see me & seductively close,
        deluxe,
the lighted-up minutes, desire breaking
through fixations, making me
glad I'm old, glad they don't hold

no more, letting him, body against mine,
turning & turning over—but going
too fast—doing too much too fast—not
loving the time, slower, better next time

never get any closer

2000

Veracruz

In Veracruz, city of breezes & sailors & loud birds,
an old man, I walked the Malecón by the sea,

and I thought of my father, who when a young man
had walked the Malecón in Havana, dreaming of Brazil,

and I wished he had gone to Brazil
& learned magic,

and I wished my father had come back to San Francisco
armed with Brazilian magic, & that he had married
not my mother, but her brother, whom he truly loved.

I wish my father had, like Tiresias, changed himself into a
  woman,
& that he had been impregnated by my uncle & given birth to me
  as a girl.

I wish that I had grown up in San Francisco as a girl,
A tall, serious girl,
& that eventually I had come to Veracruz,
& walking on the Malecón, I had met a sailor,
a Mexican sailor or a sailor from some other country—
    maybe a Brazilian sailor,
& that he had married me & I had become pregnant
    by him,
so that I could give birth at last to my son—the boy
    I love.

2000

Daryl Hine, 1936–

Lines On a Platonic Friendship

Virtue was the sunset creeping in the grass
Or fireworks supplied with paradise;
But surely the day has come and gone,
Like regal chestnuts burning in the ice,
When you could hold my face in the burning-glass
And flash a hole to China through my flesh.

You will search the skies to bring me down
Because I shall escape to other suns
Reflected in a geographic calm.
It seems to me your love was like a gun
That could break into the blind, myself,
With a racket like a hunter falling down,
Showing us how to capture through the trees
Palaces to house the widowed fox
And Captain Courage dead among the phlox.

Whenever I wished we used to talk of vice,
Holding his chessmen balanced in the glass
Or suddenly illuminating flesh,
While a bee for beauty boomed behind the grove
Exploding comments on the world of love
Above a hill that shone like bone,
Not as you would think, white and smooth,
But a mangled affair of feathers, guts and blood
In the wide and waveless waters of the wood.

The sun will set among these sacred pits
Filled with gillyflowers and with cats,
Rephrasing silence till the silence fits.
Sleepers will wake upon a precipice,
Their beardless faces sunburnt by the glass,
Guides or strangers in my place.
And you, whom virtue beautifies no more,
Where the print ends like a wave upon the page

Will indicate a comment in the margin:
"Love's a shadow like a current in the garden."

1954

The Wound

Tomorrow will the wound be quickly healed,
Or mutual. You will then be well,
Or we united by a common ill,
Division from the womb be reconciled.
But see how slow it bleeds!
Beside the heaving impasse of the boar,
Whose tusks he once preferred to Eros' reeds,
Under Venus' care Adonis bleeds
Of the wound he suffered at the kill.
See how she bends above him still
And takes what he would not bestow before!

In a while the bleeding slowly stops:
For the time being you are cured and whole.
For that duration who will comfort me?
We profit from each other's injury,
We change with wounding, wounded are transformed.
The oriole, they say, sings best when blind;
For ostentation is the peacock penned,
And everyone knows about the chrysalis,
That time's limp is his aggrandisement.

The hurt you entertained, you say,
Was like the mark an arrow leaves in exit:
Round and not too large, contagion's portal.
The target that the arrow makes is joy.
My own mutilation as a fiction
I sustained, I thought alone, for weeks,
Until by habit turned in your direction,
I felt the shared blood running down your cheeks.

1956

Sestina Contra Naturam

Who would ever suspect there were so many vices,
A tribute, I think, to the imagination
Of some who, in these abominable Cities,
Ill-famed for unimaginable perversion,
Inhibited only by the limitations by their bodies,
Could put those bodies to such various uses?

Many, accused of unusual abuses
Contrary to nature; while indulging phantom vices
In the lupanars of the imagination,
Have so far escaped the same fate as the Cities
Of the Plain, rebuked for innocent perversion
Through the spirit's envy of unthinking bodies.

In view of the known misuse of nobodies
One must confess no bodies have no uses
Except as diabolical devices
To indulge seraphic imagination
Not content with negative capacities
Or paraphilias in their paper version

That make a metaphysics of a perversion
Of the physical science of foreign bodies,
Their experimental uses and excuses
And ultimately unimaginative vices.
Love is the faculty of the imagination
That theoretically debauches cities.

For heaven's sake have pity on such cities,
And pardon that omniscient perversion
That contradicts its own created bodies,
Which are the chosen instruments grace uses,
Alchemically reforming virtues from their vices
To refurbish a heaven of the imagination.

O where is that paradise, imagination,
First and least corruptible of cities,
If not in the heavenly kingdom of perversion

Where angels have no sexes and no bodies,
Speech no words and innocence no uses?
None enter there who do not know their vices.

Number your vices in imagination:
Would they teach whole cities of perversion?
Forgive us our bodies, forgive us our bodies' uses.

1961

Summer Afternoon

Emerging from the naked labyrinth
Into the golden armour of the day,
Glittering with salt, a wrestler
With the sun in his fierce palaestra,
Every drop an angel and a man,
Adept at the being that becomes a god,
You pause before the simple backdrop, look
And listen not to the abstract ocean but to me.

At our backs the breakers serially
Beat a tattoo upon the flat-bellied beach;
In our faces the minutes wait to strike and yawn,
And now the afternoon is nearly gone.
Meanwhile we sit absorbed and precious to each
Other, for the time being where and who we want to be.

1968

A Visit

Le bonheur quel ennui! Mais l'ennui, quel bonheur!

With you the days were scarcely three hours long
Like winter days within the arctic circle
On which a brief and splendid solace shone:
What did we do on which? Let's see, on Monday

We went out, on Tuesday we stayed home
Before the imaginary fire, and read.
From time to time the cat got up and stretched and settled
On a fresh lap, encouraged by our anatomy
To resume the briefly interrupted nap
That is a cat's life. One of us turned a page.

How slow, how infinitely gentle then
Seemed to us the clumsy flight of time,
Like one of those birds, barnyard or extinct,
That flap from branch to branch but cannot really fly.
Each tick of the clock was noticed, weighed
Like a pulse beat at its proper value.
Thus in no time it was dinner time
And, ah soon after, time to go to bed.

Now I can't remember what we read
Or said, or even how it felt
To have you here, near, within sight and hearing,
Neglected as a treasure is neglected
By its owner, secure in its possession.
Time's deliberate pace, too, was deceptive
For even then in retrospect it flew.

What of the other days, for there were several
Sped in a variety of ways,
Spent like unreplenished capital
To the present starvation of the senses?
It is painful to remember every morning,
Mornings too intimate almost to record,
Rich and various as a paisley scarf:
You emerging towelled from the bedroom,
And us later, together in the shower, masked
In soap, slippery, lascivious as fish.
Too intimate, and yet I keep a record
Of what we did and how and when and where.
Friday you lay back upon the sofa,
Sunday I awoke within your arms,
Thursday you bestrode me like a statue,
And it is as if in all of our embraces
The universal was made personal.

Now: now I need to stop and think a minute.
What have I left out? Oh, everything.
It is like looking at a map of, or seeing from the air,
A neighbourhood where once one was at home;
Like reading a menu, after, of a meal:
Is it, or in what sense was it, real?

Poets must have something else to write of
Than their own tragic thoughts and epic feelings.
But what? Will a comic interruption do?
The scramble, worthy of a bedroom farce,
When the delivery boy rang the bell, the sudden
Sinister breakdown of the telephone,
Which now, like my anxiety, seems funny.
Or your silent tears? The stories of the service
In which you shone with an ironic virtue
Maladroit, touchingly inferior, and wise?

The very muchness of the world disgusts me
Some times, when it comes between us two,
And suddenly I lose all appetite.
At others it is all we have together:
Like the moments on the bus, to me terrific
(You never guessed with what courage taken)
Before we said goodbye again. You proved then
How much can be included in a look,
When the fleeting sun illuminated
As it set the shining fancy of your flesh.

1968

Point Grey

Brought up as I was to ask of the weather
Whether it was fair or overcast,
Here, at least, it is a pretty morning,
The first fine day as I am told in months.
I took a path that led down to the beach,
Reflecting as I went on landscape, sex and weather.

I met a welcome wonderful enough
To exorcise the educated ghost
Within me. No, this country is not haunted,
Only the rain makes spectres of the mountains.

There they are, and there somehow is the problem
Not exactly of freedom or of generation
But just of living and the pain it causes.
Sometimes I think the air we breathe is mortal
And dies, trapped, in our unfeeling lungs.

Not too distant the mountains and the morning
Dropped their dim approval on the gesture
With which enthralled I greeted all this grandeur.
Beside the path, half buried in the bracken,
Stood a long-abandoned concrete bunker,
A little temple of lust, its rough walls covered
With religious frieze and votary inscription.

Personally I know no one who doesn't suffer
Some sore of guilt, and mostly bedsores, too,
Those that come from itching where it scratches
And that dangerous sympathy called prurience.
But all about release and absolution
Lie, in the waves that lap the dirty shingle
And the mountains that rise at hand above the rain.
Though I had forgotten that it could be so simple,
A beauty of sorts is nearly always within reach.

1968

Commonplaces

Places have no memory for faces.
This nowhere landscape like a windy corner,
Not the sort of spot one would have chosen
For a rendezvous, distinct, unpromising,
Metaphysical, featureless, flat, frozen,
Where anyone might feel a foreigner,
Has been somewhere one day none the less.

An accident, perhaps, such as occur
To anybody anywhere like home,
Or a meeting—who cares to recall
Of their first encounter the inauspicious setting?
Everyone, equivocal as we all
Are about sacred places, Mudville, Rome,
Texts whose true reading must remain obscure

And possibly corrupt, a palimpsest
Of names effaced or scarcely legible,
Initials which do not need to be completed,
Transitive four letter verbs that sing.
Thus literature is phrase by phrase deleted
As time decides which words are eligible
For honour, and erases all the rest.

1975

What's His Face

The god that is leaving me perhaps has left
Already. Bereft of his presence I breathe lighter.
What was his name? Apollo, Eros, Zeus,
As he hinted? Or one of their attendants?
By turns appalling, erotic, zoomorphic,
He might have been some petty local demon,
His divinity unrecognized by the tribe next door,
His attributes demonic to a fault,
Ithyphallic, pushy, mischievous,

Totally undependable, adept
At deceit while he denied he led me on.
Impalpable, incomprehensible,
He appeared in the flesh—what? half-a-dozen times?
Smiling his cryptic, unforgiving smile,
Saying little, glimpsed in intervals
Of sleep or at a distance, domestic idol
Destructive of peace and quiet. Now he's gone
Life is private again, desecrated, dull,
Without his infrequent fraudulent manifestations,
Without his unconvincing oracles.
His image, which was cast in terra cotta
And clumsily, though not unattractively, modelled,
Smashed, and his untidy shrine abandoned,
Having given nothing to his votary
Has he turned his face toward the dawn?
Is he visiting with the Hyperboreans? God
Forgive me, what made me think he was a god?

1975

Editio Princeps*

Austere and unforgiving spring
        Overshadowed by malaise,
        Precocious, tantalizing days
Protracted into evening
        By the sun's reluctant rays,

Everything you touch awakes
        Unenthusiastically,
        Such as this stark, naked tree
That, awkward and unsightly, breaks
        Out in the throes of puberty,

Or these modest, backward flowers,
        Inhibited by circumstance,
        The genitalia of plants,

More delicately fleshed than ours
        In their coloured underpants.

With seasonable tardiness
        As subscribers we enjoy
        On the doorstep or nearby
Two leavings of the daily press
        Each flung by a different paper boy:

First the surreptitious one,
        Unencouraging and cold,
        Then, open as a centrefold,
His buddy, in comparison
        Forward, foul-mouthed, fresh and bold.

The lad who brought *The Morning Star,*
        Shy and silent with the dawn
        Unobserved has come and gone,
Unlike the more spectacular
        Youth who brings *The Evening Sun*.

* First edition

1990

Edward A. Lacey, 1937–1995

Quintillas

In city streets, obscure with rain,
obsessed by hunger and regret,
of an old land no wars forget,
I saw the face that brought me pain
in pauses of the level rain.

Ruin and youth shone from the face
of a boy who, as I passed by,
leaned watching me, with shaded eye,
against a street wall: feral grace
and the corruption of that face!

We knew each other: he spoke to me
a language that no words convey,
ancient, in hips' and body's sway,
the language of my anarchy;
and then he stirred and touched me,

light, on the arm; I stopped for him
(I was young too) and turned, and smiled,
and saw my ruin in those defiled
fair features mirrored; there in the dim
light he signalled; I followed him

into some intricate recess
of patterned buildings, where with him
I entered into congress grim
and lovely, felt his manhood's slim
mastery, his boyhood's loneliness.

And in our heightened senses' swim
we lent our litheness to each other's whim
desire dictated: all the air
was thick with mist and darkness: there
our bodies rolled, limb with limb

intertwined in a sensual dance;
of rain without no drop within
fell on the moment's circumstances
(cherished for that); only the din
of far-off drops curtained our sin

as, harbouring no thought of loss
or separation's lonely cry
we played our game of pitch-and-toss,
then rested, till, in a greying sky,
morning: an ash of snow fell, dry,

on another earth: we rose, shook, smiled,
two young boys met a night, and then
I went out to a world of men
and never saw his face again;
he had the eyes of a little child,

tortured and lost; we made our way
by separate paths out of that place,
a sort of courtyard, foul by day,
where neighbouring skyscrapers embrace
and mingle, leaving lust a place

to seek out from the winter cold,
in cities where love is bought and sold.

Late 1950s

Anacreon

for Robert Finch

Age discerns only the lost angel grace:
the suffering and the pride remain to them,
who wear their youth as blind men wear a gem:
and always run, and always lose the race;
and youth's cool eyes know only age's rages
of impotence, but not the appetite

for life that makes these vampires walk their night
and turn to page-boys as years turn the pages.

Age seeks in youth the kindling of false fires,
youth sees in age the mirror of false fears,
none reads the message of the passing years,
that tongue which for deciphering requires
the art that no man has proved guilty of:
to say "I understand," and not "I love."

1959

Delicate Equilibrium

You will be this way just a little while,
Then you will change.

A year, a few months, between boyhood and adolescence,
You will retain that grave and self-possessed

Beauty of face, the litheness
Of body that lays my summer dust.

A year, a few months, going up and down,
I will see you, at work or play. Your serious kid eyes

Bent over your bicycle, or looking through me,
Living in a world far enough away from mine,

A world of beefs, of hustlers; already you put on
Your black leather jacket, poor child. Thursday nights.

A year, a few months, you will change away,
Though I would keep you, as a eunuch singer,

You will alter, you will grow gross, you will be another.
Already the pox of change is at your face.

1965

Eggplant

Eggplant, berenjena, beringela, aubergine, melongène, boulanger,
babaganush,
Baigan,
juicy names, full of labials and linguals, luscious voiced vibrating
consonants
—what is it that they remind you of?
See them glowing darkly on the corner fruit-stand, or in great purple piles
at the downtown market,
fruit of the Latin, Semite, Hindu and the slave,
fruit of the dark hot peoples, third-world fruit,
lustrous long cylindrical protuberances,
so black that they glow bluish, like Nigerians.
Take one in your hand now, squeeze it, feel its thickness, length, its
spongy yet
unyielding quality
—what is it that it reminds you of?
Peel it, boil it, mash it, eat it now,
soft cream- or green-coloured, laced with sesame seeds and oil,
warm, almost liquid, melting in the mouth
—what is it that it reminds you of?
Food is sex is race is history.

1973

Canadian Sonnets

1.

We were the land's before the land was ours;
the snow, the rock, the cold—they were all here
waiting their victims, countless thousand years
while we were still unthought, waiting the hour

when Cartier should sail down the shining stream;
and the laws—yes, the laws were also there:
thou shall not laugh nor drink nor fuck nor swear;
this above all, thou shall not sing or dream.
They say this was the land God gave to Cain;
it'd take Cain's God to give a land like this,
a God at once of vengeance and of pain,
to whom our shrivelled lives are incensed bliss,
who carved his laws upon Precambrian schist,
and stamped that schist into the human brain.

2.

The brown Brazilians asked me: "What is snow?
Is it sand-white? Or sky-blue? Or sun-gold?
Does it smell like flowers? Is it good to hold
and feel, like skins of women that we know?
Does it taste like the fruits and foods we grow?
Does it sing like birds at morning as it falls?
Is it to you what suns and carnivals
Are to us?" And I answered soft and low:

"Snow has no taste, no colour and no smell,
nor joy of touch, and speaks no syllable;
snow is the flower and quintessence of no;
snow is our rule of churches, work and laws,
our reticence, our loneliness, our pause,
the emptiness we live in. This is snow."

3.

They say the snow has really gone away
—for good this time—and with Pierre things are swell;
cocksucking's legal; you can go to hell
in any but the old religious way;
Toronto boasts its first outdoor café
and Sunday drinks; Montréal has a hotel
which looks out on a court of palms; all's well,
the ice has melted now, come back, they say.

And they are wrong; something is setting in,
but snow turns ice and hardens as it thaws;
the frost was in the people, not the laws;

winter is on the lives, not on the land;
sadder than snow, irrevocably damned,
a Puritan people without sense of sin.

4.

Old God of Calvin, Thou art mighty yet;
Thou hast left Thy people free to fornicate,
drink wine, eat caviar, smoke hash, masturbate,
with but one *ne plus ultra* by Thee set:
that there shall be no joy in aught they do;
that they shall seek and take their pleasures sadly,
knowing that life is grim and all ends badly;
that they, and not their Sundays, shall be blue.

Now, with Thy blessing, to the moon and on.
I think the moon is much like Canada,
Calvinist and Precambrian: God and Law
are waiting there, no doubt, with cold and stone
to welcome us. And so I end this song,
dreaming of love where the nights are two weeks long.

1973

Réjean

On his chest he had tattooed *"vivre,"*
and I knew *just* what it meant
the night he sat down uninvited
at the table where I was drinking
in the dear, dead Altesse Tavern.
He spoke absolutely no English,
but we got along well enough.
Son of a poor farming family

from the country near Trois-Rivières,
he had come to the city,
like all boys, trying his luck.
His long black hair was lustrous.
His smile was young and mocking.
His cock was pale and urgent.
"Je suis aux hommes," he told me.

He stayed with me for one winter,
a season of discontent
(like all seasons in Canada),
and at night his pale candle consoled me
for my sun-skinned South Americans.
He cost me a lot of money,
for he liked to wear fine clothing;
he liked steak and seafood dinners;
he frequented PJ's nightclub,
where he joked with the transvestites
and drank *crème de cacao*
avec du lait (I paid,
but I got my *lait* for free).
He smoked a lot of dope,
and he dropped a little acid,
and he caused me all sorts of problems,
for all his friends were hoodlums
who belonged to *la petite pègre*.
He was a good boy, basically,
but eighteen years old, and crazy.

He stayed with me all winter,
and in the spring I left him,
because he cost me money
and he caused me many problems
and his feet stank most disgracefully,
and I grew tired of his penis
—as I grow tired of everything;
so in the end I left him
—as I leave everybody—
to go on with my searching.

And God knows what's become of him.
Réjean. His motto, "*vivre*."
And lived for a while off me.

1978

Desencuentro

A boy is waiting for me tonight in Santiago.
He does not know he has seen me for the last time.

At nine, under the university clock, I told him:
I'll take you to dinner, and then we'll find a hotel room.

He walks back and forth under the clock, smokes a cigarette,
Stares after the passing buttocks, wonders where the *maricón* is.

But *maricónes* are always late, like women,
And, anyhow, where else could I find a man like him?

He has brown eyes, brown skin. He's—let's say—a mechanic.
He was passionate in bed. I think I liked him.

At nine-thirty he decides he'll give me fifteen minutes.
At ten he definitely decides to go, but yet...

I gave him food, I gave him money, I gave him my body.
I even gave—I guess—affection. But I could not give him my time.

He's tired. It's getting cold. He's out fifty pesos.
But he should have known. A *maricón* is a *maricón*.

He stands under the clock in Santiago.
He knows now he will never see me again.

1978

Abdelfatteh

You put your hand on my shoulder
and *n'aie pas peur* you said.
Hot windless night. We were watching
a street fight in Marrákech.
You smiled at me, young hill-boy
(who thought that you were twenty,
but you just might have been eighteen),
and you showed two broken teeth.
We drank tea on the corner,
where you taught me Arab letters,
and we ended up at the *hammam*,
where you rubbed me down and fucked me.
Then you told me your life story,
all about your mountain village,
how you once had been a student
but had fallen out with a teacher
(lost promise of your family),
and you'd been expelled and now
you slept nights in the cafés
and smoked kif all the hot day
and scoured the town for tourists.

I went with you to your village
in the mountains near Marrákech.
I saw the barren hillside
(though to you it was blooming).
I saw the *bordj* you lived in
with the stable underneath it
for the camels and the donkeys,
and the sheep, the goats, the turkeys.
I met your grave, stern father,
upright in his blue djellaba.
I drank tea and smoked kif there.
I met your other mother
(as you called your father's new wife).
And you washed my hands with water
poured from a silver pitcher
(the custom of the country),

and we slept on Berber carpets
that were woven by your sisters.

And so I came to trust you,
and so I took you travelling,
and then we fell in prison
in a town called Mogador.
And *n'aie pas peur* you told me,
maktoub, it was all written,
but, *inchallah,* we'll get out,
though you yourself were frightened.

For two long months we rotted
in a prison by the seaside,
where the gulls laughed every morning,
and the muezzin wailed at daybreak,
as the key turned in the iron door,
and the lice and bedbugs ate us,
and we lived on beans and lentils,
and you sold the shoes I'd bought you
and the blue shirt you were wearing
to get more food from the kitchen
so that I could eat "European."
And at nights you slept beside me
(on the cold floor, rough wool blankets)
and you put your arms around me
to protect me from the others
(for there were forty others).

Days, we walked around in circles
in the courtyard with eight olive trees,
hand in hand, like all the others
(the custom of the country),
sat and listened to the imams
(though of course I understood nothing),
while the armed guards prowled the rooftops.

The last time that I saw you
was as I was leaving prison
And we kissed each other on both cheeks

(the custom of that country),
while my police escorts looked on,
and you grabbed my hand and told me
"Remember, I'm your brother,"
and I marched out of the doorway,
for I was being deported.

Now, back on your *douar,*
you send me Christmas cards and little letters
(decorated with calligraphy and flowers)
in your funny French, saying things like this:
Mon cher frère, si tu veux m'aider, aide-moi
à ce moment, n'importe de quelle chose,
de l'argent, si tu peux, ou des vêtements
anciens, ou une cartouche de cigarettes.
And I sometimes send you money,
and I hope it makes you happy,
for I won't be going back there.
And I wander,
from country to country, purposeful, purposeless,
but sometimes
even now
at night
in my hotel-room of dreams
I hear across the darkness *n'aie pas peur*
feel
the small protecting body close to mine,
warm arms around my waist, quick, quiet breath,
the hard cock pulsing, saying "Let me in,"
brief spasm of union and separation.
Abd-el-Fatteh.
Servant
of the Open Door!

1986

bill bissett, 1939–

a warm place to shit

awarmplacetoshitawarmplacetoshit
awarmplacetoshitawar mplacetoshitawarmplacetoshitaw
armplacetoshitawarmplacetoshitawarmplacetoshitawarm
awarmplacetoshitawarmplacetoshitawarmplacetoshitawa
rmplacetoshitawarmplacetoshitawarmplacetoshitawarmp
lacetoshitawarmplacetoshitawarmplacetoshitawarmplac
etoshitawarmplacetoshitawarmplacetoshitawarmplaceto
shitawarmplacetoshitawar mplacetoshitawarmplacetosh
itawarmplacetoshitawarmplacetoshitawarmplacetoshita
warmplacetoshitawarmplacetoshitawarmplacetoshitawar
mplacetoshitawarmplacetoshitawarmplacetoshitawarmpl
acetoshitawarmplacetoshitawarmplacetoshitawarmplace
toshitawarmplacetoshitawarmplacetoshitawarmplacetos
hit

1973

eet me alive

thn inside th bush thru th steps
up down nd inside inside th flesh
th opn beam push in in nd
furthr in nd mor hands on
me bhind me cummin
thru th branches th orange
half moon th tendr
meat nd stond
eyez cum
blind
me
to see
only ths
take off my buttons
caress my chest th fingrs

uv th moon my pants
dropping to my
knees ankuls
push my
cock
in

th sea stone me th
gatherd creatures in th
dark my tits enlarge
press against my
thighs mouth
down on
me my cock
inside th beam light
thru th window nd in th
shuffuling dark th tendr
creatures embrace th
floor turn to
gold to sand to
eyez soul heart
awakening
nd i cum upwards in
side th round flesh my legs
shaking branches rub against
my face nd th moon fall
into my mouth

1974

i was on beech avenue in vancouvr

wher th canada gees gathr with a boom
mike intrviewing th canada gees abt
theyr life styles if yu show feer they
hiss n honk yu away

i was asking them how cum they choos to
mate for life n what happns whn n if

trianguls develop   dew they have divors
n trial separaysyuns

is th purpos uv life mating to ensure th
stabilitee uv th food chain in theyr
peer groups   continuitee for th goslings

i told them   we with our techologee n
entertainment n compewtr science have
lost th reeson evn for valid short term
mating n sumtimes think we have evolvd
byond needing it but not reelee from
wanting sum romance   can gees go cruising

i showd no feer n they wer gathring around
me   i sd we wud like to know from them   i
undrstand yu have great longevitee duz yr
passyun surviv th yeers n attensyun spans
obviouslee it duz bettr than ours bcoz we

oftn forget who we ar with n go with othrs
evn out uv forgetfulness   or absent mind
idness   curiositee   changing times   can we
lern from yu

i showd no feer but they convergd on me
almost hissing n honking sputtring   who
is ths fool   who is ths fool

1985

i can remembr a corvet

driving past us   always pulling
ahed   neer peggys cove voglers

cove   ovr th line   xtreemlee gud
looking peopul in it   yu have to

b to b riding in a corvet in
nova scotia it was my favorit

car wud i evr ride in wun on it
undr it inside it at nite yeers

latr in vancouvr by th watr th
necklace uv lites undr th dash

bord getting out i lookd at th
car i hadint realizd had no time

bfor so caut i was by th eyez
pulling me into th front seet

fuck i notisd getting out uv
th car that had caut me thats

a corvet all thees yeers iud
dreemd uv making it getting it

on in a corvet it was red god
n th willow treez wer sweeping

th stars like serchlites sum
recognishyun private ths event

was almost enuff for me

1988

my first job

in halifax my fathr got me
pumping gas dewing lube grees
n brake jobs i was 12

th assistant managr wud crawl undr
th car aftr me whn i wud be working

on th undr bellee uv sum general
motors product   try feeling me   he
wanted to give me a blow job

cumming into th washroom   wch was
also my job to kleen up aftr th
whol citee made a mess in ther
seemd like

i kept avoiding him   n my fathr
saying i cudint quit   wondring what
they all wer trying to proov   they
was sumtimes veree big in my mind   so
i wud start to scrape brand nu buick
whil filling gas

by wrapping th whol length uv th hose
around it to get to th fuel tank hole

dropping burning cigaretts   neer pools
uv gas iud spilld   got wun whol side
uv a nu chyrslr scraped to hell

th managr sd he didint know   whn i
startid out   i was so great now i
was so clumsee

i sd   i didn't know eithr

1988

inkorrect thots

WARNING   each wun uv thees
pomes may contain inkorrect
thots   thees pomes have not
bin kleerd by th ministree
uv korrect thots

ths book contains reel storees
that have reelee happend   th
mysteree uv pain has not bin
adequatelee xplaind 2 us why
memories can cum crashing down
on us robbing us uv our present
or why we lifting grasp hold uv
a suddn laffing idea   baloons
us up   n what we lern from memorees

i cum skraping across a glacier
bringing yu ths burnd flowr   see
its petals bleed as it opns   all
ovr our plans   our mesurd safetees
see its tabula filling with such
wondrous snow

falling   falling   on th beautiful
wounds th uncared for moaning in
allees   undr cardbord   whil othrs
walk by   going 2 sumwher not
stopping   a tree is a tent   us   a
molecule   longing is   i think
recentlee deleetid from consciousness

ther ar an infinitee uv thots being
xpressd heer   ths is langwage   nd an
infinitee uv thots not being xpressd
heer   ther is silens   ther is yr mind
is it   th ministree has not prepard
us for evreething   what is not being
xpressd heer   may b inkorrectlee not
being xpressd   not being xpressd so
inkorrectlee   as 2 hous an infinitee
uv words   ther is no control ovr
wht is not being xpressd

ths hous is on th moov   ther have bin
apolojees bfor   they have alredee bin
made   for th peopul who are not heer
we apologize agen   ther ar word games

signifiying much word ecstasee   within
th langwage   n its momenta resembla   a
word uv cawsyun   its own music   sumtimes
inkorrect thots may b byond our control
each wun uv thees pomes may contain an
inkorrect thot

these pomes have not bin kleerd by
the ministree uv korrect thots   we have
no control ovr what is not being xpressd
heer eithr

byond ths sign   yr on yr own

1992

my fathr in his bed room th morning i left

in a weird way i was starting 2 like him he was
loosning up a bit   thru th greef uv my first mothr
going 2 spirit n his feeling less pressurd now by
doctors   n operaysyuns n was th worst ovr yet

maybe he was starting 2 like me   my boy frend who
i was in love with   wud stay ovr upstares with me   in
th green attik   fathr wud b nice 2 us both   i still wud
take his cookeez n milk 2 him   b4 he was going 2 bed

at nite as always sins my mothr went 2 spirit n he
wud say up th stairs gud nite 2 us both he wud still
skreem at my oldr sistrs me yelling at him 4 them tho
he left his estate 2 them i dont know what it was nowun

evr told me he was yelling at them less tho it was all
mor thn i cud undrstand   always had bin tho i tried
2 sumtimes   blamed him 4 most uv it   othrwize iud
blamd myself wch i reelee oftn did internalizing th
pressurs   n whn wud he start skreeming   n blaming
us agen   th erupsyuns wer unpredicktabul   n uncawsd

like th patreearkal god   but ther was a parshul tendrness
beginning   n i was leeving me n my boy frend getting
out   we had reseevd 2 manee cawsyunaree messages
subliminal n overt   tales uv what it wud b like if we wer
2 stay ther   in halifax 2 soldyeer on   with our love ther

told fathr i had a job with his frend who ran general
motors in calgary it was erlee morning no warning he
was getting up now in his pajamas i sd we wanted an
erlee start   on th road   whn th rides wud b best

he sd gudbye son   i think he knew ther reelee was no
such job at general motors in calgary with his frend

me n my boy frend wer going 2 leev western civilizaysyun
n b happee 4evr   how different was th rest uv th world

1999

swallow me

========= swallo me its sew hevee outside uv yu =====

=== swallow me its sew hevee out heer ==========6666

****

swallow me its sew hevee outside uv yu **********

*************** can yu make me disapeer in yu ******

but eye still love gettin up in th morning ##############

####### runnin out on th medow seein th birds flyin 00000

#####*** roun n heerin

theyr song +++

n i still love typing all day bout th mystereez uv=====

======= langwages n wher th bodeez lay ###############

############################## n eye still love going 2 sleep

at nite ===== dreems uv my lovr in my hed boing boing boing

zonk out=== boing boing boing zonk out zonk out zonk out

1999

i dreemd i livd with keanu reeves

he was sew in2 me we had met at an
xcellent partee he knew my work
lovd it by th end uv th nite
he lovd me n i lovd him
hello

we livd 2gethr brillyantlee i helpd him
with all his appointments etsetera i was like
batmans valet quite a bit evreething was
alwayze wundrful my life was devotid
2 him we slept 2gethr evree nite n
almost alwayze had breakfast at leest 2gethr
xsept whn uv kours he was away on a shoot
or on th road with his band dogstar

thn wun nite he askd if i cud stay in th
east wing we livd in a huge palace 4 two
dayze or sew he had sumthing he needed
2 get in 2 on his own i sd uv kours n
whn we rekonveend on th third morning 4 brek
fast i didn't say aneething or ask aneething
did not bug aneething it was great 2 hang
with each othr agen

n that night we made love got it on
like nevr b4 sew wundrful n i woke up
sew arousd wun uv th best dreems evr

in my life

2004

Michael Estok, 1939–1989

Ordination

Doug,
I imagine you
(being red-haired, mad)
wore nothing once but a canoe
on your shoulder,
following

the Shield's
impossible slopes
from Nipissing to Ottawa,
your eyes and muscle pitched
for balance into water
shadow folding pine
and mountain
fall.

I stalk
the track your body left
for stretches of lonesomeness
or love.

but somewhere
along the way you disappear,
ambushed between vertigo colours of sky
and subtle single
rock.

maybe
your paddle's flash
profaned some sacred shore, or you felt
the spirit mark of a slaughtered totem,
the stare of a quick bush cat
you could not leave
behind.

For later,
your shape was collared
by a witch in a book and eaten
organ by organ down to skin and nail
bleached whiter in your reading light
than bones on a northern
beach.

Now,
Sundays,
we use electronic magic,
our love is football formal,
tasteless in the mouth as a pebble clean
from a stream brought back
to tell about.

Imagining
something there,
oaths we said in secret,
a beast battle old as the stars' teeth,
scars of manhood,
I see
nothing,

nothing
but a riddle, a doll,
this crude map
I make:

here
is the forest felled
across the place where I waited
for you to walk out of the lake
like a Huron
sun.

Here
are fire blackened
stones,

this
blank space
is where we first touched land.
I put it under my finger,
already it has shrunk
to an imaginary
dot.

Every
island lessens as we slide
away.

I look
into my cupped hands,
unable to fix the contours of love
before the last mouthful of water I hold
up to morning slips
into river, into
sea.

A mad
uncovered ghost
glares back at me,

my kiss unclothes him
like a burning
tree.

1987

as the crisis deepened

the authorities incited crowds to riot in the shopping plazas
after that it was easy to impose a curfew and street patrols
hourly bulletins of the casualty figures made parents demand
that schools close, trucks carried off children to military camps
but the contagion spread, hooded strangers blew kisses
and the taverns stayed open past time to service the troops
the faces of the authorities glowed like tiny television furnaces

as the public debate staged on the crisis ticked on like clockwork
with goons in blue suits cruising the stadium corridors
and fresh-skinned young women standing up to applaud
crueler punishments: white-coated technicians demonstrated
the theory and use of insulin shock and cattle-prod

disposal of corpses, as always, proved the most urgent problem
nobody wanted to lay a hand on them once the authorities
had made the correct political diagnosis by removing the genitals
a clever reporter suggested that shots be taken with a vaselined lens
relatives preferred these keepsakes to the actual remains:
the mantlepiece is easier to decorate than a grave

in prison, poets starved themselves into gullible silence
tapped out drainpipe reassurances to imaginary friends
or scratched coded messages at night on the cold stone
the authorities listened in, smiled, and doubled their sentences
encouraging these most compliant of inmates to pin their hopes
on the promise of a star beside their names in the holocaust lists

1989

hydrangeas

heavy with September rain
grow out of old graves at the end of Sackville Street
Thick roots like rough tongues suck the rich rotten blood of the dead
caress loosening sinew and bone till they dissolve in blossom—
great ruddy rose and cream white blooms engorge, distend themselves
declaring in their sexual arch and droop
the flushed victory of that outrageous androgyne
sweet witless nature—

do these
pale convenants of harvest or of doom
serve as blunt warning or as invitation
to the ghostly troop that wanders here each night
to lean and lie among the stones?

new deaths
outnumber those the tall branches
of the hydrangeas have softened with their shadows—
now they multiply faster than the children left us by that
  vengeful god
for punishment when we scorned his other, tidier garden
a murmur rises to heaven from the stricken—
throng on the wrong side
of the fence: "what then
must we do?"

what else but be sly
and blind as the wreath
oblivious of its own brazen waste?
let grief fall away like a blood-coloured leaf
let us lie down in the wet grass, lie down and love
cling to each other till we have touched the final lamp of summer
into cool, deliberate flame: love and forgive
even as we feel the last defiant shudder of our flesh
draw death up
out of the cold earth

1989

Stan Persky, 1941–

Slaves

Gay pride is the opposite of the slave fantasy
homosexuals are given a parody of
in the club that holds a slave auction or
in the society that demands I have a slave
mentality
Politically simply: the half-hearted tolerance
afforded by society cuts across and disguises
the category of social class. We are taught
to internalize it in an absence of community
substituted for by the ghetto that gives us
the imagination of owning a slave.
In a capitalist society where the slave class
exists only as a metaphor the slaveowners
want us to imagine we want to own slaves.
These owners of production and production-
numbers never knowing that in history
We real slaves of the Greeks
Were mainly agricultural workers, textile
producers, musicians, silver miners, history
teachers, and poets.
Sometimes I think poetry is the benumbed and
limited expression of the limited space
(of a ghetto) we're given. Expressing real pain.
My master, also a slave, taught me this art.
Contrary to myth like the Greek slaves are contrary
to Greek myth
Poetry isn't inspired-fuss like they say it is
in school.
True, autobiography gets in the way
(For instance, I wanted this poem to express the pain
I felt last night when you went off at midnight
not wanting me like you haven't wanted me
anytime but once and I beg, abject as a slave)
True
Autobiography gets in the way
But now that I'm a master and slave myself, like

the crafty man who taught me, I don't believe
as he did, that I'm simply the instrument
of a message that wants to get through
from a source we can't know
These messages come from the actual conditions of
slaves. I don't have pat answers to
explain the messages, like: gay pride, that
I transmit but don't autobiographically feel,
because I feel real pain.

August 21, 1973

Hockey Night in Canada

It is not justified by the men being beautiful
or their faces showing agony. If you love men
they are beautiful in the street and everywhere.
I'm not talking about when we play soccer by Trout Lake
on Sunday afternoons.
It's not justified by someone pointing out that what's going on
a million miles below in the rink is a mini-order
reflecting the order of the universe.
The relations down there are the same as the relations
of production throughout capitalism. This is hidden
by announcing tonight's attendance over the public
address system.

It isn't justified by the moment of beauty being swallowed up
in the roar of the crowd.
It isn't justified by the beauty of the perfect play.
The athletes are used up and left with scars. The men
I slept with were always more beautiful than the most
beautiful.
This surprised me, but I didn't stop to understand.

It isn't justified. No capitalist sports are justified.
If you weren't tricked into cheering for something else
there would probably be some loss of beauty

but there would be a gain of truth. Turn off the
set.
I'm willing to sacrifice the beauty that occurs in these lines,
even go without beauty for awhile (though it would hurt)
to gain
the truth that will have a beauty that's unknown right now.
Anything human beings do against human beings defending
capitalism
is justified.
Remember the hot night they were playing in Philadelphia
the ice fogged up engulfing the players and they had
to stop the game. It was beautiful.

August 16, 1975

The Red-Headed Boy

so much of it, of who I am now, in any situation, I find myself behind a door

and someone beneath me, so something moving from under, the red-haired kid, red-genitalled, a door such as closes one into the darkness, of a shed, or passageway, you can do anything you want, with him,

I'm 11 or 13, we play softball in the lot by the factory, we're on the blue carpet in my mother and father's bedroom, struggling, his head by the toy-chest with everything in it, the softball, come on up, we'll get it, the tightening all through my stomach and arms and neck,

who fought who behind the what kind of factory, I'm 6 the ditches frighten me, then the factory is built, there is a space, an alley, between its wall and that of the viaduct, with railroad tracks on the viaduct, I'm 4, Pat's father makes lead soldiers, I try to squeeze them through the windows of the toy train like the ones I see when I look out the window, their arms waving from the windows,

the red-headed boy, squirming, we have him, in the grassy slope on the other side of the viaduct, someone driving, in a car, down the street, would not notice, anything other than kids, scuffling, the grass hid us, we slide off his pants,

there is not much more than that, not yet, it is strictly visual, the pleasure, I feel it rip, the satiny lining of my jacket, in the jostling and pulling, my arms moving, like my desire, in a blur—

1977

Walter Borden, 1942–

Ethiopia the Drag Queen

RECORDED VOICE: WELL, NOW WHAT YOU'VE ALL BEEN WAITING FOR. THE QUEEN OF TRAGEDY: THE EMPRESS OF REMORSE: THE HIGH PRIESTESS PATHOS: LADIES AND ... FIGURATIVELY SPEAKING ... GENTLEMEN, THE PIECE OF RESISTANCE OF THE EVENING ... MISS ETHIOPIA!

(*ETHIOPIA enters amid wild cheering and the beginning strains of "All By Myself." When the noise has subsided, she seats herself close to the audience, microphone in hand, and begins to sing "All By Myself." ETHIOPIA will be seen in full light until she begins her monologue. She will then be lit with a single spot.*)

ETHIOPIA:

An image / passing as a human being / contorts a frown into a smile /
& telegraphs a message of *HOW ARE YOU* to my mind /

An image / pretending to be me / confuses fact & fiction
by responding with some
BULLSHIT
saying / EVERYTHING'S JUST *GREAT-GREAT*
GR-ea-t
graaate
graaaate /
that's the sound of a heart / draggin' into overtime / the sound
or the song / some ancient mattress sings / while whiskey-flavoured
promises are pledged / with panting slur / & climax into
hush-a-by
lull-a-by
peaceful time is here /
off to bed / sleepyhead
let emptiness come sneak into my solitude / & ravage all my
dreams / & bittersweet rememberings of yesterday / when all my
thoughts were young as innocence itself / & love & understanding
flowed from me like *MAN-AH* was completely in control / & *HAPPY
DAYS* / unsanitized for early primetime viewing / meant more than
suckin' lollipops out back behind some diner / but no one really

thought that he was fuckin'up / TRADITION / cuz
no one saw
no decrease in
the surplus population
&
charcoal grey apologized /
discreetly / for the presence
of the colour pink / that
brightened up our wardrobes / then
someone read between the lines of jesus love me /
this i know /
for the bible tells me so /
& found that it was not ap*PLIC*able / to faggots / according to
the christians / but not to dr. kinsey / who advised the church
& state that
OVER-ZEALOUS STRETCHING
OF THE BOUNDARIES OF CHOICE /
RESULTED IN LIBIDO
SCHIZOPHRENIA /
& Vindication toppled Vaseline /
& All my friends were normalized / statistically /
& dr. kinsey opted for a sex change / & emerged as dr. ruth /
& I became a shadow in that s
o
l
o land
convention deems
FORBIDDENNNN /
where the semi-hemi-demi-folk / on one square mile of anguish /
are doomed to dance the midnight mass to madness / as it boldly
stalks & preys upon the hunted
& the hunters /
who give themselves like
sacrificial relics
to some unrequited passion ooooozing from the acid queen /
in neon never never land / where amyl nitrate castles kiss
the sky / & snowflakes mound
around
my tears
to form
an image ... of a pumpkin ... that can change into

a honda / or
a lincoln / or
an epic fairy tale of those men who wander
straight into some pansy paradise /
every evening / after sunset / where
they wrap their guilt in fantasies
of mounting virgin maidens / & everybody
knows that *GETTIN'* blown don't make
you queer / cuz
that's really that just
benign
PARTICIPATION
that seduces *HOMOPHOBIA*
in all those eager washrooms
where the corporate heads
go
down
to meet
the public
made of frantic fathers fingering hipo*CRAZY*
& someone else's son / while looking for an
all-night store / via short-cuts through a
graveyard filled with
hearts that have no beat /
yet do not rest in peace
because
they're waiting /
like i am waiting /
for a gentle touch
which even desperate places
sometimes give / when i find
i am so very much
All by myself /
Don't want to be …
all by myself
Don't want to be …
all by myself—all alone—
Anymore

1987

Keith Garebian, 1943–

Sapphic Interlude

He loves my 'Zapata' moustache; I love his boyishness, small fingers in my dark Aztec hair, and fat breasts that Sappho would have relished on her island.

It is an island I know, having sailed to it after picking flowers from a zona rosa, *joy bursting from me like a sudden wave. Pita Amor greets me ashore, and our tongues taste of months we share together. Ah, great love falls into our skirts and we reach up to spread the stars across the night dripping rich pollen. Desire is doubled and is tasted between our legs. The noise of foam lashes the shore with the smell of jasmine.*

He goes on working and fucking. He loves me in his own fashion, and I can't stop it happening.

2004

The Life of Art in Thievery

Artists aren't prostitutes, he claimed,
they're thieves, remembering Apollo's lyre,
Cavafy's bed-boys looking like Cocteau,
and a candle he'd stolen from a Roman church
for *Caravaggio*. What was the film if not a theft
of the Renaissance for his own biography,
no mirror held up to nature,
but a penetration of the self and structures
of power. Everything built around paintings,
each image of the man, his *semblable*,
so close to the paint and canvas, the camera
breathes him. Step back and you have
a likeness, similarities rightly poised,
a social world, not a film set.
Only inner landscapes
for two nocturnal backroom boys—

him and Caravaggio.
A self-portrait that's not the painter's life,
but that life stolen as a filter,
inheritance gratefully accepted,
light to alter a ceiling, if only
by suggestion. Something meets the eye and mind,
in gestures and interface,
ineluctable, shivers of recognition,
the life of art in thievery.

2005

Untitled Sound Poem

Sometimes light can open your eyes
with sound. A torch in St. Bartholomew's,
doctor's commands dilating pupils
where lesions are caught
in blinding terror.
The world's last night anticipated
in a camera flash,
your eyes becoming a planet
with diseased geography.
Eye-drops sting in flashes and flares,
you can go blind with light.
Sometimes the worst of the illness
is what you hear
but don't see. Seashore-rusted
metals and their melodies,
spectral noise of waves,
fingers at a keyboard,
washing machine churning,
HB drawing the blinds before leaving,
room filled with voices—
Tilda, Brian, Nigel, John
melding, switched channels on the telly.
You don't catalogue the winds
in Dungeness, nor the light
that reaches you. Can't hear the blue sky,

only darkness of the tide.
Somewhere a dog barks, sheep pass
in tinkling bells.
Somewhere in shadows, the condemned
man awakes to a jailer's jangling chains.

2005

Note: "The Life of Art in Thievery" and "Untitled Sound Poem" are drawn from a work-in-progress about the late British filmmaker, Derek Jarman.

Michael Lynch, 1944–1991

Survivors

i.

You stretch out on the other bed, big
and unrefined as a W.P.A. sculpture
called *Big Boy Reading*.
You are a big boy. This is not poetry.
You read a book on children and their
parents I gave you with my marginalia,
jotting with a hotel pen your own.

We have assembled in this divisive
capitol a little reunion of three:
Bill from Toronto and me from New York,
revelling in the warmth
that shocks the Washingtonians,
you from San Francisco griping because
you miss and hoped to find some snow.

ii.

Your legs transect the air like the
Lines outside the Hirshhorn. You sway
them practicing your teenage-
hood which begins too soon
next week. This trip as never before
you chasten my quirks that might
embarrass you in public, but sitting

beside me in a cab, or on a marble bench,
or anywhere, you rest
one hand on my knee or throw an arm
around my back and say
how glad you are we're
together even if our feet
are sore.

iii.

Say what they will, this town was made
to torture feet and thus the human frame.
Measure a civilization by its capitol,
but measure a capitol
by what it does to the feet.
London I suddenly respect,
not that the English care.

Washington lets nothing be measured by feet.
Washington measures by yards. Even when Vermeers
hang or stuffed birds perch together
we are weary getting to them. Because
D.C. ennobles distance
and denigrates the near, I love
your tramping close beside me down the Mall.

iv.

Tonight as we dawdled along Connecticut Avenue
yakking about cabs
a shopwindow backlit you and cast on me
your figure, grown:
a sculptured pickup idling
by my blousier sedan.
The line of your chest brooded

as the black of the rectangle
in the Rothko we saw today
shook against vividest apricot,
the outline of your chest our future
if I'm here. Tonight marks four weeks
of coughing, I've begun
to fret: pneumocystis, its velocity.

v.

I couldn't tell you this, only
Bill who doesn't panic

but knows the possibilities.
He says by joining us
how much he misses us,
his sweetness pleasing us
but scaring me: does something in him know

it's our last time together as us three?
Everything's gone so well
these hints that the lab reports lie
run to my face like the inversion
spurring a cadenza: is
our first walk through Washington our last?

vi.

At the airport you hold on to me as if
you too knew something
but today I bury that thought, think
how sweet it is to be with you
looking at topaz and chrysolite. I never knew
stone had so many ways
to capture light. In the hall

of evolution you curl your tongue,
from your mother, I roll mine.
The hall is vast. Survival
of the fittest has thrown us up
against these polished rocks. We leave
on different planes at the same time.

vii.

Eastern channels me from gate to plane,
from forty to thirteen. I pass my father
drooling, shying his eyes
from me, his liver already stone.
He knows. I buckle in
my rage at his decay
and his protection. Once, he would wake me

with the sun and in a conspiracy of two
we'd slip from the sleeping house
to Rhode's Pond to feed the sheepsheads
breakfast. Mostly we caught eels.
No, mostly we caught each other while the sun
broke over the water and winds died into day.
When I was afraid I could hold his hand.

1989

Cry

Morning through a city garden widens
its swath. Shiny eyes of cinquefoil
azure eyes of myosotis, bruised lobelia
refuse to blink. Intruders trapped in the cross-
stare harden, crumble into fine
dustings because our sympathies
will not adapt to sun and cinquefoil: our world
steel and concrete, oil and song.
We hoist our lives high over the drone
of traffic and screwing gulls, hoist bags
of soil to terraces at the setbacks; set out
cinquefoil, watch its leavings, count
its days. Some days we doze in the sun
and dream we too are cinquefoil or lobelia,
blowing and blanching without demur.
The pneumocystis breaks.
We open our eyes to that skyline we incised
and know as a jet cuts through cloud that
cities are our gardens, with their stench
and contagion and rage, our memory, our
sepals that will not endure
these waves of dying friends
without a cry.

1989

André Roy, 1944–

Saturdays and Saturday

towards the end the Saturdays were
in better shape, your skin too, perfect skin,
adolescent pink, lips parted, well moistened
when affirming I have the nicest penis in
town becomes risky but your tastes are
divided. reasonableness of the day,
the notion of flesh as though we'd declared
we were not too worried when
we were quite worried in appearance:
unhappy Saturday passion Saturday.
the best part of our pride, blue eyes for life
and let's never say "Your body is an asshole
or just about" or clumsy Saturdays
when you try not to mistake your
feelings: certain just qualities are attributed
to me during caresses and much attention,
but pride is there to resist:
I want to hear everything
embrace everything
naked Saturday but we are naked in our
refusal to wake up to disappointments
(we can die so stupidly). slippery slopes of
anguish: the bodies rolling, rain of dreams,
several persons he loved, the ensuing ten-
derness and its wealth, the story of ten-
derness still to be written, he has made it his
specialty just recently.
Saturday that accumulates or a day too
narrow for two when the snow for mood is
better than the rain.

1979 *Translated by Daniel Sloate*

Like in the Movies, Like Making a Scene

in the room not able to sleep
because softly soughing in the tongue
trade, crossbreeding salivas, you pushed me away
with a few love words no mystery in them the way
it happens in the movies: edited sentiments
and a pile of affects I call to mind what I said
about your skin too delicate too familiar or broken
in as regards effects, or innocent,
   the extravagant bed
I recall in that night suddenly racing past us
when I was a pretext for tears:
   it's the kind of scene
that works fine once in awhile for
a confirmed bachelor like me.

1979 *Translated by Daniel Sloate*

Far from Montréal, far from
all that made me gentle and wounded,
or far from dream, from the holes that are left
where the wind blows, the slips of the tongue,
the meetings bringing lovers: 1) a penis is so
different without its accessories; during the voyage
we caressed you, it was snowing, we were sure
the days would open their doors on other
foreign words, flanked by misgivings naturally,
so we may be your new heroes, your needs
in terms of memories and expenses: 2) the
cultural efforts, the six proud inches when I'm
hard, a really fine effort of mind and body,
tomorrow will still be interested in the.
Ejaculation, what we would admit: the language
of the times, ideas and musics in order to say
the new world will have the second name of
our Modernity.

1983 *Translated by Daniel Sloate*

The Surrealistic Sex Hunter (penultimate version)

the years of ashes are over
I imagine time has shed its spices
(though without mingling it with your one-time blondness)
it was a time when love was a part of nature
your heart, lacking air,
had imprinted a large stain upon my sweater
life flowed, your sex was a big teacher
ashes are now a part of my vocabulary
the bedroom, this cathedral of heat, this burnt city
now inside I assume the position
of having a happy past
of splitting myself in two so I can write as before

the sky is blond throughout
the sky appears difficult
what happened to the spectacle of the world after you
I'm a little afraid of dying for others
now that others are nothing but bodies
mine is pierced, primed in the past
even if my sex still knows from experience how to explode
with a silky sound

skin is light, skin is natural
adjectives colliding in moments of ecstasy
ideas long ago visible
here they are speeding through the poem
a room long ago unknown
now space is speeding up here
a night from the past for the little cat
—I am still weaving cats into my texts—
that I hear purring in your belly
sometimes there are only words for love
they were so alive in the mouth
the happy mouth of the creator of clouds

boys come to enjoy it
boys are happy in my place

I think for them, I hammered my words into their flesh
my flesh, your flesh, his flesh
cut in two, dear, I've lapsed into error
now I utter the pronouns more slowly
I find in them the exuberant oxygen
and the structure of chance
necessary for my dead writing

without question these were the years of ashes
the sky was spiced
(though your blondness carried no astronomical price tag)
the sperm left a large stain that changed colour hourly
upon my belly, your belly, their belly
the room with the storm of tears
and the conception of prolonged kisses
I caressed you here as if I had been unhappy
now I am dividing myself
to be able to disappear while writing

I no longer escape the sense of the fluid
times past allowed us to love just anyone
but not just anything
I ate adjectives while listening to you
the sky had a face
the sky was not tired
now it was the bed of clouds
and the long dicks that from the front and at right angles
showed the exact position of the Big Dipper
handsome blond, young cannibal
what has become of your sex that I'd already pictured
exploding with the sound of a rose in my eyes

the years pass us through fire
I imagine that time let me fall
dust, ashes, clouds
writing was a part of the culture
(the metaphors gave voice to the little cats in the poem)
permanently saving the adjectives of times past
to describe *ecstasy, experiment*
of the sexhunter who did not escape the law of error

nor that of illness
I understood it was the joy of loving you
that brought me the unhappiness of loving you

1992 *Translated by Jonathan Kaplansky*

The Future

Repercussions of the illness: certain words
burned inside us like dragons
that the night could abandon
upon the old snow
illness caught the life
that had created it
did I have it within me to write the end of it all
to speak of the last time that I kissed you
beneath the stars dying
one after the other in general indifference

1992 *Translated by Jonathan Kaplansky*

The Sexuality Professional (Close to Night)

Sexes, decked out in all colours
adorn the abundant skies
that shift above us
and still leave us unsatisfied.
(Images in relief against the limp air.)
Multiple shapes slamming against my chest
with force, going at it with such passion
that we'd say they were in the way
on a battlefield.

Examples of kindness
and dreams of language,
sexes know we like them large and gentle
inside, outside, everywhere.

Reality suspended beneath the clouds,
reality just like eyes.
Gauging the speed of the senses
for many of them run across my belly.
Sexes appear quasi-miraculous,
as if they had been born in spring.

Music awakening certain sorrows,
going back in history …
We do not ask them to prove they exist
even if sexes often act as if unknown
to smugglers exiled
in the night where we hide
and that sustains us.
Sadness will one day come down from the sky,
and dwell among us for a long while.

Behold the night in scents and objects.
Music returns; it can imagine us
in these unjust times;
touching us,
recording the surrounding disorder.
Sexes breathe
and play our part,
we swoon for them.
The sky is not as high
in poems written
below, in the cold, on earth.

Ideas fixed to the landscape.
A sex younger than the time
left to us
becomes a metaphor of the night
that again begins imagining itself an acrobat.
("And you will look like this boy breathing his last
beneath the white upsurge.")
Sexes, making ready for brilliant things,
will shine among the stars
fixed to the sky's raging vault.

Rocket. Whirlwind of intelligence.
Solitude upon the body.
Dead thing, but strong
as soon as we address it,
as soon as we care for it
as if it were our shadow.
Sex could produce thought.
"Write it right, write for me,
who hammers a heart
into each word."

Miracle of the heavens, colours
outlined in the fluid landscape.
Images fall from each body,
and each body will hold fast in the disorder
that has already come to pass on Earth;
images plunge into the unbounded air
I watch sexes because they swell,
because they claim to be gentle objects,
because they claim to be powerful objects
next to others, upon others, in others.

We possess but one sex, the sole friend
who tolerates us.
("Write about the science of life
that awaits you each evening
before vanishing.")
("Write about the weight of the firmament,
the exhaustion of stars forced to shine.")
Your sex straining like those of others
will converse with our gentle and difficult aims,
it will shudder, a reality that dreams.

Structures of intensity, sensitive substances,
do sexes have a soul?
"A night already full, that sharpens
once meeting you is in the air
in the world marked by sin.
Just the stars, just the sky and you with your flesh."
(Poems with hard-ons unfurl

and burst in the battle over meaning.)
"Open your soul to the word delicacy."
Tenderness claims to be a ghost
as if looming up from an old movie
that we would still like
in our thoughts.
Race toward the good object, the well-endowed object,
the one most visible on bodies
wanting to struggle to live.
(In the dissolute night, each sex is a planet,
all things are great and natural.)

The night like a house of pleasures;
tender thought thick and fast in ribbons.
"I have an exacting passion for liquids,
especially if the liquids spring
live from your body."
Time is restless, night looks around,
desire takes hold, reality is embedded in the landscape.
(Sexes lived because they desired us
several times over and over.)

Beautiful sex,
it explodes like the way we love you
when we meet you
in the night that listens to, touches us
and desires us for itself alone;
it allies itself with a unique destiny
(because a sex is like a sex and it looks like a sex)
and all the abundant words of abundant boys
are appended to it,
only to it,
that knows how to burst
at an unjust time.

Sex, dense and sentimental object
with energy only for itself.

I call it "the soul's sensual delight."
Tears in the night because we divine
that night requires diverse forms of melancholy from us.
("You look so elegant when you come.")
Our sexes consent to certain poems,
those written while thinking about your life.

All is sex, all is miracle.
Here is the light that guides us,
witnessing our abandon
to the natural goodness of the senses.
Sexes full in a world ever so large
that stretches every night.
"Write all the names,
sew them on your skin."
The sky departs, returns, always ready
to welcome the stars
deserted by God.

Poetry's images modify
those entering and exiting,
the enterers and exiters of life.
Night provides a structure
preparing us for the earth's
endless fear of heights.
"Your sex grew with each new word,
I will not forget it
when I am ready to write."
Sexes imagined everywhere,
inside and outside us
we possess them
because they will possess us.

1998 *Translated by Jonathan Kaplansky*

Ian Young, 1945–

(Poem)

On rainy afternoons when we would share cool music
          in this little room
I've thought of that blond boy you liked
and asked myself if you could ever lean against me
          and be still
or draw down sleep to keep us from our rainy grieving.
And yet I've wished that he could take my place
          beside you here—
For him you had hands and yearning
and your heart's warmth hurt in its cool centre.

1969

The Mutes

Centuries ago
we too
spoke,
until the others
swallowed up our voices...
Now, we hail
one another
with uplifted arms,
still,
across the distances
dividing...
Touch a cheek
or shoulder,
one of another...
Speak the soundless speech
of eyes,
hands...
No language that
we can remember...
The others

talk around us
and
do not understand
our silent changes and
our mute encounters...
But at times
seeing us,
the others
fall also
into dumbness...
Our gestures
have, perhaps,
a grace to them—
consecrated
by our quietness....

1969

In My Café

In my café
it is always raining.
(The rain is
outside the window and
behind your eyes.)

In my café
I have your body to myself
(across the biscuits),
and it is very quiet.

(Sometimes,
André Gide is there,
dining alone.)

1969

Rob, Polishing His Motorbike

He pulls his T-shirt over his back and head,
folds it slowly in a wad and finishes the job with it.
Sometimes he sees his own reflection in the black surfaces.
Polishing smooth metal with delicate fingers,
he is surprised at his own face: human, white, not normal.
Something does not fit. Apart from his machine, he is no rider
but something individual. An intelligence. Someone.
He throws his shirt onto a pile of spanners and mounts the cycle.
Now he is just in jeans. Tonight he will wear leather and drive fast.
Speed coddles him. "You don't have to do anything,"
he says, "You're just there.
If I get killed, what will you write about me?"
He was a white body, wearing black, or
He died fast and took his time about it.

1976

Photography

for Ron Yourkowski

What is it? This person with a black box, yourself,
waiting to make a border around what occurs,
or keep it, small and absolute,
between the stiff covers of a book.
Friend or lover,
laughing group, party camp or public building,
no matter what the subject, there is always
something erotic about it.
This lens, poking erect into another's world,
invading his being, his glance perhaps resisting
or coy, pretending to resist.
That image of the other, threaded
into the metal works
and etched
invisibly on virgin film.
A mutual penetration.

The soft, firm pressure of the finger
on the shutter's cold
consummates. A click.
Conception takes itself.
Then the development in a dark place, closed,
uninterrupted, warm.
In soft, red light, the stillness of heavy air,
you can hear the body and
the picture, an utterly new thing, ascends, ascends
in fluid with amniotic scent,
the womb's fluid.
Gradually it emerges.
Tongs, forceps, guide it to the surface,
to the world,
surprising always, no matter how expected,
pictorial flesh
resolving into black and white.
Then it is washed, gently with slopping sounds.
The dark warmth is still.
With both hands
you lift the image up and gaze and gaze
into your own longing, that will outlive you.

1986

Sex Magick

My boyfriend is a magician.
Once when I came home unexpected,
I saw him leaning forward, hands on his knees,
talking in growls, whispers and low mutterings
to a little man made of smoke,
odd-shaped like a cloaked dwarf,
dark and hovering in the air,
made of the air but looking like a thing of ink
at the bottom of the sea.
As I opened the apartment door, the being
twisted suddenly like a cape
caught by a gust of wind and

dissolved, filling the apartment
with grey smoke and a
lingering smell,
burnt, but delicate, like scorched jasmine or
lavender.
"Stove acting up again?" I remarked,
sniffing and hanging up my coat.

My boyfriend is an enchanter.
The day I met him I
stopped in my tracks,
forgot the day's errands and important meeting and
turned back
only to encounter him.
Yet I had not seen him.
It was when, magick book in hand, he
peered through a bush at me
like Priapus piping in the Arcadian trees
I knew he wanted me.
I didn't know for what.

My boyfriend is a high priest.
Robes hang in the bathroom. Wands
lean in the hall, incense burning in brass.
The basement walls are covered with jars holding
powders, herbs, salts, dried things.
It was his spell
brought us to this house so
it's only right I juggle words and numbers
to keep it. Were we to leave,
the landlord would be puzzled
at the strange circles painted on his floor,
runes marked on the wainscotting,
talismans over the door.
Our landlord would try to examine them
(to find out how to remove them of course).
He would spend a great deal of time over the problem.
He would become more and more absorbed.
His wife would begin to worry
about his state of mind lately.

Slowly, the markings would begin to take shape for him,
would alter him. And then...
But our landlord and his wife are definitely
not ready for this.
So of course we stay,
and make ourselves at home,
with their co-operation.

My boyfriend is a shaman.
When his black cat died, his familiar,
something went out of our relationship.
I can't replace Pootz but have tried
to take his place
and my boyfriend, I think,
knows this and
works magick through me.
Because of it and out of
deference to my wishes, he
refrains from filling our house with snakes,
weasels and other small creatures.
Instead, there are stuffed bears,
teddy bears in his bedroom,
library and on the stair.
Hello Providence (head wedged between the bannisters).
Ah! Mephistopheles, face down in the towel pile.
All his bears have names.

My boyfriend is a conjurer.
Sometimes I feel myself more
like a winged horse than a man
when he wants to ride me.
And sometimes he just makes me disappear
in a traditional puff of smoke
for a few moments or
a few months at a time.
When he brings me back,
a little dazed but
more or less ready for action, I always find
the joints he's rolled for me on the mantle,
just behind that blank, gazing white Egyptian head.

My boyfriend seems to be a yogi.
One Saturday morning when I was elsewhere,
he phoned (how did he know where I was?)
and asked if I was coming home and
would I bring (as usual) his *TV Guide*
to see what old movies are in store for us this week.
When I arrived we got cozy in the sunroom and he
unbuttoned his jeans and presented
his cock to me, impaled
with a needle he'd
run through the skin beneath the cock-head and
replaced with a golden ring.
There was no swelling and
only the merest speck of blood,
powdery and dry like a spot of rust.
He soon had me leashing his cock like a falcon
at my hand till he spilled in it;
and all that night he worked sex magick through me.
People came up to me in the street,
I was proposed to by women and men,
boys looking for their first adventure
would find *me*.
And my hand on the jacketed back of a student
burned, he said, like a hot iron.
My boyfriend had made me literally hot,
body temperature at fever point yet
I had no fever...
When I walked into a bar the first person I saw
was a quiet young man from the same
English suburb I grew up in.
He came home with me and was transformed
into a living incarnation of the wolf-god,
eyes flashing and hooded, growls
deep in the throat, rain-damp
fur standing on end,
and in the black focus of his eyes as they
commended me,
the image of a young Pan
trampling the erect earth in antic joy.

My boyfriend is a sorcerer
and in our garden there is a circle on painted stones.
Once, at night, I thought I saw
tiny figures
holding some miniature rite
under their darkness.
But when we are there,
my boyfriend's white blouse and trousers
catch the moonlight in a way I cannot forget.
And I am Pegasus again,
his name for me.

My boyfriend is a man of impulse.
His hands alter the weather
(he can rearrange small clouds like chess pieces);
he travels at will. In his need
he can wound me
but only once has failed to match his word to me.
He was with another man and I was in Central Park,
worrying. A sudden storm,
hail, lightning and hurricane wind
smashed through the park,
levelling trees and
turning the paths to rivers
and the monument steps to waterfalls.
My back, hit by a falling bough
sheared from a huge oak tree
was bruised black and cut, my hands
scraped and raw, my neck ripped.
Others were sure my boyfriend had tried to kill me.
I knew otherwise. It was the gods
warning him
of his power over me,
of how easily he could hurt me.

My boyfriend is a philosopher
when he is with me
of a morning in the sunroom,
listening to music, smoking dope and planning…
There I am his amanuensis and

make marks on a paper as he speaks to me.
Sometimes I don't understand what I write—
runes on a cryptic wall—
but I type them up, the letters
jumping about and
changing places with one another
until they are his and mine,
the way he wants it.

And when he is not in our house
and I am here alone to water the cats and
feed the plants and inhabit,
when he is not here,
when I wait for him
the house is always in shade.
There are few sounds.
My typewriter seizes up.
The record player utters only a tiny tinny voice,
essential things disappear until he returns
and there is a cold chill
in certain areas of the basement.
A creak on the stair,
a tap-tapping in the pantry, but
no one is there.
Only I am there, left
with these papers, these words.
Left alone
in a house of bears.

1986

Jean-Paul Daoust, 1946–

Egyptian Poem

I'll write a poem for you
In the Egyptian style
On your skin
Hieroglyphs of love
That our fingers will decipher
I'm going to mummify you
Wind you in wrappings
And kisses
Our careful ritual gestures
To keep you
In my eternity
I'll stretch you out
In the core of my heart
Where no one can go
Its beat is like music
To soothe you
To lull you
Love you
In the desert
Flooded with light
Our skin burning like sand
In the shade
The two of us
With our erections like obelisks of sacred light
Jealously guarded by the sphinx of love

1982 *Translated by Daniel Sloate*

from Magic Boys

He's making love right this minute, I know. With someone else. What can I do about it. Except stare at this motionless fog where the evening is vanishing. His silence. This burning moment that's consuming me. Don't panic. WHATEVER YOU DO. Otherwise disaster time. Wait. For it to be over. For him to come back to me. For him to want me. Plant my teeth in his neck to scare his blood. Clutch his hair. My claws unsheathed. Another swan is dying. May apocalyptic fury be celebrated on our tongues. I walk delicately through the apartment. I explode at the least squabble. I'm an atomic bomb. Crazy crippled telephone there. Old thing. Deaf. Dumb. If he were here obviously everything would be just fine. Obviously. I'd be bitchy to him though. Like an *extra large all dressed* pizza with a double of order of anchovies a *Chinese dinner for three* five St-Hubert BBQ chickens obscene telephone calls a telegram singing: *Fuck you. Fuck you. Fuck you. Fuck you. Fuck you. Fuck you. Fuck you. Fuck you.* But my body is eating the silence. Barely moving except to grab a rum and coke. And put it down like a piece of ebony. Very chic I don't even wipe away a tear that starts down my face. Lava. A new wrinkle. Because of him. The TV is on. I can hear it buzzing. America and its mechanical presence. I'm so anxious for him to come home so we can both laugh. At us. The hesitation before the first kiss. More tears will follow. The heart is in eruption. His transparent dross. He really is making love to someone else. Maybe he's in love with him. Maybe not. And when he comes back he'll have that champagne smile of his. He'll bury his lying eyes in my skin. But he'll come back. Until then all I can do is wait. Everybody's lived through what I'm going through. So what's the matter except my pain. More poems are stuck in my throat. It's not that I'm afraid of comparisons. *I know who I am.* But him. So far away suddenly. Perilous sirens sing in my tears. Sad eruptions from the eyes. The WE is foundering. Night. A punctured eye. But there's no big deal. He's just making love with another guy. My words are submerged in tears. Angels with damp wings can't fly. Alone. My heart as it writes screeches like fingernails on a blackboard. The picture is empty. Eyes blaze in the storm. And the day is rising. Its crooked smile. And those immaculate sheets. Like a shroud around a death-stricken heart. Mummified.

1986 *Translated by Daniel Sloate*

from **Blue Ashes**

I learned what love is
While the other children of my age
Were learning to recite their lessons
I was learning how to inflict pain
At the alphabet age
Caterpillars butterflies ants
Grasshoppers give me juice or you're dead
I made him suffer when I'd not show up
When I told him never again
When I'd run away for no reason
Fear
Of him of myself of others
I'd run to the lake
Screaming my terror
My rage
At him
Sentenced to silence he watched me run off
His big hands in tears splitting the wood
But not as precisely as I chopped his heart
A love story
But I was only six and a half
He was in his twenties
I'll never forget his body
Whenever I saw him
His body's smell in the shed
The sweaty wood
That I never found elsewhere
In the sterile air of the elementary school
The nuns like wax statues
At times the stale air in the confessional
Would hint at his perfume
His shoulders broad as church portals
Where I loved to be
The ritual of our caresses
Always in a chiaroscuro setting
The paintings of Caravaggio
That I understood the minute I saw them
Except it all took place between the rue Tully

And the boulevard du Havre
In Valleyfield
Where the bay is the stage
For the most beautiful sunsets in the world
Clouds in a frenzy behind the belfries
Of Notre Dame de Bellerive Church
Tipped over the tables said the priest
But the water of the lake
Blessed by Satan
Where I would plunge after lovemaking
How could I purify myself
At six and a half
How could I purify myself in those waters
Gothic cathedral mirror
Condemned excommunicated
I was preparing for my First Communion
My heart full of you
But my soul was very light
It's a love story just a love story
So banal
How to make it believable I loved him but
There is nothing to tell
You try to understand you know afterwards
It doesn't change much of anything
Six and a half years
Time to be happy
He loved me
He wasn't a relative
A young neighbour in his twenties
Tall and strong and beautiful and tender and passionate
His hair was black and curly and long
His eyes blue like lakes mirroring the sky
A smile like a ship all lights ablaze
Shoulders where I could sit and ride
A torso thighs a penis
A body that still excites me
When I was a child Reason awakened
Deep in the heart
He gave me what others
Would try to take from me

He was only twenty
And a few years more
I was six and a half
He loved me
I loved him
I loved burrowing my face in his chest
I could hide all of me there
No one could ever find me
Sheltered from every stupid thing
It was always noon with him
We were in love for years
But I grew up
And he didn't change
I left him
In the fire
Calling him names
The way we do to those we think
Are hurting us
He loved me
And I loved him
Does he still love me
In his bouquet of ashes
I will always love him
Despite the call of other bodies

1990 *Translated by Daniel Sloate*

Enjoy!

for Maurice Tourigny

Through the amber veins of the streets
I'm strolling along very Proustian
Finally a tourist of myself
Night suits American cities
The bigger-than-life anthology of their bodies
The restaurants the bars
Where wall to wall angels wait
Words on fire in the evening's ink jostle and jump

Shhh! Enjoy! whispers the spring breeze
Streaked with dark flashes where the young and beautiful
Parade like bold bits of blue from heaven
Shhh! Enjoy!
From beyond the evening's grave this ritual
Love trail on Lavender Lane
Booming from the loud speaker of my heart this voice
Shhh! Enjoy!
On the luminous canvas of New York
The full moon seems so small
Alfred de Musset would probably rewrite it
A dot on a gigantic I
Out of an open door like a cat
A jazz tune slinks its way
The sax notes fall in golden rain
On a beggar slumped on his bench
With a hood on his head
Looking like a lost monk
Beside him a man noosed in his tie
Is reading Zen Comics
Over his head crucified on a tree
A poster for heroin addicts
Call us when you're ready to get off your high horse
But in my ears the wind keeps repeating its mantra
Shhh! Enjoy!

1996 *Translated by Daniel Sloate*

Live Epitaph

Two beautiful boys are kissing
They're young
They're beautiful
They're thin
They have AIDS

Do you want to be cremated?
And you?

Well we will manage to die together won't we?
Yes my love
So let's drink to that!

I listen to this epitaph live from the Tunnel Bar
Completely   Incredulous

1996   *Translated by Daniel Sloate*

The Air in Your Mouth

I breathed in the air from your mouth
Superb as the full moon in July
I drank in the water from your mouth
Superb as San Francisco Bay
And I laid claim to your body
To keep death at bay
I swallowed your soul
So deeply time vanished from the horizon
And the song of our hands
Like constellations high in our heads
Where we'll be able to contemplate
Their impossible return

1996   *Translated by Daniel Sloate*

Song of the Serpents

I'm starting to like the shards of sky
Screaming the blues rotten-to-the-core of the clouds
And the dead stars shining in vain
Just as I'm growing fond of acid rain created in man's image
Asphalt roads splitting like chunks of intimist despair
And the subways and taxis and jet planes all spoiling space
Where the ozone's tunnels are travelled by the Death Express
I'm starting to like the superb decadence of our effete selves
And those recipes for multiple cosmetic lifts to the soul
I'm starting to like everything with no purpose at all

Unless it's to pay the taxes of the moment's stars
But since we love to give to stupid gods
The candor of our torments
Like this beautiful country with its worthless flag
And like everybody I love to love so let's all love
With moronic litany let's toast our failures
Applaud our exploits of an evening and our mistakes too
Aren't we the discoverers of beavers bears and tribes
Aren't we the astronauts of this misunderstood planet
I'm starting to like the end that's jeering at us
The sooner it happens the better
I know love at times can be rotten
And the cosmetic smile can be oozing with vitriol
So go and scrawl lipstick kisses on your mirror
Go to your homes and educate the monsters
Of the next millennium for a paper fiction
I'm starting to like not having to do so anymore
Sleep well good folk because in those far off times past
A whole show was in preparation
And the resonant poetry of ontological coochie-coochies
The anal aphrodisiacs of the executive branch
Contaminated like all the rest and I'm starting to like
What I've already written like
The Apocalypse is tap-dancing on the planet top
Is it tango or rock'n' roll or heavy metal or losers' chagrin
On AM FM from one ear to the other it's just a question of tint
But I've always like instant eyes
Near-sighted caresses and the safari skins of evenings
Especially evenings of readings seemingly so sophisticated
Ah I'm starting no doubt to like the impossible
Because they run so fast so mindless after the sauna bargains
After the toilets the bars the flea-market stories
But I'm just starting to like maybe
A gothic clown's lyricism
I haven't anything more to lose just like the country
I have no real regrets except one or two lovers
Of maybe none at all
Or maybe we're starting to love maybe
I have no clear boundaries or taboos
And bodies to make even a pope erect are welcome

In fact I've nothing I can call my own
But these words like an open wound
I love the sound of ice in my glass in the evening
The peaked twinkle of the Pole Star
Through the so-called light of a skylight
Can one enjoy being the barbarian for others
My tongue is sharp and ready to scalp their brains
My eye of lynx can detect sentiment's lost souls
My mouth is toothless as a starving wolf's
But as efficient as ever
My arms are lean from too many programmed hugs and holds
But I'm starting to like to repeat old forgotten things
And which it would seem are now forbidden
For you know there are ideas that stink like churches
Something like gestating corpses you have to keep lashing
I can hear the rough mauve from a mouth just dead
Presto I lasso the soul and tether it loose
On the dance floor of a university campus
I'm starting to like the literary horror films
Profs lacerated by all their moronic questions
And without a move unless it's an arching eyebrow's
Cap with a circumflex the nose you circumcise
Of a reader of good books in his pyjamas
We all have demons to be burned
Let's take our time it makes hell last longer
I'm starting to like fictions about phantoms
With their sparkles and travestied words and proud of it
I'm starting to like the wind in thermal windows
The swirling snows that bring poems to mind
And how to forget your lips so alive with kisses
At night especially when you came knocking at my door
Like the sound of an indecent wind
Because of all that and lots of other things a poet
He's become and announces it to others he loves
At the time a poet more decadent than you'd believe
Was learning how to sing the song of the serpent

1996 *Translated by Daniel Sloate*

Stephen Schecter, 1946–

from **David and Jonathan**

And so to the south.
Two days later.
Jonathan lies asleep
in the crack between night and day.
Roe eyes stare but belong to a man
who is wet with dew and shivers.
He shivers because he does not know
if the man asleep will rejoice to see him,
will take him in his arms
as he now wants to be taken,
having seen, again having seen
the black curls and the powerful arms
and the legs that open and close like scissors,
and that face that bares its neck
as much to a knife as to God.

David pulls himself up to the edge
and does a little reckoning:
once,
twice,
how many times can you leave a man
and return?
But when Jonathan opens his eyes,
he blesses David as he blesses his soul
for returning to his body.
And now for once, just for once,
black and red blend
in this castle parquetry,
the lust and fear that run to the colour of loathing
for once left outside like dead quail,
only the sleek and dripping limbs
of a man who has worn the woods like a nightshirt
allowed into the chamber,
the bed,
the still open aorta of love.
And for once, just for once, they are happy.

Hours later they wake up.
The sun high in the sky melts anything in sight.
In the space hollowed out of the wall
Jonathan sits
and looks into the garden.
His friend stands near, a fox on his hind legs.
They watch the earth at work, though nothing moves.
Fronds smile crazily. The trees keep guard
like a one man army. Shrubs that flower
disrobe.
Jonathan reaches for David's hand
and places it on his shoulder,
there where it flows into his neck;
in lieu of the words
he does not have to say
points to the grasses pushing their way
through the fire-baked earth
and into the fire-baked air,
bent by genes to the eyes of men
and a halogen sky,
and starts to name them:
calamus, cinnamon, thyme,
and the man whose fingers knead the word-soaked flesh
talks to him of the whereabouts
of love's other fruit trees:
the almond and the pomegranate,
frankincense and myrrh;
and so they sit and stand
in the shadows of stone
wedded to the murmurs of their bowels,
lords bestowing praise
as if theirs was the kingdom.
It was not.

1996

Intimacy

There are people whose lips you want on yours
and whose cock you want up your ass
and others whose lips
you are content to brush
and whose cock you want only to feel.
There are people you want at arm's length
but whom you are happy to hold
and others you only want to know
with a table standing between you,
others across a room
and some people not at all.

Is this how God feels
about the children of Israel:
sometimes a lover, sometimes a bride,
sometimes only a sidekick,
sometimes the union
in labour negotiations,
sometimes a promise
and sometimes a great disappointment?

Blessed be God
for falling in love
and blessed be the chosen people
with whom He fell.

2005

Waiting For a Boyfriend

What shall I do while I'm waiting?
Think of you? Dream of you?
Conjure you up like a boy icon
gazed upon in the Metropolitan Museum,
or the Titian portrait in that house
fifteen streets down Fifth Avenue?
Maybe even write a disquisition

how the exquisite buttocks of a headless youth
could only have been wrought by an artist
who did not live in an empire?
For once, at least,
I'd be right where I am,
pen poised,
the alphabet about to flow into words.
And maybe for once the words will not be
about love trapped in stone,
nostalgic as the sunset
that four centuries of science later
still storms the sky with its paint box.
No Turner, no Proust,
only the wonderfully clear Vermeer
who said this is blue, this yellow,
this a captain, this a letter,
this a map on the wall,
and all of it, like you,
a perfectly adequate idea.

2005

Richard Teleky, 1946–

The Hermit's Kiss

Touch me. My wound is for your hands. If you prefer to pray, remember that I cannot hear. Listen to me instead. They thought I emanated a sense of death. How can I know? I spoke reluctantly.

One historian—his name does not matter, for he, too, will die—wrote that "Mongol movements across previously isolating distances in all probability brought the bacillus *Pasteurella pestis* to the rodents of the Eurasian steppe for the first time." And from there, to Europe. To Piacenza. In northern Italy.

This search for causes, sources, origins, has never interested me.

My life is the history of plague. My body, my shell, is made of plaster and wood. Bones, flesh, blood—they felt the same. The carver had a name: Eugenio. He loved dogs, the scent of baking bread, mushroom risotto and young men with strong arms. Which may explain why his knife and hands formed the mass that became this body with such patience. Ignoring my pain, he gave me health and beauty. Did he dare whisper my name as an endearment? It was eighty, ninety years ago, no matter—a short time to me—and anyway, I probably forgave him.

My bones, of wood, were covered with plaster in order to absorb color: *indigo, cremisi d'Alizarine, terra di Siena bruciata*. I can't recall the painter's name, if I ever knew it. I believe he preferred the dog to me, just another man in robes. Dogs were rare, he didn't get one every day, the sentimentalist. So my cheeks are too flushed and high-coloured, more like the heroine's in a romance than a feverish man's; my lips—a sweet bow—could leave their print on yours.

On Sunday mornings children always notice me. I am the saint with the dog. The dog who carried a bread roll in its mouth.

Even as a child I preferred solitude to the company of my family. I liked to walk in the hillsides of Montpellier. The scent of thyme and rosemary still clings to me. I never missed great rooms, fine tapestries—my life was not to be wasted.

My people, wealthy merchants, lived as aristocrats might. They valued safety and comfort. Mother often kept a bowl of rose water in her chambers; she liked to stay in bed all morning, even into the afternoon. I believe she was praying.

As I grew older, I remained in the hills overnight. Eventually people frowned, as if I were fanatic, yearning to be part of the family of saints; even then, the world had no place for me. But I knew the wisdom of refusing all temptations. The flesh is not easily exhausted. I would pray for an hour or so before going to sleep. At night I liked to watch the stars.

Hermit, pilgrim: only words.

Across the street, this Corso Italia on another continent, peacocks shop for Versace sweaters, couples drink *latte macchiato*. It is the Christmas season when fresh snow fills the trees and gentle plump women buy the imported sweet bread called *panettone* in its bright blue boxed stamped "Motta" in gold. "The original Milanese recipe," proclaims the box, but I wouldn't know about that; I never saw an orange, much less candied peel. Such delicacies you have at your finger tips! No one visits me on this cold Saturday afternoon.

So the truth appears in details, you say? Are details facts? I leave that issue to others. In 1346, several years before I was born, the bubonic infection returned to Europe. (I died from it at the age of thirty.) This was the plague's second appearance, now as the Black Death. According to historians, the last previous mention of the plague by Christian writers dates from 767. Almost four hundred years after *Pasteurella pestis* found a home, its ecological niche, as you call it, in the burrows of the black rat, whose fleas carried the plague. Rat; flea; man, woman, child. Flea bites, at first, then by human contact—touch me!—and through the air, as you inhaled the contamination of coughing, sneezing. Soon vileness surrounded us. Our air bled with it, our bedding stank. Even the soup we ate tasted of death. No, I will not tell you how ships carried the infection across the Atlantic, or to the remote ports of Europe. We never knew, and you already know enough. There is always a plague brewing. And I am always dying of it.

At twenty, after my parents died, I sold our land and set out for Rome.

The roads left me breathless. I began to cough, with a pain deep in my chest. Many times, men could have killed me.

Outside the walls of each new town, corpses piled up. Inside, I heard rumors of witches, and of executions. Once someone gave me a piece of leathery sausage, but I tossed it to a stray dog. I could have lived on wild olives.

Often I wondered where I would die, and how. The torch-lit processions passing the lane where I slept usually meant another funeral. Bells rang continuously.

The afternoon passes as usual. A young girl visits Mary: Does she have a vocation? An elderly man dressed in black dips his fingers into holy water, makes the sign of the cross on his forehead. After looking about—perhaps for Father—he leaves, frowning.

Gradually the church darkens.

Then, out of nowhere, a woman with long greying black hair stands before me. She focuses a camera while the bearded man behind her left shoulder comments, apparently in a low voice. But I can't hear, as I said before. With one hand he gestures toward my wound. The camera tilts upward.

I believe they are speaking of light.

I am embarrassed that my leg thrusts out like a chorus girl's (I know about them—eternity isn't static). My wound glistens, its hard pink lips a wild rose, the *vagina dentate*, the Sacred Heart. It burns me, burns me.

Roch, Rocco, Rock. Try and remember.

One year, after visiting Rome, I met the plague in Piacenza where, tradition has it, I was fed in the woods by a lone dog. And I cured fellow sufferers miraculously, before returning to Montpellier, and my cruel uncle. This seems a reasonable account, if you can believe that a man dying of plague would walk from Italy to France. Why not? What you believe is of little consequence to me.

My uncle would not see me. Denied me, even. Had me imprisoned as an impostor. Could he not see? I watched him kick his horse once, a foolish man.

The making of a cave—every hermit learns now. Rule #1: Keep

possessions to a minimum. Yesterday's newspapers told of a nameless old man who died under a bridge, where he apparently slept. Around his body police found his few possessions: an empty rye bottle, several foul shirts rolled into a ball, torn magazines, half a dozen wire hangers, a chipped mug, a bag of stale doughnuts, an unopened jar of peanut butter, three books of matches, a plastic bag stuffed with other plastic bags, all carefully concealed under another plastic bag as protection from the rats who shared his home. He understood how to make a cave.

The winters are cold in Piacenza.

A hand, dipping cloth into brandy, smells of the sweet old wine we used for cleansing. Each sore has a stench of its own. I have watched hands move around the wounds, over and over, pity in the touch. Whose hands were they? Mine? I have seen too many wounds, yet what I wanted most was another.

Several days after the flea bite: swelling glands, headache, nausea, vomiting, bloody diarrhea, blotchy red skin rash. Then the first bubo appears, one to four inches in diameter, in the groin, or the arm pit, or beside the neck. But usually in the groin. Tender, at first, it fills with yellowish liquid, a mixture of puss and blood. Now chills, fever, rapid pulse, even delirium. If death doesn't occur, your infection might spread to the lungs, which develop abscesses. Death by pneumonia. Or—for there always seems to be an or—the buboes might be infected by other bacteria. But I won't elaborate. These are the things you become. God's tokens, some called them, the buboes. Or, simply, tokens.

Some say I died back in Montpellier, others cite Lombardy. Relics were claimed across Europe, from Arles to Venice. Look me up in any dictionary of saints, under Roch—you'll see. A cult emerged, and I became patron of the plague-stricken.

And then the Black Death died down, taking with it a third of the population of Europe. Two hundred years later, people no longer needed me, although revivals have happened. Outbreaks of cholera in the nineteenth century found me again. Remember, I am always waiting.

And the dog? Of course there is no truth to the story of the dog. Is that what you want to hear? You want me to say that he belongs to legend, to fancy? You would be wrong. There were always a pack of dogs barking furiously.

You do not understand miracle. No—I said miracle, in the singular. Miracle is a place. You can live there, if you like. I once lived in miracle: that is the nature of prayer.

The man and woman prepare to leave. After taking one more picture, of him at my feet, she puts her camera into a leather bag, then buttons her coat; he pulls on gloves. They look about the empty church and nod to each other.

Darkness quickens my memory. I will myself to forget.

Thyme, sage, rosemary.

Across the street, rats come out to play in narrow lanes behind the vegetable stores, restaurants.

Stay with me tonight, for one whole, single night, as if it could go from sleep to death.

2006

H. Nigel Thomas, 1947–

Boy-Child

"You're special,"
I was told;
"you're a boy."

"Your wife's given you four boy-childs;
you should love her,"
a woman cousin told my father
after a disabling flogging he gave my mother.
If she'd been *his* wife, my father said,
he'd have sealed her mouth—
forever.

Later, living in my grandparents' household,
I was told a boy-child
keeps the family name in hold,
is its gold.

Most children at my school
had their mothers' names,
because, my grandmother said,
asking God's forgiveness for saying it,
they were illegitimate—
a word my seven-year tongue could not lift,
could not spit out,
a filth-filled word
holding the whirlpools of a frothing Atlantic.

At eight, I learned
at my last brother's birth,
that before he's seen the sun,
a boy-child must not see the moon.
A bad omen, they said.

My attraction to the moon's mutability
and power to turn ugly landscape into silver sea
(a secret, since a boy-child must admire might)

presaged my predilection for the night
and queens whose crowns are poetry
eschewing might.

Today, Fundamentalists tell me
I pervert my role:
they say I'm Yang,
who's abandoned Yin,
(whom they've placed outside me)
crying for control;
and a boy-child becomes a man
only when he's added to the fold.

The Rastas want my head removed
because I'm 'scepterless.'
Truth, they insist: Levitical light.
'Perverts,' they add and nod,
are dragged to deserts
and stoned.

1999

Unfulfilled Desire

To be the gristle and bone
scraped from the plate of
last night's dinner
is reality my Caribbean upbringing did
not prepare me for—but there
I pined in cells of conformity.

Here or there one hangs
still
from the horns of desire,
unable to shut one's ears
to syrens shrilling cacophony within.

Scapegoat or commodity—
one or the other—

unsated desire is
insouciant of metaphor.

1999

Nigger-Kike-Honky-Wop

Dear Roger, you ask me to plunge into
your loneliness,
hoping I'd not know I'd be its fuel.
But I do,
and you explode with
"Nègre! Nègre!"

You, who're charged to expand appetite for industry,
must know that *kike* and *nègre*, *wop* and *honky*
are cries from an agony
few—I'd hoped you were one—can cure.

Now you circle a
cluster of prepubescent men
like a revolving door;
they insult;
but tonight you prefer their curses
to the indifference
you'd otherwise endure.

1999

Gilles Devault, 1948–

from *Ferns of Ash*

when a cat leaves you
is it by chance that the wind rises up
that rain suddenly showers upon the windows
that with one swoop autumn sweeps in
reaching even below the sheets

this animal we let go away
must it still remain inside us
          like an empty room
this other silence we are no longer able to hold
this other cat inside us
          that lets us sleep no more

how many nights will it take
          let the dead trees moan

*

sometimes it is a dream motionless as two trees
          side by side
scarcely moving   speaking to each other from
  their fingertips
taking advantage of the time together
          that stirs their leaves

rain-like restlessness beneath cold sheets
when dawn awkwardly crumbles
          its rocks of mist

sometimes it's your mouth or your heart to consume
biting into me in the morning
          the hairy fist of boredom

the laziness of a dream
that lingers before eyes close
makes my hands fall suddenly silent

the inside of your skin dizzies me
this desert that lets itself be cradled like desire
when night has nothing left to tell

sometimes your whole body mingles with mine
            and falls silent

1993   *Translated by Jonathan Kaplansky*

from *White Eye of Sleep*

opening your eyes will settle nothing
the night will not erase
the sea is always the same
always the same relentlessness
the pain has not shifted
I still keep your heart in my hand
against the roaring waves

sometimes the murmuring is so strong
we no longer hear it
the murmuring is so strong
it sounds like an archangel perched on the din of death

I keep your heart warm against my hand
I hear sorrow beating in your sleep

do not wake yet
dawn is still not here
wait a little longer
it is not yet time to awake

burning sings against your cheek

let the sea be calm
let the shore once more fill with light
let new stars disappear

at night I like to look deep into the skin of your face
in your face I like to look deep into the night at the end of my fingers

your skin appears moon-like
a landscape sleeping beneath the mirage of your eyes

I like the weight of your hip along the nerves of my thigh
I like to sense we are sleeping together
in the desert of our dreams
I keep this secret sleep entirely inside for your return
the night is a lie in the hollow of my shoulder

*

sleeping against your belly
fingers linked on sweating thighs
lulling you to sleep with liquid amber
lips half open to sleep

recounting scents to you
palms quivering upon the moss
wings rustling beneath the racket of crickets
dry twigs in the hollows of folded flesh

faint prayer
breath riffling through your body hair
slight fever
in the nest of the world
where my mouth falls silent
where my eyes rest

sketching the bitterness of lips
over your marble skin

caught in the morning's wool
cheek sinking into the swelling of your flesh

at your centre
dreaming of cliffs

of islands as well
trail streaked with colours jarringly bright
pearls beneath seaweed green

weathering the downpour
caressing the sea bream's prickly back

curled upside down
in the terror of desire
standing up silent beneath the storm
a pirate longing for sweet scents

milk discharged burning
dream's rough skin
beneath a bank of heavy snow

half fainted
white with pale nights
breath slow beneath your skin's coat

and nothing
your hand far above
strong as it approaches my hair
and sleep
far beyond
without weight upon my shoulder
just that
my mouth half open on the shaft of your soul

1995 *Translated by Jonathan Kaplansky*

BERTRAND LACHANCE, 1948–

send me those eyes again

send me those eyes again
dreem up anothr one boy
send me those eyes again
dreem up anothr one boy
send me those eyes again
dreem up anothr one boy
send me those eyes again
dreem up anothr one boy
send me those eyes again
dreem up anothr one boy

send me those eyes again
dreem up anothr one boy
send me those eyes again
dreem up anothr one boy
send me those eyes again
dreem up anothr one boy
send me those eyes again
dreem up anothr one boy
send me those eyes again
dreem up anothr one boy
send me those eyes again
dreem up anothr one boy
send me those eyes again
dreem up anothr one boy
send me those eyes again
dreem up anothr one boy
send me those eyes again

dreem up anothr one boy
send me those eyes again
dreem up anothr one boy
send me those eyes again
dreem up anothr one boy
send me those eyes again
dreem up anothr one boy
send me those eyes again
dreem up anothr one boy
send me those eyes again
dreem up anothr one boy
send me those eyes again
dreem up anothr one boy
send me those eyes again
dreem up anothr one boy
send me those eyes again
dreem up anothr one boy
send me those eyes again
dreem up anothr one boy
send me those eyes again
dreem up anothr one boy
send me those eyes again
dreem up anothr one boy
send me those eyes again
dreem up anothr one boy

send me those eyes again
dreem up anothr one boy
send me those eyes again

dreem up anothr one boy
send me those eyes again
dreem up anothr one boy
send me those eyes again

1972

Jean Chapdelaine Gagnon, 1949–

Do Not Reveal This Word

XII

Do not reveal this word that an indiscreet tongue could have let slip. Do not reveal this word; the sea hears it so well and pulls it taut between each of its waves, cradling it. Let this child's word, this word, this song, travel instead from the mouth to the heart. Do not awaken the ear, let it sleep, let it ripen, with no vibrations to disturb it; keep it on key the way you would a silence, sure and hushed, driven by the sole desire to never betray anything more, to make itself dense water, a halted gesture, expectation.

XI

Do not reveal this word that I used to weave in a halting tongue, that I began anew like a stutterer his sentence or Penelope her weaving precious and rare. I made it my distant maze where I could cover myself with noise, lose myself in my tongue. Hearing myself too much and never finishing, I had become a secret for myself, an indecipherable enigma. By wanting to reconstruct me, against my will, can't you see that you were offering me up like the accused for whom a word too poorly weighed would cause to perish in the flames like a sorcerer, like a woman. That a blunt, innocuous word would decree my death far better than a sentence.

X

Do not reveal this word
That like so much could
Escape you
Seal your tongues and your lips
Cement them
So that none of your gestures betray
What was entrusted to you
In veiled words   between cupped palms
Very close to your ear

Conceal this word spoken
Do not make it a song or a refrain
Sift it through

IX

Do not reveal this word held back till now beneath the glottis as if stifled, this world that nourished you and that sustained me. And why not hesitate to say it and utter it, why feel guilty for not disclosing it? Why would it not be for you, resounding for you and in you alone? Are you not entitled to words, entitled to have a secret and to not reveal yourself? And who could claim, tell me, who could give himself the right to open you up, to assail you so that finally this word would be expelled from you, this aspirated word, this troubled gaze?

VIII

Do not reveal this word of harmony impossible to understand. The reverse has already cut lines in the glass. The goal is to hide, to conceal the splinters and broken glass. When the shape is perfect, no one has the power to hear. Above and beyond fragments too fine for anyone to notice, I urge you to be silent. They will blame you, they will make you matter or modelling clay. Dream with no sound other than that of a cat. Do not move a fingernail, an eyelid or this sharpened thread, which could turn against you, that more than anything could inflict upon you a wound impossible to heal. Snuggle beneath your swaddling clothes, make yourself a fetus again and go back while there is time.

VII

for Lorraine Bénic

Do not reveal this word, this word, this sound, this reverse side of the letter where any joy would erroneously run counter to asceticism. And this silence you surround yourself with, where you take refuge to better fend off the dull, heavy rain, sudden ice jams that give way, I want it to envelop you completely, perfect like an enclosed space where no opening is possible—like an endorsement, like a tomb be silent; make yourself a wall, fence, belly and reservoir, so that no leak can touch you. Make yourself a wall, town, partition and why not a prison, so that nothing escapes your understanding and so the echo in you and you alone can grow stronger.

VI

Do not reveal this word
Far too sombre and deadly
This word that grapples
With your bodies   with your lips
And that awaits from you but a gesture
To take from you   to swallow
The white space of a letter
Where you went to take refuge

V

Do not reveal this word
That slips between us
Garrulous restrained and driven by a letter
At its best a naked Mona Lisa
And silent
Frozen as if readying to utter a word
That cannot leave her
Her lips pinched and stitched together
Like a Medusa at the sirens' seductive song

IV

Do not reveal this word
That takes shape
Winding its way from you to me

Do not reveal this word
Similar to all others
And yet not like
The ones that are forged among all other words
And come undone
Different and perhaps still the same

III

Do not reveal this word
Someone could hear it and appropriate it
Someone could take it
And keep it for himself
Someone with a thousand masks
Could stretch out upon it
Curl up
Like a shell on its core
Or its mollusc
Like a sea in its conch

II

Do not reveal this word
Like water lengthening
Do not make it a stream running into the sea
Double over your bones your flesh your skin
Pull yourself taut   Hold back your tongue
Do not nest
Like the ringer in its far too loud bell
And that at the slightest start
Loses itself in echoes   thrown off centre
Abandons its belly to the desert winds

I

Do not reveal this word. I wanted it to be held between just us two like an offering, like a magnet from my mouth to your ear, heard by you alone. I wanted no one to suspect its existence, no one to question me and for it never to fall in the mouth of the Echo. But who could have deceived our silence and watchfulness, who could have seized this language spoken by us alone? Between my mouth and your ear, it has disappeared, has eluded us to deliver both of us naked to the words of those who heard nothing and who would take pleasure in throwing us to the tellers of tales.

1985   *Translated by Jonathan Kaplansky*

Your Name of Love

I

I do not know you by name
Other than the one your voice dictated to me
Many centuries ago it seems
And your body even more than your face
Vanishes
Like a morning hurrying to give way
Not to day but to night

II

In the kitchen the coffee goes bitter
Without your mouth to drink it
Without your lips the cup has lost for me
This taste of you
Before I set it down
Disappointed
At not having met you

III

I no longer find you
Not in your words nor in my places
That have become foreign to me
Already I see you as a stranger
Despite the everyday despite
This promiscuity
Poorly shared between us for so long

IV

I know I know you can't bear me anymore
My presence weighing you down
Like a sin
Carrying me the way we carry our deaths
At arm's length or at thoughts'
You can no longer bear my wandering
In the house not outside

Never with another
You can no longer bear my fidelity
Like a silent reproach

V

Without you
I no longer go to the mountain
To see the sunrise from the lookout
Each morning
And never anymore do I watch
This rapid shift to night
As the city blushes with sleep

VI

I no longer make love since then
As if all of a sudden I had forgotten what I'd learned
For a long time I stopped keeping track
Of your absence
I am but a fallen man

VII

Each time I hear a motorcycle I rush over
You know it isn't you
It is never you anymore
Knocking at my door
On the telephone never you
And I even forget the sound of your voice
I sometimes forget even your name
Of love
In my night

1988 *Translated by Jonathan Kaplansky*

from *Île de mémoire*

Upon your face my father
Sometimes are blurry imprints
Of other men's features
Loved in love or friendship
Loved also sometimes with hate wrongly loved
And whose faces like yours
Crumple up a bit more each day

Of some there only remains
Just a smile wink frown
While all the rest is eaten up by forgetfulness
Oval jaw bridge of the nose
Prominent forehead and cheekbones
Shape of the lip
Chin square or dimpled
While their soul persists
As clearly today as a thousand years ago
Venus in the night

**

Four months later when I call Étienne
I seem to be hearing my father's voice
A voice I can barely hear
That the wire seems to have trouble conveying
It sounds so frail
Throaty voice with no breath in it
Voice wearing out its chords
Like a violin abandoned by its soul

At twenty-five Étienne has an old man's voice
Worn by a century of excess or hardship
An impersonal voice
Even sexless with imminent death

**

Twenty-nine days after this brief conversation
—The time that February takes—
Étienne died

Strange coincidence that at my kitchen wall
Daylight inexorably fades the ink
Of a drawing that once was dark
Today sepia
There where a vase a key two irises are shaded off
Their withered stems make me think of
Two birds ready to topple over head first
On the painter's work bench or on the easel
Of master Espinet

1997 *Translated by Jonathan Kaplansky*

from *Tu*

Whom do you see in me
Son or slave
A wisp of straw or a vase
That poorly withstood the test of fire
A work partly finished
Half a man aspiring to be God
Who turns his back on you as soon as
You avert your gaze

2000 *Translated by Jonathan Kaplansky*

Blaine Marchand, 1949–

Travelling Alone

Take it, you insisted.
Your *Michelin* guide to ancient Rome.
Flipping open the pages carefully,
the spine broken from being well-thumbed,
you said the best ruins are the ones
you marked. Your hand lingered on mine
as I took the book, tucked it
carefully in my luggage,
smiling, imagining one day we might travel
as lovers.

Once off the plane, the taxi hurtled me
through the quiet roadways,
early morning shadows dark as priests in cassocks.
I checked into the hotel, unpacked the guide, set out.
It took my breath away,
the Coliseum, there, at the end of the street,
a broken honeycomb through which the sun poured.
You, an artist, were right.
The light here beautiful, exquisite as saffron.
From some cavern inside, pilgrims sang the *Te Deum*,
their voices careened among the stones,
exposed as if the venerated corpse of a martyr.

Then on to St. Peter-in-Chains. This you gave three stars.
It was dark and damp. Scaffolding everywhere
as if it were about to collapse on itself.
But off to the right, the unfinished tomb of Pope Julius,
Michelangelo's *Moses*. A tourist clunked a coin into the meter.
The light against the sculpted, muscled arms a shimmer of
water.
I thought of you stepping out of the shower
after we had made love. You bent to the bed,
a pool of drops gathered on my chest.
For the first time, I felt the isolation
of the tourist travelling alone. Fatigue made me skittish.

I turned back to the hotel where, although only noon,
I fell into the dead of sleep.

All week long, each day, after work,
your choices guided me into basilicas,
down the Spanish Steps, through the Terme di Caracalla,
but also to less-travelled sites.
Feeling out-of-place,
among the elegant Italian men you raved about.
I thought about you and me, so similar,
craving beauty everywhere. Soothing the pain.
All our life walking among the remnants
of our past, rendering, transforming them,
the way floodlights at night
accented the monuments,
gave them surrealistic splendour.

By mid-week, I imagined us in bed once again,
waking from the brief drowse men fall into
after sex, comparing insights, impressions.
But although the plane brought me closer,
you withdrew, kept retreating,
always a last minute change of plans.
I sought guidance, explanations,
confused by your tactics, your cryptic signs.

Now I willingly wander
among the monuments of my own city.
I stare up at the flank of bronze soldiers
in the arch of the War Memorial.
The sculptor has them advancing,
a battalion of heroic men
marching through the eye of a needle.
I, too, have finally chosen to pass through.
High above, on the arc of granite,
winged Peace and Freedom hold up
a torch and laurel to the open sky.

1995

Subversion

As a young boy I loved
a priest who hid
his longing for male flesh,
sought it in the company of altar servers.
His desire burning like a coal inside a censer,
which, once doused with myrrh, smouldered,
the air suddenly acrid.

You advise me not to use words
—cock, crotch, cum—
that my poems are complex, layered
and such words only get in the way,
are voyeuristic, too explicit,
far too political.

Should songs of love be only
ambiguous, discrete,
shadows falling across bushes,
or with curtains drawn
masking interior scenes?

For years, I said nothing,
though I could not deny
the voice that spoke, if only inside,
longing for hands,
the thrill of fingers at waistbands,
anticipation of wet mouth against flesh.

And it would not be quiet
even when I pierced my skin
with pins, conjuring
the image of a gaunt saint
in a desert cave.

Even for a child, sex
can be pleasurable,
what is not
is the lesson

that grown-up words
are treacherous,
double-headed coins,
—on one side, the mouth begs for release;
on the other, it cries shame.

A child shapes his world
by what he experiences,
learns to be cunning,
risks uttering certain phrases
even knowing there will be
the tang of soap in his mouth,
a slap leaving
a handprint across his cheek.

By trial and error, language is mastered,
the child subverted becomes an adult
who confides only in private
and when disabled by truth.

Some poems about love dare
to speak of the body,
unafraid of its dangers.

1995

The Carver

In this man's hands
Wood becomes liberated
From itself, shavings flying,
Ebony birds at dusk
Clattering in the concealment of a tree
Then leaping into the air,
Released over the veld,
A fine thread drawn through limitless sky,
Unbound from the comings and goings of those below.

In this man's hands
The heart of wood is unfettered.
The flow lines of its grain,
Unhindered by bark,
Now saturate the surface
In channels the augur's blade
Has scraped. Incised fibers
Smoothed and polished to sheen,
To a concise delineation
Of skin and bone.

In this man's hands
The wood becomes other.
Ochre of earth, midnight of wood ash
Rubbed roughly into pores
On forehead, nose, mouth and chin.
It becomes, after decades of weathering
By relentless sun, endless drought,
To stand, ingrained. Now, through it
They become, released—their voices forged
Their limbs congruent in dance,
They, no longer boys but full-bodied men.

2003

Doug Wilson, 1950–1992

There is a thingold
youngman
who holds
your head between his hands
hands like antique gold
cool and glowing
against your hair
your flesh shines
with his touching
this is no Midas
there is a kiss like a balm
upon your brow
the room darkens
the metal tightens
on your flesh
you have awakened
alchemies.

1977

there is poetry
in our lying here
the jumble of flushed
flesh and blankets
the sharpnessess of hipbones
the swell of ribcage
the lolling sex
I notice the small things
a pulse moving
in your throat, the veins
in your hands,
the bedlight gilding
the hair on my arm
details important only
in that they are now
recorded
but changing as we

move, as we change
as others replace you
as others replace me
there will be poetry
in the lying here.

1977

I dream often
of angels
silverswift young
windmen
they come to me
on moonlight
never speaking
great wings folded
they enter me
fill me
are me
I fly
I am angel
I will come
to you on moonlight
dream of me.

1977

Sky Gilbert, 1952–

Assfucking and June Allyson

(I can't believe I got them both in one poem)
You know what it's like when you start to argue with them
I mean really argue
And they're twenty-one years old (just turned)
and then you start to fall in "like"?
It's that night when you first think
I'm going to remember this night and I'm going to look back on it
and I'm going to think about how he got so gleefully energetically angry
And then the fight
And this night the fight was about assfucking without a condom
theoretical—no really—
not that we would I mean ... really engage in (gosh!)
But he's twenty-one years old and he only came out three years ago
and he doesn't really understand what it feels like
or what makes it so wonderful
And I realize it's as important
as remembering June Allyson's voice
to describe to him what it was like
So just pretend you're twenty-one years old
and you have incredibly blond hair
and you've never ever heard June Allyson speak (except on those golden age diaper commercials which don't really count!)
You don't even know who she is
and so I have to somehow describe how
June Allyson's voice sort of came from down there
sort of deep and very felt
but it was sweet
and harsh
and when you needed it most
it was always there
And sometimes you hated it
sometimes it got on your nerves
but then when you got down to it
there was nothing quite like June Allyson's voice
And that's what it was like to fuck somebody in the ass without a

condom
And you're twenty-one years old
and you'll get mad at me for writing this poem
and you'll probably want to scratch my back with your incredibly
long nails
but that's alright
because some day in 1999 when they've found a cure for AIDS
I'll actually shove my dick up your ass without a condom
and you'll open your mouth, meaning to say
"What the hell do you think you're—"
and instead
you'll end up talking like June Allyson
which is, as I said
sometimes painful
but more often than not, incredibly, incredibly wonderful

1995

Winnipeg Farts

for Ian

no one farts in Winnipeg
it would wake the geese
only toques can make you happy
and the bathroom floor is heated
everything goes on forever
until you get to the end

then it stops

I want you to love me desperately
but please don't do it in Winnipeg
you promise, don't you?
I saw a boy in Winnipeg
his arms were soft and hairy
I listened to some music in Winnipeg
but nothing could pierce the vast grey sky
that painting belonged to my grandmother!

and the people are so friendly
or so they say, but still—
it's Louis Riel you long for
as you understand why their Puritan passion
just had to wrench the life out of him
(one imagines he had erections, after all
like any Frenchman)

the next time I go down on you honey
will you make me forget I ever went to Winnipeg?

I farted quite publicly in Winnipeg
and no one seemed to notice

but somewhere far off, in the lonely forest a bird died
such is the power of wishing and wanting and wallowing
in a place where even despair is muted
by wheat

yet beige is not my colour

do your eyes still sparkle, in spite of Winnipeg?
when can I see them again, my darling?

oh when can we wear pajamas
and jump up and down on feathery beds
make stains, and celebrate our bodily functions?
not in sunny Manitoba, please
far far far from The Prayeree

2003

Something Else

in my dream I keep moving into different rooms
of a very large hippie household
it's miles from the gay ghetto
(how will I ever get home late at night after the bars?)
some of the apartments are spacious and homey
I can wander around the crumbling capacious halls
my straight neighbors are rarely if ever home
or they're vicious
the landlord is some sort of cheat
some of the apartments are very dark and dirty
there is a communal kitchen
suspicious substances stuck to an old pan.
should I move there?
or should I stay in my tiny apartment
so comfortable in the heart of my own gay community?
in my dream I waver, back and forth
visiting one apartment and then the other
and then I meet Cavafy
who is lounging in a chair, his shirt unbuttoned
every inch the satisfied Daddy
and he curls his finger and beckons me to his side
"you needn't live above a brothel, even though I do."
I love everything about him
especially his charming Greek/Brit accent.
"you needn't live above a brothel,
as long as you have a brothel in your mind"
at that point, a naked young man, wet from the shower,
wanders carelessly into the
livingroom, toweling his hair
"although actual proximity has its advantages"
Cavafy and the boy don't touch each other
and for a moment I wonder, is it because they already have?
or is it something else

2003

Daniel David Moses, 1952–

A Bone in the Balance of Moonlight

The moon, that heavy weight, pulled you out.
You'll never underestimate her
again. Had you ever thought her light

might lead you far into the dark or
hold you there so long the neighbourhood
park would empty? Why no one even

walks a dog! So maybe the moon's walking
you—has got you out of doors to do
your business. But what sort could you do

and with who when we're talking so poor
this gleam of pennies on the pavement
can also distract you? But the moon

knows who you are and where you belong
in the exchange of heavy and bright,
knows who among her daughters and sons,

the many and few, might benefit
from prowling the town with her, up for
all comers, after midnight. And, boy,

she's done more than a few blocks and talked
you through to clarity before. Don't
blame her if you won't see what she's thrown

as more than bones. Her conversation
from now on concerns the currency
of blood, must be just with her daughters.

She'll give you no quarter, won't let you
go back to your room with her or alone.
You're here to spend those moons off the ends

of your fingers, to break the shining
line that pulled you out off in a spill
of silver. *Find the friend, the stranger,*

the eyes, she says. *Toss them like coins. Heads*
or tails, spit and sweat, you'll soon get to
put a new down payment on the night.

2000

Offhand Song

I do not dare compare your hand
with those of a woman or boy
or with the closed wing of a bird

at rest on the table. I do
not dare compare it there even
with my own so open here as

we talk it could hold or cover
yours up. Your hand has the power
just by touching your chest to slow

or suspend the beat of your heart.
What need then would it have of touch,
of a nest or father or man?

I hold on to my cup, hold off
finishing the coffee up, not
wanting to dare the hand to hand

comparison of goodbye. There
I might be taken by the need
to embrace or follow or fly.

2000

Cowboy Pictures

I want to send away
to California
for pictures of the sun.
That state of the Union
is famous for its light.
Even in black and white,
the glamour of young men
who've oiled up their skin
till it shines with the sky
is bound to make my day,

to say nothing of night.
I can't imagine what
colour could do. Or what
those guys go through to get
to that estate. Mountain
passes, the Great Salt Plain?
A still-hostile frontier
might explain why most wear
cowboy hats black and white
as the pictures. But what

explains them lacking all
other clothes? A couple
are trying the wild
Indian bit, child
faces looking paler
under the cheap feathers
and war paint. And of course
this grown-up guy as Horse
needs some explaining too.
Or at least a lasso.

All the other rules seem
the same. Whatever game
they're playing, the only
difference seems to be
the gold there was in them

there hills is now a gleam
of silver bodies, still
as any mineral.
Gold caught in shades of grey,
never aging. Will they?

Picture yourself that way
in California,
some green rancher, say, out
riding your range, without
a thought for what sweet heart
you left across the Great
Divide. Or maybe be
the little lost dogie
he cradles to his chest.
So the pictures suggest

some sentimental ways
of bondage, yes, of boys
being boys. Shining with
the sky, in skin and breath
and eye, they're the picture
of youth—their six guns are
shooting stars through the bars
of the dark that covers
more than half the planet.
Try to bite the bullet.

2000

Ian Stephens, 1954–1995

Wounds: Valentine's Day

Some guy put a lit cigarette into my shoulder in your storeroom. That was in October, my first time in Montreal.

When I was released into the back of the city I had five separate burns in an arc on my shoulder, so when I got back to McGill I thought about you for months, even in Rochester, my home town; it was always sore; I never really healed, always somebody scraping them open, making me bleed.

And Winnipeg, the sadistic Indian with whom I thought I was in love, soft-skinned, soft-spoken, he too made me bleed, chewing my shoulder as he shot.

But when I left him I came back to you. St. Valentine's Day, empty-hearted at last, on a perfect day, perfect for you, with the wind blowing ash off the hood of your Buick, with another boy auditioning on stage in your empty club.

I used to think that your eyes were blue.

I used to worry about love, where it hid when the fires tore off the door, when the rubber hands squeezed the pale thin throat.

I watched him jerk and look sexy to the disco beat and the mirrors but he took off his g-string with shaking hands, his half-hard unskinned cock escaping into light, squeezed at the base by a red suede strap. I knew that within a week you'd beat him and make him do anything for you just like you had done to me.

You lowered the music. Putting the cigarette in your mouth, you stepped over the braid onto the stage. You held the boy's elbow, instructing him, pouting at him, telling him to pose a little longer, take it easy, the customers liked that. This went on for a few minutes until you laughed charmingly.

Without being seen I ducked down into the toilet.

Waiting for you to come back was like waiting for the drug to kick in, knowing I'd be somewhere else, would be someone else. And I could watch it all.

Finally, you showed up. I was waiting in a cubicle and I saw you pull out your cock and spray the back of the urinal. You saw me and grunted, almost laughing. I followed you into the alley, I took off my boots, jeans and shirt and threw them into the back of your car and waited.

Like I had the first time.

After putting on your gloves you told me to get in.

I don't know this city and I don't want to. We drove through a tunnel and soon we were through the suburbs and into an industrial park on the edge of the country.

Near a river, under a bridge you taped my ankles together and my wrists behind my back, you wound tape over my eyes so I couldn't see you.

You pushed me down. The ground was wet, cold but clean.

The only thing you said was, "The Lord is my Shepherd I do not want...."

I didn't care. Even then I knew he was going to kill me; I could smell the knife as clearly as I could smell his ass. He put his cock in my mouth and knew he was going to slit my throat as he came because that is what I wanted him to do.

Roughly he shoved and lifted my legs so that he was over me with his smile poised and ready over my hole; he licked it, hit it, pulled his fist back and slugged it, then bit into my skin. I was numb when he threw his cock into my ass. He had no trouble ripping my hole and pushing it in all the way. He fucked me for a minute then took it out, put on a condom and started again.

I could feel warm liquid dribbling through my crotch. I heard ice floes on the river cracking under each other. Gradually, I forgot what was happening. The tape started to come off my eyes and I could see lights, some buildings in the dark distance.

After he came he emptied the condom on my head and kissed me, his thin lips wired with nicotine, sharp nicotine, tongue so warm.... I could feel his juice sliding down the neck over my throat.

He took out the knife. He cut the tape off my ankles and hands.

But I don't care about freedom. Not when I'm with him.

Without a word, I knew he knew but it wasn't going to be easy. He shoved me towards the car. "You can work in the basement tonight."

He wouldn't let me touch my dick even though it was dark

red and harder than cement. He gave me a blanket and told me to be quiet.

I started shaking as the street lights slid over my shoulders. I could feel the salt burning where you had scraped me. I knew that my arc was now bleeding and probably wouldn't heal. Ever.

You put on a tape; ChemLab—the music tore through my ears as we tore through the tunnel. I mouthed the words as Jared, the singer, shouted "I Still Bleed, I Still Bleed" over and over. I knew that song, it was our song, darling, our song.

I looked down and pulled the blanket away from my groin. I slid forward and my cock throbbed like a fat fish on a plate. I knew that you'd like to cut it off and eat it. I knew that you were going to shave my crotch and make me lie in the shower in the basement on a leash and drink a hundred men. As a special treat for all the members. And at dawn you'd let me be fucked by twelve men, friends or rich ugly bastards and when it was over, when even the young boy who auditioned this afternoon had shot his thick load over my back and screamed, slamming his balls over my wide open hole, that you'd burn me, perhaps in the same place, perhaps on my face, perhaps when I was unconscious, perhaps when I was open-eyed and hungry.

I looked over your face as we emerged from the underground. Except for the scar, it was unlined and content. At that moment you could have been my younger brother Jeff, the one working at Kodak as a mechanical designer, the shutter specialist.

I wonder what Jeff would think of his brother, the burn-freak, the queer. Or if he'd care. I can't remember ever thinking about what he does with his dick.

I'd rather hear slashing guitars and feel a cool orange butt on my flesh, the incense of flesh, flesh and smoke....

I don't want to ever shoot. I want to be hard for you always, naked, taped tight and burnt for you.

I still bleed, I still bleed.

Such is my love, my love, my love....

So my cock burned. At a traffic light you looked at it and slapped it hard, hurting me. When it wouldn't go down, you squeezed my balls and it hurt too much. I almost passed out.

Almost, almost.

On the edge.

Of *never.*

I thought I was going to die until I didn't think at all. My brain was full of pain and there was nothing else.

As it was when you burnt me, on my shoulder, on an arc, five stars.

1994

Bill Richardson, 1955–

Nothing Like a Dame

The story I'll tell you is all about Al,
A mountainous man who had mountainous pals,
With gym-sculpted bodies unsullied by toxins:
Their calves hard as granite and necks thick as oxen,
With hillocks for chests and with statuesque shoulders
And biceps the size of conventional boulders,
With tummies that rippled and thighs made of thunder,
And as for the rest—well, I'll leave you to wonder.

They all had Camaros emblazoned with dragons,
And brows anthropologists might call Cro-Magnon.
In every way masculine in their deportment:
Oh, never was seen such a macho assortment.
Hallowe'en night was again on the verge
And Al and his pals had the fun-loving urge
To deck themselves out and do something inane.
"I got it," Al ventured. "Let's go out as dames!"

"Yeah! Dames!" said his buddies. "Va va va va voom!"
One snickered, "Hooters!" One chuckled, "Bazooms!"
They drove to the thrift store and swiftly took stock,
They bought hideous wigs and rebarbative frocks,
They tried on the shoes and like madmen careened
From pillar to post in their pumps, size 16.
They dashed to the cash and unloaded their carts,
Then went home to practice the womanly arts.

Big Al, on arrival, made haste to put on
His black *crêpe de Chine* and his hot pink chiffon.
He looked in the mirror and liked what he saw:
His nice way with scarves, his complexion *sans* flaw.
He was big, he was butch, and devotedly hetero ...
But still he was thrilled to be sporting stilettos.
He felt like a diva: Tebaldi or Callas.
Thus Al was transformed, and before him stood Alice.

He stood breathing heavily, misting the mirror,
He lurched back a step, teetered nearer and nearer,
And then just as surely as push leads to shove
Allan and Alice fell deeply in love.
Yes, surely as borrowers look for a lender
Al was enmeshed in confusion of gender,
And surely as knickknacks belitter a shelf
Big Al, at a glance, fell in love with himself.

Hallowe'en came, they all had a great time,
And when it was over his buddies consigned
Their dresses and girdles, their borroweds and blues
To attics and basements and Sally Anns, too.
Al, though, was different. His buddies were stumped
To see him keep purchasing boas and pumps.
His father was puzzled, his mother depressed,
But Al wanted Alice dependably dressed.

Psychologists doubtless could try to explain
And give Al's condition a clinical name,
Reveal how his fondness for ladies' emporia
Signals some kind of a gender dysphoria,
Call him regressive or else narcissistic.
Labels, however, are simply simplistic.
Al thinks his life has been latterly great.
He never again needs to look for a date.

A touch of mascara, a girdle and bra,
A dress, matching pumps with a clutch and *voilà*!
In just half an hour he's changed and he's ready.
Alice and Al, quite content going steady.
Perhaps you will think this is simply absurd,
Dismiss as apocryphal what you have heard.
All fellows, at some point, on some Hallowe'en
Will smear up their faces with mom's Maybelline,

Will put on her shoes, even colour their hair
And next day are nothing the worse for the wear.
So why then should Al, quintessentially normal,
Now go out to restaurants bedecked in a formal?

He just knows for certain that self-dating's fun,
He's Al and he's Alice: a couple in one.
The moral is simple. I close with this lone word.
Dateless this weekend? Then angel, look homeward.

1994

David Bateman, 1956–

stark insane voice on some liminal horizon

hawk moon nights misspell imitative
as cowboys find disproportionate surprise
among high heeled leather boots
lipstick brands on cowhide
and the faint masculine gaze
of their forefathers

It was never Lana Turner
It was always me

sleeping with husbands demands
a particular nostalgia for someone else's
present

Hitler's intervention kept Esther Williams
from the Olympics
doomed to cinematic glory and aquacades
she developed no capacity to embrace
cross-dressed lovers

long line bathing suits as cages for
vast tracts of flesh and land
are always situated
on the horizon of desire
polka dot bikinis are islands
that are easy to get to
by delicate boat-like footsteps

Clumsy presidents with sons the size
of the Saskatchewan River
deface this rocky stare
John Wilkes Booth was a tragic actor

for years Cher believed that Mount Rushmore
was a natural phenomenon
and I believe in Cher

clothing is a verb
as raglan-sleeved cowl-necked
jumpers race and interfere
with majestic hysteria

bumper stickers cry out
"I date your husband"

inflected grief like the
stain of a very ripe peach

that part of "Imitation of Life" where Laura
throws herself on her mother's coffin
and takes all the blame for John
Gavin's whiteness
never fails to reduce me to a
particular kind of over-educated
undernourished weeping
early twenty-first century faggot
who misidentifies with Lana Turner's glamour
and the poems of Emily Dickinson
sung to the tune of
"The Yellow Rose of Texas"

in the nineteen sixties I was much younger
than I wanted to be
named my first cat after a thin fashion model
went to a masquerade as Twiggy
and was asked why I didn't wear a costume
eyeliner like vertical tears inscribes
itself upon my expectant glare

and when the past comes back to haunt you
where does it come back from?

Samuel Goldwyn was no match for
a tall faintly masculine female swimmer
who would go on to love all the wrong men in briefs
and uniforms of over-evolved masculinity
butterfly strokes disable small winged creatures

slur their speech
flying into opaque surfaces
on the horizon of desire
they are easier to reach than the translucent glass
of a reflective present

Pale green is the colour of my love
standing in for emotion
blue, blue
watered down haikus
soup, light
an impressionist painting
and some forms of courage

I dress myself in adjectives
that describe the way I feel about everything
absence weaving shawls of
delightful degradation

2005

John Barton, 1957–

My Cellophane Suit

I used to wear a suit of cellophane
snug and
clear as a surgical glove.

My mother grew it inside her
stomach and dressed me
in it.
When the time came

I popped out like a black
tap-
dancer singin' *mammie*
at the top of
my lungs.

As a kid I shone like silver
under my mother's touch.
My suit buffed up
just right.
I was a bright kid, yes,

I was full of light.
When I was big enough
I outgrew my clothes.

I went to school.
But my suit of cellophane didn't
stretch and I felt

the strain.
Soon it had shrunk so much,
it pinched my groin.
Just once some jerk

one desk behind ran
his hand down the back

of my neck.
My suit of cellophane
went with a bang
like a balloon held
to a flame.

And with my skin
exposed like this

it's all guesswork.

1990

Vancouver Gothic

This house is an attempt to make the family nuclear free.
Though a mother and father
stand at the centre.
And though not my parents their love is explosive.
Vancouver gothic: Mary holds Anna
on her hip like a sack of groceries
bought at the health-food store down Commercial Drive;
Tom ties on a carpenter's apron,
sawdust mats his hair.
They meet at the kitchen doorway;
they are about to have words.

Down the hall Stephen has been half awake all morning,
lying in bed, unwilling to take a leak;
it's too much work
to stumble to the bathroom and the sheets are so warm.
In a few hours he will close the book
of new-age mystics he dozes over,
rise, relieve himself, begin to pump iron.

I sit in the living room and down pots of tea
or close myself into the study,
write letters to those of us already moved down east.
A vanguard before us they take their chances

with opportunity, exile, and grief.
Often I stir a pot of soup I concoct from scraps for lunch
(tomato, mushroom, sometimes beet) and I wait.
Vapours clean the windows and the stock clarifies,
but seldom the reasons why some of us stay.

Refugees from unemployment we divvy up welfare cheques.
We sit in the dining room and divide
equally the costs of our living
here in this wind-razed house where somehow we feel
the world, inner and outer, does not impinge.
Back and forth, Anna, our modern-day abacus,
skitters under the table
between us, demanding and portioning love.

Through a cracked window sun breaks across a Chinese rug
worn from use, unfurled over damaged floors.
Loose thread snagged between delighted fingers
Anna scuttles ahead of Stephen or Tom.
The pattern ravels.
Even under this uneasy shelter of warped laths
and flaking paint, we make
room for comic relief.
Though unlike laughter rain falls,
collects in buckets in the four corners of the living room,
moves debris into deltas of the cordillera.

1993

Parallel Lanes

We meet underwater, swimming in parallel lanes.
Both of us rising out of the breaststroke,
hands forcing the water apart.
We meet like this, length after length,
our trained bodies dreaming
a way to each end of the pool and turning,
coming up for air to breathe only,

the black hair matted across your chest
a flag that rises, that falls.
Later in the shower room,
after all the other swimmers have left,
we exchange something more furtive than glances,
something more gentle than words
as we talk, soap lathered onto our skins
and into our hair, washed
off with such pleasure, a common
language of bodies released from their stories
which we will tell each other over coffee
after we dress, underwear that is the beginning
and end of seduction, the well-worn jeans,
the red shirt that a sister made you
tucked in half-unbuttoned while drying your hair,
the dark flag of your chest unsettling
as you bend to lace up your runners.

On the steps of the Champagne Bath, we are suddenly ourselves.
Brightly coloured jackets resist the cold
air come between us as March blows off the river.
Walking into the Market, snow catches
in our hair like sparks, sparks that melt and go out.
Already you are telling me about some man
I will later watch you talk to,
leaning into the phone booth, laughing,
mouthing into the receiver: *I will be home soon,*
as you have been for eleven years.
Crossing a restaurant crowded
with empty tables and chairs with bashed-up legs,
you smile inwardly, navigate
among all the abandoned coffee cups
and the slow-burning candles between us.

Stripped of the heavy clothing of this snowy night,
I want to be held as the water holds you,
swimming in another lane towards and away.
I want to hold this man of yours as you do,
want to know, in one lasting embrace, how to hold a man
forever in the sure arms of this, my only life.

1994

Saranac Lake Variation

I am mainly preoccupied with the world as I experience it,
and at times when I would rather be dead the thought that
I could never write another poem has so far stopped me.
I think this is an ignoble attitude. I would rather die
for love, but I haven't.
—Frank O'Hara, September 1959

Boxing Day 1993,
alone in my hotel room, reading
City Poet in the bath, (Bruce calls it
Brad Gooch's *I-do-this-I-do-that* life
and times of Frank O'Hara),
water hot and replenishible to my armpits,
toe blocking the overflow,
                                        and I think of you,
far away in New Brunswick, (yes, it *is*
important) with your family, the frozen
Northumberland Strait outside
the window a ghost looking in
while you dine, no doubt,
on leftover turkey and mince,

and I think of Frank's love of the unrequited,
the longing

and invention he needed to articulate his poems,
those windows.

The Adirondacks rise outside my hotel window
into grey light, your chest pushing
against my hand last
week as it slid, a cross-country skier
                                          down and across
the plateau of your stomach, fingers coiling
round your cock in clouds of snow,
my mouth a blizzard about to
                                      touch down, which you
sometimes becalm, afraid (I am not sure)

of my teeth or tongue or what
you may or may not pass on,
the springs of your bed
sighing beneath us, a stand-in
in some menage-à-trois (I said to
make you laugh), though you want this
variation (not the laughter)
hidden from all those who listen.

Something Frank never worried about
in the 50s, the emergencies he meditated in
the midst of (despite McCarthy)
more *automatisé*,
generations of Abstract Expressionists at the Cedar
apprehended by his conversation and surreal
appetite for straight men, Irish
tears and bourbon, jazz,
                                        spontaneous poems
dribbled unrevised
on the backs of coasters in 10 minutes flat
for someone in their circle (the nerve
of those private
asides drawing the rest of us—his future
readers—in) before he headed out
onto 8th Street drunkenly at 2 am, alone or not alone,
love with a Manhattan skyline a sentimental
disease of his cruisy,
immuno-deficient (ie. vulnerable) spirit only.

In our time love has become a slogan, a cold
wind howling in the streets
of liberation, something we keep before the courts,
a paper coolly delivered at seminars
worldwide where doctors,
scientists, and activists compete
on how best to shield the sick
and unsick from variations mutating
like wind-sheer in the blood and in the minds
of those who wish us
dead, hate

no less virulent than in Frank's time—
only how the language is used
has mutated,
has kept mutating since his death,
though how it mutates and the aesthetics
of mutation (a.k.a. The Tradition)
allow it, chimera-like, to persist in secrets.

Frankly speaking, as Frank would say, the discourse
from the bathtub should be direct

(hot or cold), ie. ________,
find me irresistible, though I can be
a klutz, for instance nearly
dropped Frank in at least once so far;
the sodden pages might well have frozen
shut and cut his story short
(which would be sad since he died
(not from love—on Fire Island
a beach taxi ran him down) at 40).

This afternoon the wind has been too
unspeakable and crystalline
for anyone to skate for long on Mirror Lake.
The wind-chilled glass in my window
changes steam rising from the bath
to frost and now I can't see
myself, so am lost and ready to confess
that I, Frank's pale imitation (Bruce says
I echo his looks), wasn't straight

about you with John and Lorraine
this morning over breakfast, invoked you
not in conversation by name
(who am I protecting?),
only as someone's son who came here once,
not my lover lured by the fleeting
weekend leaves with your parents to stay
in this hotel, perhaps sleeping comfortably
in the roomy bed where last night I dreamt of you,

where you might have once
dreamt about someone like me,

anticipating our bodies, a variation
on the unconscious,
therefore primordial and beloved.
Desire takes many forms, but perhaps what
is unspoken cannot be
edited out and (sweet ellipsis) becomes
the content of the poem—
                                        windows blown out
by winds loosening chance
ecstatic needles from stands of white
pine on some far shore even
a city boy like Frank would walk along
for lack of anything else
new to write about.

1998

Hybrid

The wineglass we broke
last night recalls

its bell of flawless
light and fills with sun.

Before we slept
you told me about a hybrid

poplar, its system
of roots made

to lure radioactive
elements from the earth

to branches far-off and tousled
by fingertips of breeze.

Your hair at midnight as we made love.
The moonlit leaves.

The dark snare
of capillaries drawing

fever from the wetlands
my forehead glazing

with sweat while we slept
beneath scalding

sheets, your agitated
fingers warping my back

the wineglass ablaze
with light, shards

fusing round spilled
atmospheres as we woke

and wake refreshed
poplars torn up from

nightmare and burned
to containable ash.

2001

Him

after Ron Mueck's Dead Dad, *mixed media, 1996–1997*

There is no rhetoric in an open mouth, the lips caught
mid-breath, nothing left to expel, his last few rasps

etched in my ear, a moth against wind-rattled glass
as dusk grew silent, the perpetual thrum of traffic

unheeded, no pulse. He was a man who grew small
in my eyes, how else could I remain a nonbeliever

until his features petrified into a mask no one lifts off
chin canted downwards, eyes stoppered into unscanning

ellipses, his pajama redundant, an inscrutable shroud
—if this is love, I have learned it too late: little stays

private when hands are held with the dead, my life
leached out, evacuating queer ethers into his body

denying rot in the final moments of touch, my face
wiped of awareness while, in lamplight, his continues

as life-like, hair unbrushed, skin wanting soap, jaw
clenching, gaze thrown askance. His was another self

the stand-in I could not betray for men I have known
men secretive as he was about an invisible set course

gone nowhere now, time dumbstruck, a presence felt
pressures the body erases subsiding into bedclothes.

2005

Jim Nason, 1957–

The Water Trough

Beneath the open doors of the hay loft
one dry and low water trough
only it used to be the porcelain
claw foot bathtub
in that small unfinished room
off the pale and blue place
where a congregation of things collects
and hangs together dark and dusty:
above my aunt's old oak four poster bed is Jesus
and his bleeding palms and red robe
and white silk and fingers crossed and they are pointing up
towards heaven and eyes downcast and dripping
the blood must be
but never really does
and there is golden straw around the trough and
stuck in the dirt and there is a dried cow pie
and even green grass in the bottom and even a pebble
probably there in the dusty pile like a scar
or an apple seed on account of
JoBo the gelding thinks that he is a stallion
and canters and carries on
kicking things in the air to land
wherever they will while
the thunder rolls in
to the highest corner
of this barn and the light streams through and the eaves angle
and tilt and so does every particle of dust
that floats down this way and something
black and downy and falling is a bat
or a spider but it never really touches
me because I have you instead
to cover me and I close my eyes against
the thing and the sun
falling back
into the bales and piles and the stretch
of it all and thinking of taking off

my clothes like Walt Whitman would
and you and me and your beard
is itchy and the straw moves
in your divine dry lips.

1991

Shroud

The fireman, kind enough to open the door
in the hoarding so I can take a picture.

Curious tourist, thought I'd step through
the frame of September, look down into darkness,

a sixteen acre pit of twisted steel, as if a meteor
had crashed into Manhattan. Thought I'd see

something in the pit—a desk, a ring, a ring finger?
But it is flat. Ploughed over and still. As if God

mistook Manhattan for a cluttered table,
swiped it clean with the back of his hand,

left just one steel-beam cross shooting up
the middle. Whose God did it?

The misunderstood against the misunderstood.
Good and evil.

Evil and good.
I won't get into that.

*

After. I walk around the perimeter,
close to the fence. Past T-shirts and flowers,

rosary beads and votive candles.
Past the red-white-and-blue
every six or eight feet
and the firemen's hats,

NYPD caps,
the police officers, handsome

in black
like statue widows.

Smell fire, damp smoke.
Signs everywhere: *No looking.*

Stay out! ***THIS MEANS YOU!***
But that fireman opened the door.

A guide of sorts, in his brilliant yellow
helmet, let me look for free

rather than wait
in the pay-for-view line.

His heavy coat spread out like a canvas.
Built hard, but somehow soft,

a nice soul telling another his story.
I was still.

Snapped the picture.
How else could I remember

the giant shadow
of the neighbour tower

—like an 80-storey casket, shrouded
in black parachute material
waving in a cool May morning.
Clouds edge across the ground,

nothing for them to reflect into
except maybe the leaded glass
of some far off building.
That fireman's eyes.

What could have possessed him
to show me what he'd seen?

2006

Andrew

Each day new lumps, hard as pearls spring like bulbs
in staggered rows between the narrow caves of your ribs.
Each day new pain, bone pain. You moan, talk to yourself,

arms and hands float (like ghosts) away from your sides.
From the air above your face you pluck imaginary feathers,
pick apples from high branches, reach through the dark

for the light above our bed. I wanted to touch your alive skin.
Even the tumour that came forth like a Biblical prediction
turned upon one of God's best. Laughing and screaming

it came forth and the rest of you caved in around it.
There wasn't a kiss I could give or a squeeze of hand that could hold you
in this house, that bed, our room. Glass dropper against your teeth,

under your tongue, morphine, lorazapam. You go into yourself inch
by inch. Pound by pound. And your teeth come forward
as do your cheek and skull bones, and your eyes asking

What happened? How did I get like this?

The last week we slept holding hands, yours cold and thin.
Your eyes, two slits of light unspoken. And me, every eight

or ten minutes, watch the rise and fall of your chest.

2006

Dennis Denisoff, 1961–

Mid Post

the peas of Kiev are unshelled but packaged
positioned
gently lined
amongst the grid of white linoleum

by now
the window   by how
sills   the wind
spin so   nonnuclear
mixedly   thins so
everybody retires to the safety of the bed   quickly
pow   everybody has separate access to the bed
                                             post

creamy yet dry to the touch
the cheek of that frozen calf
we are told not to eat

with more news on the radio than in the world
I find the stupid church across the street
quaint warm
squarish banal

ax-
like
root
rising
totem pole-like a
mammoth Ukrainian salt
bowl hand carved, hand painted,
garish red and light crossing the
horizon and not really rising at all
it calms me just to know it calms
all those folks down
cupola brimming
with calm

a calm autumn evening
language leaping calmly
in sense as well as time
size as well as degree
9.5 9.8 9.7 9.7 9.8 9.8 9.9 9.85 9

locals busily spraying not voting
lips brimming with cum

my computer not the colour of
any nun in particular
Vancouver proper considerably
less peripheral
better supplied

I will not tolerate children who say
I hate you I hate you I hate you I hate you I hate you

as bed time is a moment
that is to say
make a sturdy life

I don't like trauma. What makes you think I like trauma?

> Each one sees one's own position in relation to the victims as most suspect. A few hope so and that's valid if you knew them, each sensing the flutter of skin inspiring the collective flaught

any group overconsumes
madam

he doesn't notice Marge
take more time than necessary
(though lacking lobes
he still inspired jewellery)
galena earrings
from the real to the realized
the real not anywhere
until warranted

some statements made while waiting for word:

> Everything took Tolstoy so long.
>
> If Tolstoy had been born in Shelley's age he would have been dead by now.
>
> My childhood recollections have never ended.
>
> Any memory retrieved, is first something forgotten.
>
> By this definition in:
> "You are late again. You did not get here in time."
>
> You do not want to learn. You are dreaming.
>
> 68 Detail of 62.

Not everyone in Québec is named Pierre.
Some are named Alain.

everything nowadays
rendered with a realism
beyond virtuosity

rear-ender brought screams
as a murder brings to mind
darkling meltdown
faith in the real

there is plenty of time for that
but not enough time for this

I pop in on Oly to look at the blender
face the colour of anything pureed
all the peas shelled
arranged
a line from the bed to the toilet
edge of a table cloth handkerchief
limpidity of snot putting me on edge

every star not used in the language
We ensure that each binary star is individually shelled

in olden days upon a time like when
assuming they even
let
you
in

Not everyone in Québec is named Pierre.
I know someone named Alain.

locals busily voting not cheating

Sophie carries on solitary talks with herself that she swears could not without damage to the integrity of the discourse be immediately translated into dialogue

holidaying in Montréal
mother notes "the subtlety of the French"

After years of research they finally began storing all the televisions with better commercials in a safe in the basement of the metropolitan library.

until a safer date such as when at which time
I'm not in on it
not in time
in time
ime
ime int
ime int not
in ont not me

The high point of his career came with the recognition that a fart sounded the same before and after the creation of language.

When the melt down does I am reciting. English text and appreciate their gifts of water and ripe oranges.

locals busily musing not cheating

a cloud track of chickadees
dead tubers
stiffed in flaught
splotched in dung
few things are like and I make no exceptions
pointing at the reindeer with a mechanical eye
more correctly translated?
not until I am told
locals busily eating not cheating

though by the window
attention is not on the sill
Oly pukes on it right away

Let me make it clear right from the start
nothing surprises me any more
except a fresh firm plum the size of my fist

1997

Clint Burnham, 1962–

Rent-A-Marxist

Oh heteroclite pessimism!

Menstruating tongues wag

i jerk off the plaster horse over your open mouth
get out the new english translation of the yellow pages
i'd like to dribble the illegal chopshop near the horse farm
  down your wrists

a debate over labourer versus worker
dicks dump dumbly all over the place

the oldest working stiffs
a tradition of metric historiography
my saliva'll dissolve the encrusted fluid
on the khakis with a hole in the crotch i got for 2 bucks at
value village

no please mark laba wears khakis
i'd rather castrate myself immortal
hit the immutable scission
if you'd let me strangle you

you like the way her arms are held back
around an olympian tower?
what are you a girl?

the rants that malcolm rodney gave us
will do in a pinch
a punch a penile colony
but don't rip me too much
i want to ride my bike later and see a movie

the will to power runs a few degrees above most folks...
ah my hairy tit i do love looking down at you

1997

An Evening at Home

reading about bachelor
dinners, newspaper
article on celibacy and
rhymes with habitat and fat

balzac and coffee

blowjobs come later

thinking about doing
the dishes: in one novel,
they say sisterfucker
in another
daughter fucker

wallah, sadhu

kingstoner: granite, broadloom (over
particle (children, wallphone
sideburns, television antenna
hardwired penis size
evolution, date rape, information

bicycles vs motorcycles
goretex vs leather
panniers vs nivea virgins

halcyon senectitude (swimming in ddt
Seneca College, Ontario senate
Kenorah
part of the problem is fishing
(microvans, mountaingoats: plagiarizing lynx

mendicant
do you want
a clean house
or dog où
sexe

neuter, tapioca, oatmeal hat trick
backwards, wisdom
teething ring, cock ring

children
sentimentalism vs
romance

love, lust, legionnaire's disease
jimmy carter, lesion

jews or gays?
that's obvious
we protest
a macedonian chorus
second generation theories of youth

1997

Brian Day, 1962–

Narcissus at the Pool

It is water, its infinity, that most compels him:
the way it opens its skin to include him;
how its face, unresisting, is unmarked by change.

He watches that face, his face, from the deck,
considers what invisibly surges beneath it,
and craving the sensuous narcotic of swimming,

hovers caressed between memory and motion.
His face on the water moves and is still,
and this is the face he diving enters,

plunging to the liquid unbroken mirror
where his image washes unseen around him
and with ease he manoeuvres, muscle through mind.

All that he knows is held here in water,
the cool of reflection slides over his skin,
and all who inhabit his life on the ground

are half-turned in light and recite the lines
of a myth that's born this moment in him.
He has never been so much in love.

2000

Sleeping Vishnu

Having inhaled his dream of the world, the dreamer
is stretched on the back of the serpent
that floats on the ocean's eternal black.
One labouring day of the world has ended,
when he wakes tomorrow will be composed,
and now suspended in sleep he holds
all fates in the rise and fall of his chest.

And what could love be if it is not this:
to find the world for a moment condensed
to a body I could look at in peace forever,
to the face that contains the rest of my days,
and to touch his eyebrows, his breath on my hand?

2000

Faithful to Him

His chest flexed, winking,
    inviting me to follow past
        the lockers and into the half-lit
sauna, where his hand slicked
    the sweat from his chest,
        he posed and smirked, wetting
his lips as I wet mine.
    Adjusting his towel, he asked
        what I was up to
this afternoon, if I'd like
    a drink at his place. Much
        as I'd like to, I said,
I can't. We voiced our regrets
    as we eyed one another
        and my hands imagined his skin.
He smiled and left the sauna,
    his back flaring with muscle
        that could have been mine to hold.
Now when we pass at the gym
    he pretends not to see me,
        aloof and all the more alluring.
And when, increasingly, my lust
    will not rest on the man
        I love, I return to his
image, unwrapping his towel and
    tasting his sweat, sloughing off
        my life to slide against his skin.

2000

The Love Between Krishna and Jesus

They approach one another with cool flowers of language,
move their mouths in the gorgeous recitation of beauty;

speak with the unpenned poetry of scripture,
the memory behind words of the blue walks of heaven.

After rage at armies and amassers of money,
each shows the other his friendly form,

withdraws from the gaping ground of his battles
to the secluded pool of nakedness and bathing;

eases to a heart as capacious as his own,
awakes the faint world with fresh adoration.

Hands trace over skin as sure sacred text,
ponder as patiently, savour as deep.

These princes of devotion, co-creators of love,
make themselves love on the plane of their skin,

blurring their words to a once-fused language,
their forms to one sinuous glistening of delight.

They meld themselves to this moist skin and strength,
retuning their limbs to the bright keys of heaven:

agape that these bodies bred from stars
could harbour such awe at the pouring of pleasure:

at skin newly lit and expansive as sky,
at the quick touch of wonder in a night of such eyes.

Krishna has blossomed as the season of flowers
and Jesus the fig tree now heavy with bloom.

They meet as the alpha and snake tail of time,
the clasp that unites bright intimate worlds.

2004

Better Not to Marry

Jesus, speaking to his intimate
circle of friends, assures them
it's better not to marry
but to wander unfamilied
in the company of men. He calls
his merry band to not-marry
with him, and conceives
of a Creator who, from the womb,
fashions this unmarrying brand of men
and calls them as prophets
in the birth of a kingdom.

Jesus extols the flexible eunuch
who sets aside his masculine habits
and surrenders himself to the wills
of men. He wishes all his followers
to be men and eunuchs, blessed
with that angelic ambiguity
of gender as they are entered
and enter the gates of heaven.

Jesus looks forward to that far
resurrection when marriage itself
will be finally moulted
and all will float freely
as bachelors and boys.
They'll drift promiscuous
through heavenly forms,
their bodies as permeable
and as shimmering as words.

2006

Norm Sacuta, 1962–

The Hills Are A Lie

Join me on this tour of the English Downs
where the Long Man is re-cut into sod,
more deeply than those pre-historic men
intended; intention the truth
easily cut into. Is this the first stencil
and so the only authority left? Forget hieroglyphs,
called down when the Rosetta Stone
turned falcons into argument.
The Long Man looks down,
a little white lying on green.

Seven horses carved on the South Downs Way.
One a gentleman thought too small
and far too hung. In 1850 he
wiped anatomy clean, made it bigger
in that big Victorian Way. He made truth.
And the story goes from there, commonly
out of the mouths of guides.
The one horse that speaks to you
and you and you.

Let's lie at night
in the hard-on at Cerne Abbas
chalk-drawn around us, those spade
made balls re-edged lovingly out of lawn,
caught between the legs of another walking
man. The fertility of you
wasted on the likes of me.

Let's lie between two rocks
and a hard place—well
on our way. *Stepping in the trepidation of flesh*
that will become myth.

2001

What I Wanted to Say

O good Horatio, what a wounded name,
Things standing thus unknown, shall live behind me!
If thou didst ever hold me in thy heart,
Absent thee from felicity for a while,
And in this harsh world draw thy breath in pain,
To tell my story.
—Hamlet

The guns shoot tonight, and light your dead shape
passed hand over hand by soldiers clumsy
in their dark armour, men too young to see
how such tenderness contradicts their fates.

They carry your body as I have yearned
to know your touch without camaraderie.
You betrothed to me your womanly soul,
interpreted my blush as modesty
then, perhaps, understood my love in all
was not something you wanted to return;
through pretty Osric you made clear my role.
And now what have you damned me to recall:

The retinal shape of death in your eyes?
Your eyes! What was the colour of your eyes?

2001

Alberta Pick-Ups

These trucks are their lives, open and honest
as the lies they tell in Lac La Biche
to wives who've come to believe the route
back from Edmonton is an hour longer
than it is.
They are without the complication
you get with a BMW or Mercedes,
so much baggage in Vancouver's West End.

Expect a ball cap—and yes—there's one,
rim backwards a kisser, forwards means business
and don't expect anything in return.

But they often return, and do
to the parking lot below
Government Hill. Summer nights
are endless. Their truck colours
refuse to fade to grey.
Anonymity lost to passing cars, they sweat
even harder across the soft leather.

Their true fantasies are of pick-ups finally theirs,
all payments made. The others are a nuisance,
required relief for something not quite right
they've always felt, but disliked.

There've been two surprises—once, after passion,
the boy from Wapiti said
Wanna see my Hummer? And he showed me.
We barely fit the McDonald's drive-through
and drove around town sipping shakes,
everyone staring, wanting, needing
his massive truck. I felt important.
His date to the prom.

The other, a cap-forward
wanting only relief,
wore a pink rubber ring
he slid off after, and hung
on the rearview mirror
like fuzzy dice.

2001

IAN IQBAL RASHID, 1964–

Another Country

All this new love of my parents' countries. We have bought the videotapes together, bought the magazines and books, all the advertisements, clothes, and each other's responses. We watch the slides of your visit. Your handsome face is tanned surrounded by mango trees, planted above the poverty. The moist beauty—which you think of blowing up and then framing, building into your walls—majesty imposed upon majesty.

Now I watch you watch Sergeant Merrick watch poor Hari Kumar. And follow as the white man's desire is twisted, manipulated into a brutal beating. You are affected by the actor's brown sweating body, supple under punishment. What moves you? The pain within the geometry of the body bent? The dignity willed in the motions of refusal? A private fantasy promised, exploding within every bead of sweat? Or is it the knowledge of later: how my body will become supple for you, will curve and bow to your wishes as yours can never quite bend to mine. What moves you then?

My beauty is branded into the colour of my skin, my strands of hair thick as snakes, damp with the lushness of all the tropics. My humble penis cheated by the imperial wealth of yours: Hari's corporal punishment, mine corporeal. Yet

this is also part of my desire. Even
stroking myself against your absence, I
close my eyes and think of England.

1991 (revised in 1995)

Could Have Danced All Night

1.

I once used to dream of being held knowingly by a man
on whom I would not look.

Then this all came again, the embrace held
in the ease of a dance, held within your hands small
yet capable and roped with thick vein.
And when I tried, it didn't surprise me
to be able to look into eyes, yours, like mine
the rough colour of night, into your shy, pie face.

Standing together tonight I long for the anise
taste of Thai basil on your skin,
your pale denim thighs and ass resplendent
in strobes of evening light.
Tonight I would dance with you across an alien landscape.
We might fly. ("I'm positive.")
But this night finds our legs rooted, knotted,
planted painfully like a flag. ("I've tested positive.")

2.

Tonight, I watch you walking away,
wheeling your burden before you into the night.
Fists jab my thighs on either side.
Fists which mean to unclench hold
fingers which mean to interlock
with yours, like pieces of a puzzle
join, into a picture of two men dancing.

Tonight movement is limited:
from hand to mouth to mind.
Tobacco, caustic laughter in the lungs,
the careful sipping of our herbal teas,
the careful sipping of our everything-will-be-all-rights.

1991

Hot Property

On the phone with you (trying heroically to save myself and failing) I hear a click—yet another call waiting. Inspiration: I decide to pretend I'm drowning, my dark body just barely visible in steam rising through a break, flailing about below a frozen body of water, helpless, unaccustomed to the cold, coming from a tropical climate and all. Save me. You do the work. But you are annoyed, won't play. You see a different kind of transparency: but no ice, no danger of freezing.

Click quickly to the next caller and become a mouth piece, confident oracle if I am believed, and I am, replete with all the wisdom of the East, a messenger (who has never been east of Montreal) false messenger, who is yet to be exposed. Even when I'm mute, it seems, this one gathers my saliva in buckets as it drips from my parted lips and strains for discovery.

I click back and you're still there watching me now as I tread water. The climate's become milder and I'm willing to swim. You're willing to pull me onto terra firma. A fair ground.

But in the same moment: I catch my dark self swimming gracefully in the mirror frame.

Tropical fish.

I see a hook.

New trick.

It's simpler to stay put and wait. Haul the fisherman in.

1991

Early Dinner, Weekend Away

Soft-footed summer girls enter
to light the candles at our table.

There is no magic in it.
(Were they so grim the other times?)
They wait for provocation
to return home as early as possible.

They spend each day preparing this room
wait for meal-times to claim their place
and displace them. But at the moment
it's just us and them
and a napkin mathematically angled,
pastels and the right number of glasses.
There is a balance now
which any change will spoil.

At home, I don't mind where I am.
All socks and books
I find places where the sunlight won't find me.
But the light that searches through this place
reaches me slightly green
through the bow window. I change my position.
Parachute my fingers into a less dangerous spot.
There is no way of hiding.

Upstairs, guests unclasp from their afternoon holds
they rise panting slightly, perspiring
shivering as their too-hot skin
meets the cool afternoon, withdrawing
stretching themselves in the too-loud rasp

of ice cream coloured sheets.
Soon they will descend and blush, their feet
making the floorboards ring.

The thrill that we are not them is gone.
I hear you cough, feel your lashes
smart, wet.

1995

Todd Bruce, 1965–

Still Life with Turkey Pie

"We find courage not with
but rather in
the tips of our fingers."

You were pretending to be
in Amsterdam, but I
know the post card
came from Victoria.
Still
your words
have punctuated my life.

What does it mean to say *still life*?

"Still Life"

Stasis, freeze frame, whip in hand, signature.

But I must tell you,

I was described as "shocking" the other day. Of course, this
came
as a complete surprise to me when in fact my life is a response
to
how shocked I am, at every moment, by the status quo.

Still Life:
how impossible it seems,
these words, next to
one another. But then
again, I have a problem
with language.

Still,
I use it.
You can tell,

of course,
I am weary, tired after all.
Tough place to be, here is.

Surprised all together
the post card
even arrived.

Makes you wonder.

Dream of ever kissing you,
the filling of your mind,
photographing you
as you come,
still life.

1993

The charm

The sun, like a cell, a cello, divides and leaves us uncertain. My face is copper, like a frieze or a coin. I am remote and my lips are gently parted, I am the boy-head of a charm that clinks and dangles from your wrist. You are my mother, orange-eyed, emitting and silently magic.

I look up from my letter and the waiter is standing above me. He smiles and asks if I would like another drink.

Two olives. The me/you olives inhaling the gin. I slide back in my chair and cross my legs as I suck them from their swords. The waiter walks away, pleased with his symbols. Of course, I find him too abstract, too unwilling, two vague in his flirtations. I fill my mouth with the martini and pick up my pen.

I remember you always. You are a memory I have not forgotten. You told me about perfection, about the riches of the soul and you shared with me the reality of your losses. Like a fog on a pond a sunrise you linger and hide and collect and you are dispersed.

He brings me another drink. This time the olives are speared by the same sword. He looks frantic and beat and his eyes are unmoving but they tap dance. I look up to him and say, what is it you are trying to say.

I asked him what it was he was trying to say. He is not at all like you. You I have never had to ask. When you shaved your head it took me weeks to notice. You, subtle as a metamorphosis. And the pleasure I took in asking who you were. Our lives together being blurred by the question mark.

I was tapped on my shoulder and reminded that time, moving, had acted like time. Cat Stevens says, trouble I haven't got a lot of time. Joni says this is a song for you, the piano being tapped as though soil were being brushed over the tops of transplants. I would like to forget this and plant us, our roots to entwine.

1997

from **Frieze (Electric Mummy)**

& I am inconsolable, irreparably dismantled because love is boundless in its hate. It attacks me like a frenzied spectre. Love blinds. Love punches me in the stomach. Not even the devil can help me now. He speaks to me in disguises fit for saints, pouring out his charms from your tongue. I am a bust encrusted with emeralds and rubies; my eyes are two perfectly bevelled diamonds, mirrors like a fly's eyes. My arms have been chiselled off, just below the shoulder and my face is frozen in ecstasy. Once, just past midnight, I could feel your fingers tracing the upper bow of my lips, and that is the closest you have ever been to saying I love you.

& that was the closest I have ever been to peace. It fell silently like dust onto my diamond eyes, brief, ephemeral, taunting. For a moment I thought I might break from the cleverly molded skin and spill like liquid to the floor, yet I remain sparkling, destitute on this wretched pedestal. I cannot drink and yet I thirst. I can only become the water's source from which you lap like a dog.

& you call to me like to an oracle from places far away, abandoning your heavy coats of armour. You look into my eyes as though they are crystal balls full of destiny, but all I can do is reflect. There can be no joy in a frozen heart, no hope without a soul, no ecstasy in the absence of flesh. At night, while you sleep, electric mummy, the moon's rays strike my bejewelled head and bands of colour imprint themselves in a kaleidoscopic conundrum across paintings of reverent men, through the tendrils of a Boston fern, over top the spines of dusty books and out through the window, back to the moon, and out the inky panes of sleeping neighbours.

& every jewel is a word or phrase you once possessed, clinging to me now like bloated ticks and iridescent beetles. The room is magnificent when it swarms, dragonflies in their stained-glass wings. But you never see these flourishes. Come morning I am still and lifeless, gawking at the sun with my parted lips, shepherding the silence of dawn into my eyes. It is only when you spritz the bougainvillea that water rests on my face and streams slowly though the creases of my eyes that I am allowed to cry.

& I am a frieze whose copper will never turn green, whose pottery might shatter, whose diamond eyes might be looted, whose emerald and ruby neck might be sold to an Egyptian prince and scattered across the floor of his bed chamber, pocketed by consorts. My lips might crack in half, never to be kissed again. Or they might remain, etched into glass or pasted into a collage as a reminder to the gods of my unwavering debauchery, my pretense of love.

& I have stopped looking for your soul (acquainted with night), through these beaming eyes. I will wait for it to return to you & if I could I would will it to. For now, all that remains is a trace of it, a veil of damp black lace, your silver heart beating beneath it like a breathing bubble of mercury. I cup it in my hands like a candle and offer it to the gods. I take umbrage with the weeds that clog your lungs, with the ghost who clings like a chain between your ankles. I can free you with one swing of an ice pick, but first I set its sights on my own bewildered soul.

& I am in pieces, shards. I am inarticulate, dumb as a drooping peony. All that remains is my bulbous centre, my petals being swept & scattered by the breeze, and the sun so bright it cannot be seen. A caterpillar gets fat on the juice of my heart.

2003

R. M. Vaughan, 1965–

Christian Bök's Max Factor Factotum

M
A
S
C
A
MISTER
MASCARA MASCARA
S
T
EMCEE
MASCARA
S
S
MASCARA MASSIMO

printemps off the rack:

revlon,
revers, LaCroix.

marabou.

pantograph pancake.

damask dahling.

1996

Lost Weekend

a playwaltz, boy to boy   only friends dance so stiffly
the last two stretches of skin left secret between us   tangle and frisk
—an accident of thighs and American love songs   blurts stories
3 years of conversation never touched on—

a Saturday with tulips and fobbed apologies   both cut at the base
    please, get to the subject (me)   I can understand any kind of love
except foolish delicacy
all mouths accept honey, all eyes take to red petals   hold me, hold me
in your arms and underestimate me

fast dancing, we boys make a near perfect circle, agreeing to its stupidiy
to the safety of no partners and hours of drink
—in another context we're a gang, a frat, the way new inlaws dance and
clap because talking is impossible—
    to notice our cocks all face the empty centre, to notice no boy spins
his backside to his opposite   to notice this is indeed a choreography
marks difference no music drowns

a Tuesday and his rigidity clears the air   shy on the phone, he sings
her body electric and I could kill him because intimacy is like a good
slap   you have to get close to smart and the touch is quick,
noncommittal   fly-blown

forgive me   I thought throwing our bodies together at high speed
meant something   meant me   in shiftless midmorning, pulling
on a pushed-off shirt, me shitting quietly, me engaged by his bookshelf
because I already read his mind   me, skanky from cum   wanting home

forgive me   I misread his sweat, mistook the press of his fingers
for Morse code   squirreled his spit under the fat of my cheek
like hard candy   took the flag and ran and held out my hand for the next
flash of primary colour and satin to see only air   only my own keys
too early to touch and iron-caked like old pennies   just as useless

I will replay this night over and soon   I'm replaying it now
because I don't believe in perspective or two-headed kings;
there is Courage, and there is not

1999

14 Reasons Not to Eat Potato Chips on Church Street

1. Every man you have had sex with or even attempted to have sex with will immediately glide forth from the shelters of smart, bi-coastal cuisine restaurants and overpriced pet food boutiques and know, know in a flash that you are getting fatter every day and those chips are not helping.

2. Because potato chips are a childhood food, you will feel compelled, like a nice boy, to share—and that's just a fast way to catch hepatitis.

3. If you have to drop by The 519 Community Centre, the tight-faced lesbian at the front counter will remind you, correctly, that queer youth of colour are being physically and verbally abused in Third World sport shoe factories owned by the parent company of Frito Lay.
   How could you?

4. And what are you gonna do with the bag? It can't be recycled (see #3).

5. Remember how unattractive you felt at that gay actor's house party when you ate all the small, broken bits of Salt 'n Vinegar at the bottom of the Emile Henry bowl and then the skinny playwright who had an affair with the theatre critic from *Now* magazine said: Don't they feed you at home?
   It could happen again, fat boy, right here in public.

6. You're supposed to be broke. So, who paid for the Humpty Dumptys?

7. All the successful gay men are eating washed green apples or Power Bars or *open-faced grilled eggplant melts with asiago cheese and fresh figs* from Spiral Grill.

You feel so alone.

8. It's bad luck. Like jaywalking with sunlight in your eyes or throwing away pennies or wearing a white shirt on Saturday night.

9. Drop one chip, just one, and you're increasing the typhus-carrying microbe population by about 2 billion. Thanks a lot.

10. One publicly consumed bag of chips is sexually counter-equal to: one flattering new haircut; 3 subtle yet penetrating colognes; any favourite, loose-fitting flannel shirt, plus a whole week's worth of consciously sucking in your stomach at 30-second intervals. Double the ratios for Ketchup flavour.

Math never lies.

11. If you can't wait until you get indoors: A) don't buy the Party Pak (278 grams!) or, failing A), B) hide your chips in an opaque grocery bag or backpack.

This advice should be obvious to us all.

12. I admit I wanted him. I admit I found him attractive. Oh, the hard kern of his jaw (sailor boy). The comforting W his pecs made, like two big smiles.

His cruel laugh I would kill to hear in my bed.

13. There is no way to construct such behaviour as legitimate radicalism.

14. Instead, you might take the 2 dollars blown on Ruffles and go across town by lazy streetcar to a kinder neighbourhood, someplace more real, a family place. Someplace where you'd meet a forthright, masculine man—maybe an engineer, or a journalist—a man who can see and, yes, even love the thousand tiny sparkles that make you you.

But now it's too late.

1999

Feverfew

A carbolic, the favourite of Saint Tomasa   who lined her
potter's cauldron   with crisped petals, her stomach with lye
and scalded primrose   A tingling root   chewed for luck,
longevity, against dry spleen or night terrors, in Mahjong heats
    This baby's clover, too bitter for nursing mothers   bruises
with pinching   (as do most bullies)   the damp switches of
fan leaves   like green coins, hundreds per stem   crease,
remember touch   (as do you)

take some in the morning, steeped in Korean corn husk
tea   swallow absently   without sugar and quickly   to the
flat back of the tongue—the dead, cold insensate patch before
the throat, a muscled plain meant to catch choking biscuits,
balls of gristle, lies—because anything so in discord with
everything you love (sweetness, bulk, artificiality) must be
improving (like exercise or books about science)   will exact
more than it adds   *eliminate, eliminate, eliminate*   you
repeat, for bravery   then swirl the mess, the crushed forest,
the pulpy runes   and squint, tilt, swallow, repeat   imagine
a bed shared   4 legs, 4 arms waking up uncovered   weekend
& garden plans   his name

2005

GREGORY SCOFIELD, 1966–

I Used to Be Sacred (on Turtle Island)

The first Two-Spirit didn't come about
because the Great Mystery was having
a confused day.
We got put on Turtle Island
for a reason—that wasn't
just to hang around the city
looking desperate
for other outcasts or acceptance.
I wasn't created
to be a lonesome turtle
crawling around by myself
(though none of these turtles
are worth beach-combing)
or duck under my shell
when someone takes a mean poke.

Just yesterday I was nosing around
at a turtle's pace
thinking
what an urban turtle like me
should do
when some big tortoise
nudged up alongside,
wanted to know
where all the best turtles go.
By his nose
I could tell
he wasn't from around here.

At first
I was flattered, tilted
my head slowly
and gave a turtle grin.
Then I saw
the red stripe on his neck

so I just shrugged, said
I didn't know.

Sure enough
three blocks later
that pushy bugger
still trailing me
wanted coffee, directions
to my nest.
Look, I snapped
I gotta big mean tortoise daddy
at home.

Pissed off, he tottered along
snorting his hooked nose.
So much for brotherly turtleship
I thought
that one would make good soup
at a Two-Spirited gathering.

Despite these beefy walruses,
cruisy sea-lions
and trendy urchins
I'm still for the most part sacred.
I even know
turquoise is a protection stone,
mined from the belly
of Mother Earth.

From month to month
I just plug along
watching my shell
doesn't get too chipped or cracked.
Often my moontime isn't regular—
though I'm a regular bleeding heart.

So what if I get too bloated
with words or opinions.
Why have to ask

who's who
and what's their story
on Turtle Island.

1996

Queenie

When first
I heard Queenie was sick
I went out of my head
thinking
I too would be a goner
in a couple of years,
maybe months, even days.

Death came to me
on a bus travelling west
back to the city
from where I was born.
I thought for sure
it would be the last time
I saw the world
with clear, undarkened eyes.

Already the funeral was planned;

I would be wrapped
in a starblanket,
my smudge feather
held between icy hands,
the red woven sash
binding my bony hips—
and the fiddlers playing
my spirit up & beyond
the Milky Way.
Queenie wanted to be
six feet deep before thirty

and got his wish,
though he gained
seven extra years
(probably the booze
preserving his insides).
Around the city
he got that name
from other Two-Spirits
who grew up on the same rez.

It was his mother's name
because she was bossy.
He was just like her, Queenie,
always telling you
what to do.

The carved silver ring
he gave me at sixteen
with his clan design
was like a wedding ring.
All throughout my teens
I kept it stashed away
for safe keeping.
Finally
I pawned it when I went straight—
although I tell people
I lost it somewhere
between Vancouver and Saskatchewan.

Somehow
they didn't need to know
until now.

In another life
I sure loved him.

1996

He Is

earthworm, caterpillar
parting my lips, he is

slug slipping between my teeth
and down, beating

moth wings, a flutter
inside my mouth

he is snail kissing dew
from the shell of my ears,

spider crawling breath tracks
down my neck and weaving

watersnake, he is
swamp frog croaking my chest

hopping from nipple to nipple,
he is mouse

on my belly running circles
and circles, he is

grouse building his nest
from marsh grass and scent,

weasel digging eggs
between my legs,

he is hungry, so hungry
turtle, he is

slow, so slow
nuzzling and nipping

I crack
beneath the weight of him,

he is mountain lion
chewing bones, tasting marrow

rain water
trickling down my spine,

he is spring bear
ample and lean

his berry tongue quick,
sweet from the feasting.

1997

My Drum, His Hands

over the bones, over the bones
stretched taut
my skin, the drum

softly he pounds
humming

as black birds dance,
their feathers
gliding over lips, they drink
the stars
from my eyes
depart like sun
making way for moon
to sing, to sing
my sleeping

my sleeping song
the sky bundle

he carries me to dreams,
his hands wet

and gleaming

my drum aching

1997

I've Looked for You

in the blackest night, calling
at the edge of a cliff
knowing, should you answer,
I'd grow wings.

I've looked for you

in the likeliest of places:
prairie cafés, washrooms in Arizona,
airport connecting countries
and lovers and

I've seen you, tall as a cedar,
reaching to the heavens,
wings of raven on top
trimmed short, neat and convincing

my hopeful eyes
till you felt their burning
and turned around.
I've searched for you

breathless and parched
as the gauzy summer,
drank your name
from water fountains

and remained thirsty. I've pressed
my face to the very moon,
cursed the stars from the sky
knowing as I do

the dark is to blame,
how big the world really is
and chances are small, fleeting
with each passing day

and yet, I am here
falling from so many edges
even the rocks below
know your silence.

1997

My Lover's Mother Laments Her Dancing Shoes

My lover's mother laments her dancing shoes,
the oxblood loafer, the good luck penny
she lost fifty years ago.
Tells us it tumbled from the car
between the dance hall and home,
landing pairless in the ditch, a loss

greater than these warm evenings in May
when the waltzing light
crouches in the corners, fades down the walls
in pastel streams.
I, too, ache for the small and not-so-small
things I've lost: my mother's narrow foot,
my grandmother's hairpins.

But tonight she brings us rosemary, parsley,
grapefruit mint. And my lover's father,
old Pie-face, the water jugs to be filled.
Tonight they are famously in love—53 years.

Some blister has been momentarily broken
and our small kitchen
is a dance hall of goodness,

a fortress of peace.
I watch my lover slip into her story,
swaying against her voice, her gestures
wanting to never let go. But
I know the shoes move their borrowed feet,
all floating, all stepping
toward the thinness of bone,

a cradle of flowers.
Inside her laughter, her echo
there is a certain unravelling,
an orchestra without a conductor.
But tonight she laments her dancing shoes,
and we cry for her
because she is our golden slipper, our goddess.

2005

Craig Poile, 1967–

Lather

This is a trick of my father's,
That I must, once again, teach myself,
Folded in the sharp hiss of steam.

First, my fingers trace
Cheek and chin melting in the shower's
Flowing glaze, sight unseen.

Then the blade comes into play,
Inching blindly along a path it completes
In a few heartbeats with a mirror's help.

I feel my way into the anxious
Thrill of cutting it close,
Remaking myself, beardless ... sexless?

Fingers stroke the throat's Gibraltar,
Its message adamant: to the touch
My imaginings are off the map.

Back at the flattering mirror,
In the curtains' sifted light
I find the job's half-finished

But easily completed. The razor moves,
Scraping. I meet my eyes only briefly, afraid
To see what's washed away.

1998

Autoerotic

Hired hands did in the scandal,
excised with yellowed veils the bits
that breed and nurse us into what

Michelangelo called
God's image. As if we'd never guess
the parts from the imperfect whole.

Below his Judgement sat holy men,
scalded white and thin, who
put on scarlet robes and Latin phrases
to masquerade as monuments
and hide the eager, mortal hand.

But for the chosen, time was threatening.
The brimming, interminable mass
dragged on like the world's last days.
Their eyes looked up, beyond the censure of
the horny finger and its ring, and turned,
full throttle, to the naked limbs above.

There's no less risk in our time, when
perfect flesh, its ripeness and sheen,
take shape in the murderous clang
of the barbell returning to the stack,
or the penitent crack and buzz edging
through the surgeon's inner room.

Hooked by a curve to worship,
the eyes carve a shape for the mind
to turn, while the body suffers
the reinvention of Catherine's wheel and
arrows Sebastian drew in like breaths.

But captive glimpses of perfection,
worked out on flesh in solitude,
will fail the test of time. Uncovered,
they're denuded, drained of colour.
Memory holds only exhibits of desire.

Don't talk of love eternal to
the drudge who stooped at Catherine's
haunch to cover up the master's art.
Lacking the timeless touch

each swathe he painted differed,
its vigour weathered by a day.

His odd job coloured in the passion
in hopes of steering the flock's devotion.
But when heaven employs my hand
to tame the lustred flames, I see
skin that's sainted, and draw in
life's deep, green breath.

1998

Accommodations

I'm stuck with the tour.
Giving it, that is. As a host,
it's a perfect way to manage the fear—
rushing in afresh with each arrival—
that I live too differently
or, worse, much the same.

I skew the directions, herd them on past
the bedroom walls, still the sorry pink we found them,
and the boxes that look dispossessed
even though they're labelled by name and room.
(We've just arrived ... is it five months now?)
But I'm guide, not guard, and one gets through

to the kitchen, a flirtatious pinch of a room,
and just as unsettling as a prelude to dinner.
A guest's turn to point: "Now that's a real sink!"
Yes, a fully functional archive, a great hulk
and fitting heir to the name Titanic. It is, as he says,
"What they were all like in the 20s and 30s."

And where's the real in that? He's found
meaning around the peeling edges, but the trace
of authenticity just leads back to his conversant
eye and Newfie grin. Rooted on the spot, a hand

on each side of the well, he's found his home, not mine.

That mystery will live and die with him.
All I've found in this spot is that agility
counts in cramped quarters and the wit to say
that our sink is the perfect size to bathe a child
(What is more agile than irony?), if only the one
my love and I dream into each other's eyes.

1998

Place Royale

Empty, still, uninviting, the park
Hushed us by design. We arrived too late.
Everyone had gone, turned tail in the dark
And left us morning like a licked-clean plate.

Near the sputtering fountain, we find chairs
Sitting in twos or threes or more, spread out
Un-uniformly, like bare-legged players.
Their poses revive what life was about

Last night, how people sat alone or knocked
Knees. We catch the angles where bodies met,
How folks laughed, touched, or argued as they talked,
The coarse tales sketched in the sand at their feet.

Uphill at Sacré-Coeur, chairs sit in rows
Below the dome that tops the city's brow.
Whispers thread the silence on the floor below,
Snapped by the creak when a body sits down.

2005

R. W. Gray, 1969–

How this begins

Thrums he does, thrums like waves breaking, waves falling over each other on their way to his feet, but who can blame them.

Up along the street the maples look awkward in their new dresses, billowing in the traffic gusts. Something, everything, has to begin.

Later we will recall this moment, though I will not speak of his clavicles and he will not mention my bottom lip. He tries to find some way to offer me a strawberry from the musky handful he picked on his way to work and I try to find some other word for clavicle but am distracted by his full-throated approach to wearing a T-shirt.

There are strawberry seeds under his fingernails. Tonight, falling asleep, a hand near his face on the pillow, he will smell strawberries and the crushed green runners. The strawberries he shucked for his and another's mouth. He will remember my bottom lip.

We will not agree. He will think it was a hot day, summer finally giving in. I will remember mostly the breeze through the open door, how spring just kept hanging around.

This will be the moment he liked me the least, but I liked him the most. He thought I was a sideways glance. I thought he was a swallow of water.

He will kiss me, outside at a table, leaning down to me as I look up, suspicious of a man who kisses me so soon and kisses me in a café.

He will wonder what comes next. I will wonder what just happened.

This is how it begins. He will not know I am on my way to analysis. That I was going to admit that I am tired of longing for longing. Tired of making up stories about picked strawberries.

2006

Flutter

It is a small moment. Dusty, the colour of dark limes, lacks generosity but still slakes the tongue. A flutter of eyelashes on my neck. I can smell his thirst, but I want him this way, thirsty against me, the sheets pale against us in relief, the afternoon light caramelized. On the kitchen counter a glass of water, now warm. He can wait.

2006

Bite

In the market at the bottom of the hill, eggplants glare as certain as Tuesday. My hands grasp them, pretend to choose, the way I can't stop myself from biting your bare shoulder when it comes too close to my mouth. Yours is an arrogant shoulder. As arrogant as eggplants stacked high, trying to deny they are waiting.

2006

Outside the Café

This morning on the Malecón, I see there are no more love letters. No one comes here for longing, to miss someone. No one.

We walk the old city avoiding hills, the righteousness of gravity, trickles among the cobblestones. A man walks shouldering a crate of tomatoes. He might know something about it.

You were here two months before me, had an affair with a man with down-turned eyes and thick lips. The city is dirty with your clumsy hands, your kisses stain walls along the market street like warnings.

Outside the café, a man with a ladder gets lost in the cat's cradle of wires strung between storefronts above him. He stands caught and closes his eyes.

Morning light plays dust across the trees, dirty as dirt. Upstairs in a room with broken shutters, a woman on a narrow street sleeps late, tired of letting go. There are no more love letters. Just the city of steps and stumbles and stray dogs. No one comes here for longing.

2006

Andy Quan, 1969–

Condensation

it has rained all week like a broken faucet that drips and stops
  and drips

it is Sunday which is never busy except when the rain drives
  people inside into waiting arms

at the bathhouse I peer into rooms sweat forming at the base of
  my back bare feet grate carpet

here he is with me all sweat and glow my chest against his
  wide back we rock one branch in the wind

my finger's indentations in his thigh I am fascinated by his
  mouth changing shapes in response to pleasure

he asks me why I'm here I tell him it is because you are away
  returning in twenty days from Shanghai which you write
  is damp and cool and crowded

and we called it kaputs quits no longer

and because I've been trying to pretend I'm healing and that
  you are not all that I think of

he tells me it is because his lover returned to Hong Kong after
  five years for work and family and sometimes it is nice to
  hold someone and be held and why do we need reasons

and he tells me lately because he and his friends have been
  saying these days how you hardly ever get what you want

we thank each other I drench my body which is moist and dry

and I miss you and I do not miss you and my body feels good
  and I am still in love

2001

The Gentle Man

Honour the gentle man,
his death in front of a
suburban train. He might
have slipped clean away
into life if not for timing
if not for a schoolboy
with fifteen hours of
grog in his blood.

Came upon the gentle man
just past noon who'd
come from a surprise
party, now changing
train lines, alone
at the station, end seat
of the platform, no station
master on duty. Privacy
perhaps he'd sought,
or quiet.

Fist raised at the gentle man
staggering out automatic
doors—*What the fuck are you
staring at?* Biceps round
as signals, a torso of metal
rail. The girls with him
a restraint: he broke free.

Pity the gentle man
the question asked again
the boy held back again
no matter, the man
jumped, ran for the other
platform, no matter.

Praise the gentle man
testaments tendered by
his lover and his sister

"record the gentle and
loving nature of
Christopher Harris."

Cry for the gentle man
Was he more scared
than we would be
to face down this
Rodney Kerr, days shy
of eighteen, now parole-
eligible in one quick
year, was this boy
scared—ever—the way
we are scared of boys
like him?

Accuse the gentle man
did drunk boy feel
himself a target
of desire direct or
faint as a sense of
someone standing
behind you.

Question the gentle man
"killed instantly": yes
or no? I've died many
deaths by Rodney Kerrs
stretched-out tracks
a railroad to
a far mountain.

Abandon the gentle man
the boy and the two girls
walked away—did they
care if he breathed
still?—the security camera
caught them
calm and unhurried.

Absolve the gentle man
did expletive boy at first
sight know the sweet
soft nature he hid or
could not hide.

Remember the gentle man
all of us who might be
him: alone on a platform.
Stand braced
for that fist to meet
with the bone in your chin
or miss, and rattle
off to another station.

2004

Crystal

By all reports, it's ravaging lives, not
everyone's but enough to make you
pause and wonder about what we trade
for freedom—this modern hag casting
spells, incanting *your hunger will not cease*
till users lose jobs, friends, everything.
A gemstone of 51 facets reduced to
a pane of glass, a personality distilled
to base parts: aggression, fearlessness,
libido, speed.
                                    But the only time I tried it
the lover-of-an-acquaintance supplier
said *that'll keep you up 'til tomorrow noon*
but all I felt was awaked-ness, the night a bit
more clear and focused, a mild itch
in my loins. The Melbourne eve was 35 degrees
and hotter than anything I'd felt
before, but ask anyone: that part is objective.

2004

Brian Rigg, 1971–

house of flies

Alex opens up his house of flies
and when we move through it
the scent of new wood
is thick in the air,
his family's presence
heavy in my throat.

the distance seems to grow
between us
with all the summers
he must have spent here

with dead cats in the barn
and a thousand images captured
by his mother's eyes—
placed in the album and colour-coded:

brown for barn life.

in the corners, he shows me
dead flies up-ended
and crisp under my feet,

in the bay windows and attic
an open mass grave, like old raisins
gathered and bathed
in pools of collected light

with him in the rain and warmth
I'm walking wounded
past his mother's garden

the tall brown sunflowers
dead, but still standing to salute.

2001

tiger lily

tonight Tiger Lily will pop an e
            let melt under tongue 2 hits
                        and when done
            putting on her face
smoke a fat one
to slow it all down

            her dress will be coded
stop-traffic yellow
there will be
a silver star
            on the front
                        and under that
will be the word fucker

she will be a STARFUCKER

she will race to the white ball
faster than
her mind can catch up

at 10:45 am
            Sunday
she will drop down dead
tired

her hair will be her own,
no wigs
for this real queen,

            and when she slaps
those black lace fans
on tight bright thighs
            snaps them open
                        and poses
one plucked eyebrow
raised
you will know who she is:

one of the last
to keep up this house
the vengeance
the fierceness
knows which school
she belongs to

and when tiger lily runways over
to that platform
boiled rice tits
cutting a path
through the fleshy crowd
no one will dare
because fame is cheap here

2001

Michael V. Smith, 1971–

Salvation

If I stood at my open window with
a strange new light falling gold
over my skin now smooth and pale
like cream, no clothes, with breasts
grown full as love, and my cock inverted
to a tight vagina, if my hair grew back
full from the forehead up and fell out
from there on down, if I were a Venus
in the window, all curves, I'd share
everything. I'd masturbate for the men
heading home, the too-tired men
of little hope, the hard workers with
unhappy jobs. They would see me and
cluster on the sidewalk, hats in hand
eyes dewy, a lump in their throats
and pants until someone brave enough
would climb the stairs and find my
door ajar and me, pleased to please.
He would have me on the windowsill
until he was satisfied and each man
from the street, each deserving man
would approach for a taste of this
transformation, so by dawn, I'd be raw
and then, by evening, ready and healed.

2006

The Sad Truth

You will only have one drink.
Friends are here toasting your buddy's
sculpture of a worn shoe, xerox-grey,
thick and nearly two-dimensional
which, everyone agrees, is strikingly
simple—common, yet complex—

making you feel you are nothing
out of the ordinary but special
nonetheless. After the first drink
a second can't hurt. The beer is cheap.
You order a third. When your body
begins a real good buzz, your date
taps you on the shoulder. Time to leave.
Across town, you attend another
get-together far more important
than this one—the wine is free.
You fill up on this opportunity
working the crowd of film people
which is your thing or which
you hope to be your thing, except—
here's the disappointing part,
here's what nudges the evening
towards disaster like a small
wind helping a traveller choose
the wrong fork in the road—
you felt better where you came from
than where you have ended up.
You cruise whatever cute men
happen to fall into your line
of vision until who knows
how long later your pal again
persuades you to leave.
Outside, the spring ocean air is
gorgeous in your lungs like dozens
of microscopic fingers pinching
you awake. Sure, you're
drunk. You don't remember
the last hour of the party, but now
you're headed home, walking
through the pooling streetlights
on a night all moon and no stars.
You need to pee, excuse yourself
to lurch behind a building and prop
one shoulder against a pine.
You black out only long enough
to find your hand warm

and what you have to admit is gooey
down the back of your pants.
A bad dream, you've shit yourself
and have checked to make sure you did
in fact shit yourself. You wish
you could wake up, night over
only you aren't asleep and your hand
has a very real problem. You remove
your shoes, jeans and underwear but
not your socks. You don't want
to get your feet dirty. Beneath you
the ground is covered with wood chips
and the fallen pine needles are softer
than you expected when you scoop
them up. You wipe your hand,
then your ass. There is comfort
knowing that this isn't so different
really from what it's like to crap
in the woods. You could be camping.
When you're as clean as you can be,
you abandon the Calvin Kleins
that were a gift anyway, pull on
your pants, and then scan
for your shoes which you now
realize you shouldn't have tossed
out of the way without noting
the direction. Again your body
ties a heavy black blindfold
round your mind. You come to.
You aren't at home. You're in the park
with your hands parting the cheeks
of an ass spreading disease
while two feet away another man
pulls at himself just out
of reach with a look that says
he costs more than you're worth.
You lurch to the curb where the old
guy with the big rings you've seen
down here before offers you a ride
in his black Mercedes. The slow

drive home, he doesn't touch you even
once which you hope is more
about respect than with how you
smell. Only in the morning do you
remember the friend you left
on a street corner waiting for you
to pee. Did he walk around
the side of the building and catch you
with your pants down or did he
give up on you as you so often
feared he would, only, this time,
that would be a blessing?

2006

Billeh Nickerson, 1972–

Why I Love Wayne Gretzky—An Erotic Fantasy

Because he knows what to do with pucks,
slapshots, wristshots, all that intricate stickwork
as he slips through defencemen,
shoots between the legs
& scores.

Because he likes to pretend
I'm the zamboni & he
the filthy ice.

Because even if he's tired
he'll perk up
whenever I sing *O Canada*.

Because sometimes my dyslexia makes me see
a giant 69 on his back.

Because he's always ready for overtime—
because he never shoots then snores.

Because he understands the importance of
a good organ player.

Because he calls me his stick boy.

Because he likes to be tied up
with the laces from his skates.

Because behind every great man
it feels good.

2000

Gonorrhea

If I could pinpoint my shame
to one precise moment
it wouldn't be the sex or
the first stains on my underwear.
It wouldn't be the day I walked to
the Public Library too embarrassed
to ask for assistance
or pulling out my cock
while the doctor told army stories,
his family looking down at me
from a framed photograph,
ten of them on a stairwell,
eight children, the mother
and the doctor.
If I could pinpoint my shame,
thumbtack it
to the cork message board
of my youth,
it would be the moment
I made him a girl,
told the doctor I couldn't remember
her name or where she lived
though she mentioned something
about the East, missing
her parents and the snow.

2000

If You Fit All Your Lovers in an Airplane, What Kind of Airplane Would It Be?

In my dreams it's a 747 filled
with sports teams,
baseball, football, soccer—
anything with balls, basically.
I'm the Captain, of course,
which means I just stick it

on automatic, head back
into the cabin to take
frequent flyer applications
in the rear.

One day it could be a 737
with enough seats
for each of my lovers
to hold one of Disney's
101 Dalmations.
At first, I'd name each pup
after the lap it sits on
but then there'd be so many Jasons
and Chrises
and Brads
that I'd just refer to them by number.

Right now I'd need a turboprop commuter,
one of those short haul affairs
with thirty seats and a flight attendant
who gives you a phone number
if you're lucky,
honey-roasted peanuts
if you're not.

How strange it seems
I once started off
in a twinseater,
no carry-on luggage,
just me and the pilot exploring
the various landscapes until
our single-engine sputters
and I realize I'll never fly
in such a small plane again.

2000

The Ultra Centrifuge

When I asked my lover what he'd done that day
    I wanted him to ask me too
since I'd just bought groceries and felt really proud,
    but instead of the usual summations,
the subsequent kiss, he just stood there, told me
    he spun people's blood all day,

tube after tube in the ultra centrifuge.
    I'd never heard of a centrifuge before
but I liked its sound so while my lover explained
    how it spins fast enough to make HIV
separate from plasma like cream gathering atop
    an old-fashioned milk bottle

I practiced pronouncing it the same way
    I repeat the names of foreign places
in case I ever go there: ul-tra cen-tri-fuge,
    ultra centrifuge, ultra centrifuge spinning
inside my mouth, my tongue separating
    each word by syllabic weight.

My lover said it's easy when you don't know
    their faces, when you don't see them
exit the clinic doors with Band-Aids
    on short-sleeved arms, when you can't feel
the warmth of their just given blood
    through your latex gloves and glass tubes.

That evening while my lover lay beside me
    I wondered how it felt
to hold the blood between his fingers,
    whether he learned to hold
my cock from holding test tubes
    or test tubes from my cock.

2000

Shane Rhodes, 1973–

Gravitas

Syntax of pull, strained
muscle guiding me down the
lines of your ribs, your
outcrop of hips. You
could well be the roust of a
much kinder geology.

Admit it, only a stoic would
think of apples. I
promise to let it all
fall for
gravity's
steady suck.

Newton said this,
of course, is what math
is for, to grasp
how the bed
wants us
to lie
in its pool
of potential.

What we have learned thus far:
Eros is geometric
extended field theory

We are preserved with salt,
vinegar and a sense of loss

If you know a shorter way home,
take it

Loneliness is dark-matter
and only birds have hollow bones

The more you weigh—the more
it will love you

Go ahead, just try and
drop me

2000

Fucking

How it was really our need we were decorating
and nothing else. The condom in my hand
everything physical and comedic   an oddity.
Twice it leapt from my hands gliding
through the air in perfect jellyfish oscillations.
My hands, covered with lube and bed lint,
scrambled for it as if it were, just then,
the very edge of both our lives.

And then it was on and we clunked
against each other's hard edges
in our closest approximation of sex.
The thing between us for we believed it
the truest point of passion and everything else
preparation. Pure lubricated fulcrum
of our rocking—holding us back and pushing
us forward. It was probably a Trojan
and I imagine poor Troy in its unbreachable walls
wooden horse covered with a sheet of latex
("ultra sensitive") ("for your pleasure")
thirty Greeks beating the door trying to get out
lungs full of nonoxynol-9 or astroglide.
The horse rocking through the night
to their blue deaththroes.

This technology of withholding
our selves, what stops us from going too far
into each other. And then both of us
ridged as something outside us

wrenched the last juices out—
The walls of Troy unfallen
and unburned. Another piece
of the future slipped by
unproved.

2002

His Hands Were Hounds Over Me

I think back to when we met. Our bodies were
younger then and sex moved through our cells
like the heat from an acid etch. It still brings me
to my knees. The only thing we didn't know of
love was the magnitude of its disappointment.
But I don't care anymore or, rather, believe
at one time I cared. Nowadays, I sit in bars
drinking beer as warm as the urine I pump out.
I talk often. I put money in the jukebox and
hear him rolling down the narrow passage. I try
not to lose my head. I try to be with men who
are normal which means I spend much of the
night alone. I am so alone. I am torn asunder.
My head floats beneath the darkening water.

2002

There is an Obvious Solution to Your Problem

Myth is only the repetition of story of a joke
so good you can't stop telling it. At the height
of the Phrygian festival of Cybele, some
men (moved by music and the shedding of
blood) would castrate themselves, tearing
away, as Catullus says, *the burden of their
groin*. Castrates became the goddess's priests.
When I was younger and worked on a farm,
I castrated pigs in spring. With legs spread

wide, head muffled in a burlap sack, I would make two small incisions between the legs and push the testicles, which hadn't descended yet, out through the slits of skin. With one quick pull and cut, I would toss them to the waiting dogs. Hundreds a day. It was like fixing machines. The fear of castration is not the fear of emasculation but the fear of becoming a *plaything*—capable of the act but not of the need that leads it. For what sex (even homosexual) is not made more consummate by the fear of *fertilization*, that I will pass *something* onto you? My fluid, my love, my sperm, my blood, my virus. *Potent*—from Latin, meaning *to have power. Potent*—from Middle English, meaning *crutch*.

2002

Orville Lloyd Douglas, 1976–

Dear Langston Hughes

Was it you at the Savoy the other day?
Talking to Alain Locke as I blurred in the smoke?
Sitting at the table I wanted to be with you....
But you already know what I desire don't you
Langston?
Were we dancing on Lennox Avenue in a twirl?
Shaking and moving to the Charleston?
Last night I loved Shuffling Along
And Josephine was amazing!
Bessie sang her sorrowful tune for all to see
Gladys was just rocking at that piano
She can really tickle the ivory can't she?
Zora had a wonderful feast last night
I laughed so hard when she talked about Godmother
Why didn't you invite me on Zora's folklore trip
South with Jesse?
All you talk about is Carl? Carl? Carl?
Yes I read Nigger Heaven and I enjoyed it
Why the reticence Langston?
When the night falls I feel your ebony hand
It caresses my spirit, it ignites a fire within me
You stand tall in front of me holding me tight
I feel at peace with you
Yet as the phoenix arises I don't hear from you anymore
You're definitely not like Bruce or Aaron
But you helped us get the booklet together
Too bad it burned in a fire
The waves of pleasure erupt as our bodies
drenched with guilt wake up
As the sky is desolate a shade of blue
Yet we are at that Drag Ball
You clapping and smiling as the queens move by
Tell Hugh Jackman, Countee Cullen, and Walt Whitman
I said hello
I can't go on like this Langston

How is Ms. Hughes by the way?
I never did get that Thanksgiving turkey in
Cleveland?

2005

Joel Gibb, 1977–

He is the Boss of Me

He is the boss of me
He gives me hugs and sugar lumps
when my heart's gone bitter
He is the boss of me
He makes me coffee
    and I write him a letter
like I'm a poet or his ancestor
He is the boss of me
He tells me where to go
So I go, I just go

He's never done me wrong
but he never wants to sing my songs
'cause he is my walrus
    and I am his blubber, his lover

He is the boss of me
We walk until we hit the shore
then we walk more,
    he walks more than me
He is the boss of me
My left foot walks to the rhythm of his
We march like we are children
    in an army club
He is the boss of me
He gives me a sensual touch
and marks a trail of human blood
    he calls angel dust

The pearl in his hand is
    the jewel that will make me a man
'cause he is my walrus
    and I am his blubber, his covers

The pearl in his hand is
    the jewel that will make me a man
'cause he is my walrus
    and I am his blubber, his lover

2001

A Miracle

Sent from god
A holy visit
I wake up in the night
"What is it"
I'm startled and I'm cold
and I believe that
    I have problems in my dreams
I feel like I'm the only one
and that I carry your disease

In my head you are suffering
In my head you are

He brings me flowers that are gold
and honey from the bees
He places a blossom in my hair
and undresses me
He tells me that I'm the only one
that can carry his disease
I'm made to be an animal by his love
and to bear his baby

In my head you are suffering
In my head you are
In my head you are suffering
In my head you are

2001

Michael Knox, 1978–

Swimming in the Bodensee

Even this soft Baden afternoon becomes a harsh glint
off water where I struggle (body surprised it's lost
its gills) out to a raft on a preposterous packed slant,
filled with German kids. You on the beach—Atwood hosts
your quiet hour while I paddle about. We came to the
other continent before we could recover our literature,
losing its framework in Konstanz mist, clear now to study
without its presence interfering. Yesterday I cured
your insomnia with a midnight bottle of champagne,
held aloft like a goose I'd caught but left me stranded
in my own sleeplessness. Ancient quiet in my ears like pain.

Water rolling gently and breaking over me, my splutter candid
a split second of fresh water shells about my ears
a perfection of will, water has decided what it will do
and cannot be swayed. Out here I discover I am not Proteus,
conscious now of my separate frailty.
                                                            And I do envy you.

I have half a mind to come to you by starlight and toast
three starry bottles to you. Swim up the moon's white trail
out to the deepest part of the lake. Say,
                                                              plant me close
to the centre; that I might become your conscienceless will.

2006

Notes to a Father

At the dusty bottom of half a box of your childhood toys
I found the root of all your problems. A quaint, stiff hardback
Morte d'Arthur slept promisingly beneath it all. Amidst a boy's
Pandora's box with your faux-metal cowboy pistols, comics,
and stalwart hand-painted figurines. Here I saw the raw models
that shaped your life after. As you cannot be blamed for your

weak father, I cannot for mine. We were never coddled,
they expected, emulated ridiculous masculinity as truth. War
and the Great Depression were enough to stifle the man who
raised you, and the figures you grew up on instead created
the man who raised me. And I sat down with a decades-stiff lasso
and the comics and that little volume and flipped the aged
pages. Here it all lay. My keen graduate-school eye picking
through every word, so deliciously archaic and different from
the gay Parisian erotica you pretend I don't study. We're all tricking
ourselves I suppose, and this volume is my proof as I thumb
across explanations of your cornball coats-across-puddles
gallantry, the barbarous high-school fisticuffs, your proud
chauvinism. All the things that have tormented you, huddled
in your bed in those dark moments before sleep, imposed
on my growing up. Irreconcilable: *your boy wanted dolls*.
But this is where forgiveness lies, I suppose. For the pugilism
and the football, and the lectures about roles with girls;
you were always too contrived, and this constituted a confession.
I always suspected something had caused you. And the cellar
held the truth of your ill-founded, obstinate chivalry. A boy-man's error.
Sad now, that I used to find you on dappled evenings, smoking a panatela
and thousand yard staring at the sunset, posing like a cowboy.

2006

Sean Horlor, 1981–

In Praise of Beauty

after Karen Solie

What we see shapes our imagining.

Poetry, clothes, a pop star's swagger.
Cologne in glass bottles.

A man with eyes the colour
Of a eucalyptus leaf turned over.

A spotlight's preference
For shimmer over shine.

For every act of daring
The astonished eye chooses to praise.

And for all that drifts: shipwrecks,
Lightning, a stranger's hello—

Beauty with edge.
Beauty with consequence.

A kind of grief that separates our lives
Into all that matters, then all that does not

And all it asks of you
Is to look, to look twice, to keep looking.

Desire is lonely work.

2007

For St. Jude, or What Gets Him Where He Is

Lists, cigarettes, his legs.
Fire hydrant, piss puddle, crack face, bus pole.
Weed.
Women, but mostly men.
Men with women.
Men with men.
A few cans of Colt-45, coat-stuffed and warming over with his every footstep north.
Friday nights and forty bucks.
The fact men are out everywhere and he's just another one of them.
E—dry-swallowed or cut and railed up John A. MacDonald-style off an apartment call-box—and jittery jaw.
The undermind of words.
Self-reflexive questions like: where will I be when I get there?
A patois-talking, jibber-jabber OD-nutcase and her ability to vanish leprechaun-like down alleyways.
Street signs.
Some kid his age, Tourette's-programmed into "Bud? Bud? Bud?" selling street-corner dime bags from a zippered knapsack and a husky puppy howling its money-maker hunger siren into the fog-horn, surf-broken night.

2007

For St. Fiacre

> *went to the std clinic, told to come back in a week if*
> *nothing changes. it didn't go away. i didn't go back.*
> —Blog entry by Anon. on *www.someoneelse.com*

This story doesn't want to be touched.
This story is wounded and silent and dangerous
in its anonymity. This story is to be read and read only.
This story can be traced back further,
partner to partner until you discover
something greater than your own understanding of it
walking through your body and finding rest.

This is the story of a farm and a forest and a man with infinity
ever-present in his mind. This story is a long conversation
of pauses—between which anything can happen.
Like most parables, this story will never tell you
what you really want to know: the name of the woman
sitting in the waiting room, crossing
and uncrossing her legs; the colour of the examination table;
whether or not you believe
other people's need will destroy you
long before your own.
This much is clear: early in the dusk of your thigh,
glowing in the midst of so much pink,
these almost moons must slip like apple seeds
under the fingertip and respond to your touch
by disappearing.

2007

Contributors

The contributor notes are composed of the following elements:

1) a biographical paragraph;
2) a compendium of the author's published collections of poetry (in the case of prolific authors, only a selection of titles are listed);
3) a representative selection of secondary source material, if any exists.

Please note that an author's key publications in other genres are identified in the biographical paragraph only.

Patrick Anderson was born in Ashtead, Surrey, England, in 1915. He was educated at Oxford University and Columbia University (New York), where he had a Commonwealth Fellowship from 1938 to 1940. He then moved to Montreal, where he taught private school and founded the influential literary journal, *Preview* (1942–1945), one of the cornerstone publications of Canadian modernism. Very active and interested in international Marxist politics and the fight against fascism during the Second World War, he also edited the short-lived journal, *En Masse* (1945). After becoming a Canadian citizen, he returned to England for a year in 1947, when he was divorced from his wife, then taught at McGill University from 1948 to 1950, after which he left Canada permanently. He taught for two years in Malaysia, then settled in England with Orlando Gearing. Between 1955 and 1972, he published three autobiographical works, *Snake Wine* (1955), *Search Me* (1957), and *The Character Bull* (1963); and four travel books, *First Steps in Greece* (1958), *The Smile of Apollo* (1964), *Over the Alps* (1969), and *Fixed!* (1972). With Alistair Sutherland, he also co-edited *Eros: An Anthology of Male Friendship* (1962). He made a month-long visit to Canada in 1971 and returned once more for a year in 1973 on sabbatical from teaching. His renewed contact with his Canadian peers reinvigorated his poetry and reputation and, after nearly a quarter century, he published a new collection of poetry, followed by a book of selected poems. He died in 1979.

A Tent for April (Montreal: First Statement, 1945); *The White Centre* (Toronto: Ryerson, 1946); *The Colour As Naked* (Toronto: McClelland & Stewart, 1953); *A Visiting Distance* (Ottawa: Borealis, 1976); *Return to Canada* (Toronto: McClelland & Stewart, 1977).

Campbell, Patrick, "Attic Shapes and Empty Attics: Patrick Anderson, a Memoir," *Canadian Literature* 121 (1989): 86–99.

Dickinson, Peter, "Critical Homophobia and Canon Formation, 1943–1967: The 'Haunted Journeys' of Patrick Anderson and Scott Symons," *Here is Queer* (Toronto: University of Toronto Press, 1998): 69–100.

Martin, Robert K., "Communists and Dandies: Canadian Poetry and the Cold War," *Love, Hate, and Fear in Canada's Cold War*, Richard Cavell, ed. (Toronto: University of Toronto Press, 2004): 208–213.

Mayne, Seymour, "A Conversation with Patrick Anderson," *Inscape* (University of Ottawa) 11 (Fall 1974): 46–79.

Sutherland, John, "The Poetry of Patrick Anderson," *Northern Review* 2.4 (1949): 8–20, 25–34.

John Barton was born in Edmonton in 1957 and raised in Calgary. He was educated at the Universities of Alberta, Calgary, Victoria, and Western Ontario as well as Columbia University in New York, studying poetry with Gary Geddes, Eli Mandel, Robin Skelton, and Joseph Brodsky. His poetry has been published in Australia, Canada, the United States, and the United Kingdom, and has won the Patricia Hackett Poetry Prize (University of Western Australia, 1986), three Archibald Lampman Awards for Poetry (1988, 1995, 1998), an Ottawa Book Award (1995), and Second Prize in the Poetry Category of the 2003 CBC Literary Awards. He worked as a librarian and editor for five national museums in Ottawa from 1985 to 2003, where he also co-edited *Arc* for thirteen years. He currently lives in Victoria where he is the editor of *The Malahat Review*.

A Poor Photographer (Victoria: Sono Nis Press, 1981); *Hidden Structure* (Victoria: Ekstasis Editions, 1984); *West of Darkness: Emily Carr, a Self-Portrait* (Kapiskasing: Penumbra, 1987 / Ottawa: BuschekBooks, bilingual edition, 2006); *Great Men* (Kingston: Quarry Press, 1990); *Notes Toward a Family Tree* (Kingston: Quarry Press, 1993); *Designs from the Interior* (Concord: House of Anansi, 1994); *Sweet Ellipsis* (Toronto: ECW Press, 1998), *Hypothesis* (Toronto: House of Anansi, 2001).

Gray, R. W., "My Own Private Alberta: Towards Identity in John Barton's *Designs from the Interior* and Gus Van Sant's *My Own Private Idaho*," *Open Letter*, Tenth Series, No. 3 (1998): 84–96.

Foster, Clarise, "An Interview with John Barton," *Contemporary Verse 2*, 27 (2004): 11–24.

May, Robert G., "'Moving from place to face': Landscape and Longing in the Poetry of John Barton," *Studies in Canadian Literature* 30 (2005): 245–269.

Jean Basile, a poet and novelist, was born in Paris in 1932, the son of a French mother and a Russian father. He came to Montreal in 1962, where he worked as a journalist for *Le Devoir,* writing about popular music (under the pseudonym 'Penelope,') and overseeing the weekly arts and letters section. In 1970, he cofounded the underground monthly magazine, *Mainmise*, which gave voice to the avant-garde in Quebec. He is also known for writing extensively as an advocate for drugs and drug culture. He published his first novel, *Lozenzo*, in 1963, which was followed by a trilogy (*La jument des Mongols* [1966], *La grand Khan* [1967], and *Les voyages d'Irkoutsk* [1970]) about underground culture in Montreal. A fifth novel, *Le piano-trompette*, appeared in 1983. He also wrote for the stage, producing two works, *Joli tambour* (1966) and *Adieu—je pars pour Vazma!: tragifarce d'après des recits de Tchekhov* (1987). He died in Montreal in 1992.

Journal poétique, 1964–1965: élegie pour apprendre à vivre (Montreal: Les Editions du Jour, 1965); *Iconostase pour Pier Paolo Pasolini: discourse poétique sur les gays, le féminisme et les nouveaux mâles* (Montreal: VLB, 1983).

David Bateman was born in Peterborough, Ontario, in 1956 and lives in Toronto. He was educated at Trent University, and the Universities of Toronto and Calgary, where he received a PhD in 2001. His influences include Spalding Grey, Karen Finley, Annie Sprinkle, Shawna Dempsey, and Lorri Millan. *www.geocities.com/godsavethedragqueen*

Salad Days (Ennismore, Ontario: Ordinary Press, 1995); *What Dreadful Things to Say About Someone Who Has Just Paid For My Lunch* (Ennismore, Ontario: Ordinary Press, 1992); *Terrain* (Victoria: finewords, 1998); *Invisible Foreground* (Calgary: Frontenac House, 2005).

bill bissett "was on th first shuttul uv childrn from lunaia 2 erth i was with th othr childrn combing th orange lite evree morning th main sours uv enerjee on lunaria i bcame 2 b heer on erth as part uv a reserch teem 2 undrstand erth wayze iuv bin heer 300 yeers in lunarian time n am getting nowher th shuttul i was on first landid in halifax nova scotia [in 1939] iuv alwayze wantid 2 xploor words lettrs images sounds involvd in 7 aproaches 2 writing lyrikul romantik sexual vizual song konkreet changing his her storikul politikul non narrativ narrativ politikul in fuseyun n fuseyun poetree pomes in wch sm or manee uv thees elements rock in th same pome kontainr i travl a lot dewing reedings havng art shows ium also a paintr have wun th dorothee livesay bc book prize in 93 n 03 n was second in th cbc poetree kontest in approx 81 have reseevd canada council grants in th 60s 70s n 90s was writr in residens at unb fredrikton 98 n uwo london ont 85-86 n writr in libraree woodstock ontario 87-88 i was subjekt uv recent bravo film maureen judg direktor n produsr heart uv a poet 06"

Selected titles: *we sleep inside each othr all* (Toronto: Ganglia, 1966); *nobody owns th earth* (Toronto: House of Anansi, 1971); *pass th food release th spirit book* (Vancouver: Talonbooks, 1973); *yu can eat it at th opening* (Vancouver: blewointmentpress, 1974); *sailor* (Vancouver: Talonbooks, 1978); *beyond even faithful legends: selected poems, 1962–1976* (Vancouver: Talonbooks, 1980); *canada gees mate for life* (Vancouver: Talonbooks, 1985); *what we have* (Vancouver: Talonbooks, 1988); *inkorrect thots* (Vancouver: Talonbooks, 1992); *scars on the seehors* (Vancouver: Talonbooks, 1999); *peter among th towring boxes* (Vancouver: Talonbooks, 2002); *narrativ enigma* (Vancouver: Talonbooks, 2004); *northern wild roses* (Vancouver: Talonbooks, 2006); *ths is erth thees ar peopul* (Vancouver: Talonbooks, 2007).

Selected CDs: *Rainbow Mewsik* (Calgary: Red Deer Press, 2001) with Chris Meloche; *rumours uv hurricane* (Calgary: Red Deer Press, 2003) with Bill Roberts; *deth interrupts th dansing* (Calgary: Red Deer Press, 2006) with Pete Dako.

Judge, Maureen, "bill bissett" (documentary), *Heart of a Poet,* episode 10 (Toronto: makin' movies, 2006).
nichol, bp, "typogeography of bill bissett," *Ganglia* 4 (1966), published with *we sleep inside each othr all.*
Precosky, Don, "bill bissett: Contraversies and Definitions," *Canadian Poetry* 27 (1980): 15–29.
Precosky, Don, "Self selected/selected Self: bill bissett's Beyond Even Faithful Legends," *Canadian Poetry* 34 (1984): 57–78.
Pew, Jeff and Stephen Roxborough, *radiant danse uv being: A Poetic Portrait of bill bissett* (Roberts Creek, BC: Nightwood Editions, 2006).
Rogers, Linda, ed., *bill bissett: Essays on His Works* (Toronto: Guernica Editions, 2002).

Robin Blaser, poet, essayist, and political theorist, was born in Denver, Colorado, in 1925, grew up in rural Idaho, and studied at the College of Idaho, Northwestern University, and the University of California at Berkley, graduating in 1955. A key member of the San Francisco Renaissance in the 1950s and 1960s, he began a friendship with Jack Spicer in 1946 that lasted until Spicer's death in 1965; he oversaw the publication of *The Collected Books of Jack Spicer* in 1975. He moved to Vancouver in 1966, where he taught at Simon Fraser University until 1986 and influenced several generations of Canadian poets. *Recovery of the Public World*, a conference in honour of Blaser's seventieth birthday, was staged in Vancouver in 1995, with the proceedings published by Talonbooks in 1999, while *The Capilano Review* devoted its Winter/Spring 1996 issue to a celebration of his work. *The Last Supper*, a libretto he wrote for an opera by British composer Harrison Birtwhistle, premiered in Berlin in 2000. In 2006, the University of California Press republished his collected poems, *The Holy Forest*, alongside his collected essays, *The Fire*.

The Moth Poem (San Francisco: Open Space, 1964); *Les Chimères: Translations of Nerval for Fran Herndon* (San Francisco: Open Space, 1969); *Cups* (San Francisco: Four Seasons Foundation, 1968); *Image Nations 1–12 & The Stadium of the Mirror* (London: Ferry, 1974); *Image Nations 13 & 14, Luck Unluck Oneluck, Sky-stone, Suddenly, Gathering* (North Vancouver: Cobblestone Press, 1975); *Harp Trees* (Vancouver: Sun Stone House & Cobblestone Press, 1977); *Image Nation 15: The Lacquerhouse* (Vancouver: W. Hoffer, 1981); *Syntax* (Vancouver: Talonbooks, 1983); *The Faerie Queen & The Park* (Vancouver: Fissure Books, 1987); *Pell Mell* (Coach House Press, 1988); *The Holy Forest* (Toronto: Coach House Press, 1993); *Nomad* (Vancouver: Slug Press, 1995); *Wanders* (with Meredith Quartermain, Vancouver: Nomados Press, 2002); *Irreparable* (Vancouver: Nomados, 2003); *The Holy Forest*, revised and expanded edition (Berkley: University of California Press, 2006).

Bernstein, Charles, "Robin on His Own," *West Coast Line* 29.2 (1995) 114–21.
Gray, R. W. "...we have to think in communities now...: an interview with Robin Blaser," *Arc* 44 (2000) 24-36.
Killian, Kevin. "Blaser Talk," *West Coast Line* 29.2 (1995): 126–31.
Nichols, Miriam, *Even on Sunday: Essays, Readings, and Archival Materials on the Poetry and Poetics of Robin Blaser* (Orono, ME: National Poetry Foundation, 2001).

Walter Borden was born in New Glasgow, NS, in 1942. He is an internationally acclaimed actor, an award-winning poet, a playwright, and a long-time respected teacher and activist. Trained at Circle in the Square Theatre School in New York, he is currently in his fourth season at the Stratford Festival. In addition to his film, television, and radio work, he has recorded the critically acclaimed CD, *Walter Borden Reads the Sonnets of William Shakespeare to the*

Music of Fernando Sor. He is the recipient of the Queen Elizabeth II Golden Jubilee Medal, the African Nova Scotian Music Association Music Heritage Award, the Dr. Martin Luther King, Jr. Achievement Award, and the Portia White Prize, is an inductee into the Dr. William P. Oliver Hall of Honour Society, and a member of the Order of Canada.

Tightrope Time: Ain't Nuthin' More Than Some Itty Bitty Madness Between Twilight & Dawn (Toronto: Playwrights Canada Press, 2005).

Clarke, George Elliott, "Must All Blackness Be American? Locating Canada in Borden's 'Tightrope Time,' or Nationalizing Gilroy's *The Black Atlantic*," *Odysseys Home* (Toronto: University of Toronto Press, 2002): 71–86.

Clarke, George Elliott, "Walter Borden's *Tightrope Time* or Voicing the Polyphonous Consciousness" (Foreword), *Tightrope Time* (Toronto: Playwrights Canada Press, 2005).

Todd Bruce was born in Winnipeg in 1965 and completed his undergraduate and graduate work at the University of Manitoba, specializing in critical theory and Canadian fiction and poetry. His influences include Robert Kroetsch, Elizabeth Smart, Al Purdy, Jacques Derrida, Julia Kristeva, Michel Foucault, George Amabilie, and Clarise Lispector. He won the John Hirsch Award for Most Promising Manitoba Writer in 1997.

Birdman (Winnipeg: dog ear press, 1992); *Jiggers* (Winnipeg: Turnstone Press, 1993); *Rhapsody in D* (Winnipeg: Turnstone Press, 1997).

Budde, Robert, "Todd Bruce: The Word Inert, Expectant," *In Muddy Water: Conversations with 11 Poets*, Robert Budde, ed. (Winnipeg: J. Gordon Shillingford Publishing, 2003): 86–102.

Clint Burnham was born in Comox in 1962. He earned postgraduate degrees from the University of Victoria (1988) and York University (1994) and lived in Toronto from the late 1980s into the 1990s, where he was active in the small press scene. He is currently based in Vancouver, where he has lived since 1995. He co-ordinated a liberal arts program for low-income students at the University of British Columbia from 1999 to 2002 and now teaches at Emily Carr Institute of Art + Design. In addition to two books of poetry, he has published a collection of short stories, *Airborne Photo*, a work of Marxist theory, *The Jamesonian Unconscious*

(1995), a novel, *Smoke Show* (2005), which was nominated for the 2005 Ethel Wilson Award for Fiction, as well as art catalogues with the Belkin and Artspeak galleries in Vancouver, including *Cop Puppet* (1999), the performance installation he mounted with Mark Laba.

Be Labour Reading (Toronto: ECW Press, 1997); *Buddyland* (Toronto: Coach House Books, 2000).

Frank Oliver Call was born in Brome, Quebec, in 1878. He attended Stanstead College, earned Bachelor of Arts (1905) and Master of Arts (1908) degrees at Bishop's University, and pursued post-graduate studies at McGill, the Université de Paris, and the University of Marburg. He was a professor of modern languages at Bishop's from 1908 to 1945. Arguably one of the first poets to experiment with modernism in Canada, he won the Quebec Literary Competition Award in 1924, received a bronze medal from the Alliance française in 1938, was president of the Eastern Townships Art Association from 1942 to 1943, and sat on the advisory board of *Canadian Poetry Magazine* from 1936 to 1945. In addition to five volumes of poetry, he published three books of prose: *The Spell of French Canada* (1926), *The Spell of Acadia* (1930), and *Marguerite Bourgeoys* (1930). A painter of floral still lifes, he participated in group shows in Montreal and New York. He died in Montreal in 1956.

In a Belgian Garden and Other Poems (London: Erskine Macdonald, 1917); *Acanthus and Wild Grape* (Toronto: McClelland & Stewart, 1920); *Simples and Other Poems* (1923); *Blue Homespun* (Toronto: Ryerson, 1924); *Sonnets for Youth* (Toronto: Ryerson, 1944).

Kizuk, Alex, "One Man's Access to Prophecy: the Sonnet Series of Frank Oliver Call," *Canadian Poetry* 21 (1987): 31–41.
Malus, Aaron, et al, "Frank Oliver Call, Eastern Townships Poetry, and the Modernist Movement," *Canadian Literature* 107 (1985): 60–69.

Jean-Paul Daoust was born in Valleyfield, Quebec, in 1946 and educated at the University of Montreal. In 1990, he won the Governor General's Award for Poetry for *Les cendres bleues.* His work appears *in* most anthologies in Quebec and has been featured on TV and in film. The editor of the poetry journal, *Estuaire,* from 1993 to 2003, he lives in Sainte-Melanie north of Montreal.

Selected books: *Oui, cher* (Montreal: Cul Q, 1976); *Les garçons magiques* (Montreal: VLB, 1986); *Les cendres bleues* (Trois-Rivières: Écrits des Forges, 1990); *111 Wooster Street* (Montreal: VLB, 1996); *Taxi pour Babylone* (Trois-Rivières: Écrits des Forges/L'Orange Bleue, 1996); *Les saisons de l'Ange* (Saint-Hippolyte: Éditions du Noroît, 1997); *Les saisons de l'Ange*, Vol. II (Montreal: Éditions du Noroît, 1999); *Le poème déshabillé* (Montreal: L'Interligne, 2000); *Les versets amoureux* (Trois-Rivières: Écrits des Forges, 2001); *Cinéma gris* (Montreal: Triptyque, 2006); *Cobra et Colibri* (Montreal: Éditions du Noroît, 2006).

English translations: *Black Diva: Selected Poems 1982–1986*, Daniel Sloate, tr. (Montreal, Guernica Editions, 1991); *Blue Ashes: Selected Poems 1982–1998*, Daniel Sloate, tr. (Toronto: Guernica Editions, 1999).

Brian Day was born in Langley, BC, in 1962 and grew up in Mission. He attended the Universities of Victoria, Trent, and Toronto, studying English, education, and theology. He won the E.J. Pratt Medal for Poetry in 1986. His influences include the Bible, the Brothers Grimm, Hindu stories, and the poetry of Rainer Maria Rilke. He teaches in Toronto.

Love is not Native to my Blood (Toronto: Guernica Editions, 2000); *Azure* (Toronto, Guernica Editions, 2004).

Dennis Denisoff was born in Glade, near Nelson, BC, in 1961, where he joined the Kootenay School of Writing. He has a PhD from McGill, was a postdoctoral fellow at Princeton, and currently holds the Chair in Nineteenth Century Literature and Culture at Ryerson in Toronto. In addition to the Soviet avant-garde, his poetry is influenced by the L=A=N=G=U=A=G=E poetry movement. His novels include *Dog Years* (Arsenal Pulp Press, 1991), which was shortlisted for the Norma Epstein Award and a QSPELL Award, and *The Winter Gardeners* (Coach House Books, 2003). He has also published a number of scholarly works, including *Aestheticism and Sexual Parody* (Cambridge University Press, 2001) and *Sexual Visuality from Literature to Film* (Palgrave–Macmillan, 2004). In 1993, he edited *Queeries* (Arsenal Pulp Press), the first anthology of Canadian gay male prose.

Tender Agencies (Vancouver: Arsenal Pulp Press, 1994).

Gilles Devault was born in Ste-Anne-de la Pérade in 1948 and lives in Trois-Rivières. In addition to publishing three books of poetry, he has worked in the theatre as a director and actor, mounting three of his own plays, *Hivernel, Magnificat,* and *Lamento* at the Théâtre de Face, where he was artistic director until 1990. He paints, has studied piano and singing, and organizes readings and lectures in Montreal and in Quebec's Mauricie region. *www.rabaska.com/art/gdevault.htm*

Fougères cendrées (Trois-Rivières: Écrits des Forges, 1993); *L'oeil blanc du sommeil* (Trois-Rivières: Écrits des Forges, 1995); *La nuit debout sur ses cendres* (Trois-Rivières: Écrits des Forges, 1997).

Orville Lloyd Douglas was born in Toronto in 1976. In 2004, he obtained a BA in history from York University. He lives in Brampton, Ontario.

You Don't Know Me (Toronto: TSAR Publications, 2005).

Clarke, George Elliott, review of *You Don't Know Me, Halifax Chronicle Herald* (November 27, 2005): 31.

Grubisic, Brett Josef, "Black Gay and Angry," *Xtra! West* (July 21, 2005): 51.

Michael Estok was born in Moose Jaw, Saskatchewan, in 1939 and died in Halifax, Nova Scotia, in 1989. He studied at the University of Saskatchewan where he earned an MA and at the University of Toronto where he was awarded a doctorate. He taught English at the University of Western Ontario, the University of Waterloo, and Dalhousie University, where he was a Killam Scholar. He spent the majority of his career at the Université Sainte Anne, in Pointe de l'Église (Church Point), NS. Individual poems appeared in numerous literary journals including *The Canadian Forum, The Far Point, The Fiddlehead, Grain, Quarry,* and *West Coast Review.* His writing delves into the broad themes of personal relationships and social justice, which his second book, *A Plague Year Journal,* integrates into a story told in searing emotional terms from the perspective of a man dying from AIDS. This posthumous collection is an important Canadian addition to the literature of the disease and continues to be a timely work.

Paradise Garage (Fredericton: Fiddlehead Poetry Books/Goose Lane Editions, 1987); *A Plague Year Journal* (Vancouver: Pulp Press, 1989).

Robert Finch was born in Freeport, Long Island, New York, in

1900 and raised on an Alberta ranch, where his family had moved in 1906. He was educated at the University of Toronto and the Sorbonne, and then joined the Department of French, University College, University of Toronto, where he taught until his retirement in 1968. He was one of six poets represented in A. J. M. Smith's landmark *New Provinces* (1936), the first anthology of Canadian modernist poetry, and twice won the Governor General's Award for Poetry in 1946 and 1961. Renowned as a poet, he was also an accomplished painter, harpsichordist, and scholar, known for *The Sixth Sense: A Study of Individualism in French Poetry, 1686–1760* (1966) and *French Individualist Poetry* (1971), an influential anthology he co-edited with E. Joliat. He was elected to the Royal Society of Canada in 1963 and received the Lorne Pierce Gold Medal in 1968. He died in Toronto in 1995.

Poems (Toronto: Oxford University Press, 1946); *The Strength of the Hills* (Toronto: McClelland & Stewart, 1948); *Acis in Oxford* (Toronto: University of Toronto Press, 1961); *Dover Beach Revisited* (Toronto: Macmillan, 1961); *Silverthorn Bush* (Toronto: Macmillan, 1966); *Variations & Theme* (Erin: Porcupine's Quill, 1980); *Has and Is* (Erin: Porcupine's Quill, 1981); *Twelve for Christmas* (Erin: Porcupine's Quill, 1982); *The Grand Duke of Moscow's Favourite Solo* (Erin: Porcupine's Quill, 1983); *Double Tuning* (Erin: Porcupine's Quill, 1984); *For the Back of a Likeness* (Erin: Porcupine's Quill, 1986); *Sail-boat and Lake* (Erin: Porcupine's Quill, 1988); *Miracle at the Jetty* (Port Rowan: Leeboard Press, 1991); *Improvisations* (Port Rowan: Leeboard Press, 1996).

Downes, G. V., "Robert Finch and the Temptations of Form," *Canadian Literature* 97 (1983): 26–33.

Gingell-Beckmann, Susan, "Against an Anabasis of Grace: A Retrospective Review of the Poems of Robert Finch," *Essays on Canadian Writing* 23 (1982): 157–162.

Helwig, David, "Robert and Edward: An Uncommon Obituary," *Canadian Notes & Queries* 50 (1996): 4–6.

Trehearne, Brian, "Finch's Early Poetry and the Dandy Manner," *Canadian Poetry* 18 (1986): 11–34.

Jean Chapdelaine Gagnon was born in Sorel, Quebec, in 1949. He graduated with a PhD in French from the University of Montreal in 1982 and works as a translator, publishing with Fides, Les Herbes Rouges, Les Presses de l'Université de Montréal, XYZ, Héritage, Trécarré, France–Amérique, and Novalis/Bayard, among others. He has published fifteen books of poetry and over forty translated works since 1979. In 1991, using the pseudonym "G. Jean" and under his own imprint, JGC, he published *Samedi chaud*, the first Canadian gay male erotic novel. He lives in Montreal.

L dites lames (Saint-Lambert: Éditions du Noroît, 1980); *Essaime* (Saint-Lambert: Éditions du Noroît, 1983); *Entretailles* (Trois-Rivières: Écrits des Forges, 1984); *N'ébruitez pas ce mot* (Saint-Lambert: Éditions du Noroît, 1985); *Les langues d'aimer* (Trois-Rivières: Écrits des Forges, 1986); *Le tant-à-cœur* (Saint-Lambert: Éditions du Noroît, 1986); *Dans l'attente d'une aube* (Montreal: Triptyque, 1987); *Malamour* (Saint-Lambert/Remoulins sur Gardon: Éditions du Noroît / Jacques Brémond, 1988); *Puis* (Saint-Lambert / Remoulins sur Gardon: Noroît/Jacques Brémond, 1989); *Île de mémoire* (Saint-Hippolyte: Éditions du Noroît, 1997); *Tu* (Montreal: Noroît, 2000); *Sur le chemin de la croix* (Montreal: Éditions Fides, 2003); *Vigile* (Montreal: Éditions du Noroît, 2003); *Cantilène* (Montreal: Éditions du Noroît, 2006).

English Translation: *Do Not Disclose this Word*, Andrea Moorehead, tr. (Peterborough, U.K: Spectacular Diseases, 1997).

Moorhead, Andrea, "Preface," *Do Not Disclose this Word* (Peterborough, UK: Spectacular Diseases, 1997).

Keith Garebian was born in Bombay to an Armenian father and Anglo–Indian mother in 1943. He immigrated with his family to Canada in 1961, where he obtained four degrees culminating in a PhD in English from Queen's University. After teaching full time in high school in Quebec and part time in colleges and universities in Quebec and Ontario, he turned to writing full time. The author of fifteen books and a chapbook, he has published over a thousand articles, reviews, and interviews in nearly eighty journals, magazines, anthologies, and newspapers in Canada and abroad. His writing (non-fiction and poetry) has won several awards, with his second book of poetry, *Frida: Paint Me As A Volcano*, longlisted for the ReLit Award in 2005. He has completed a book-length poetry manuscript on Derek Jarman, the English filmmaker, artist, and militant who died of AIDS in 1994.

Reservoir of Ancestors (Oakville: Mosaic Press, 2003); *Samson's Hair and Other Satiric Fantasies* (Toronto: Micro Prose, 2004); *Frida: Paint Me As A Volcano/Frida: Un Volcan de Souffrance* (Ottawa: BuschekBooks, 2004).

Harding-Russell, Gillian, "Points in Time and Place: Perspective and Paradox in Four Poets," *Event* 34.2 (2005) 109–113.

Joel Gibb was born in Kincardine, Ontario, in 1977. He is an artist, singer/songwriter, and leads the gay church-folk group, The Hidden Cameras, which Gibb assembled to perform his songs after the release of *Ecce Homo* on his own independent label, EvilEvil. Initially performing in churches, porn theatres, and parks in Toronto, the band now regularly tours Canada, the United States, and Europe. Singles include "Ban Marriage" (2003), "A Miracle" (2003), "I Believe in the Good of Life" (2004), "Learning the Lie" (2005), "Awoo" (2006), and "Death of a Tune" (2006). *www.thehiddencameras.com*

Hidden Cameras CDs: *Homo Ecce* (Toronto: EvilEvil, 2001); *The Smell of Our Own* (Toronto: EvilEvil, 2003); *The Hidden Cameras Play the BBC Sessions* (London: Rough Trade, 2003); *Mississauga Goddamn* (Toronto: EvilEvil, 2004); *Learning the Lie* (Toronto: EvilEvil, 2005); *Awoo* (Toronto: EvilEvil, 2006).

Barclay, Michael, "Hidden Cameras: One Nation Under A Fag," *Exclaim!* (July 29, 2004).

Sky Gilbert was born in Norwich, Connecticut, in 1952 and was educated at York and the University of Toronto, where he earned a PhD in drama. Well known as a playwright and novelist, he was the founding artistic director of Toronto's Buddies in Bad Time and is the recipient of numerous awards, including Dora Mavor Moore Awards in 1990 and 1991 and the ReLit Award for Fiction in 2005. His influences include Constantin Cavafy, Noël Coward, Frank O'Hara, and J.D. Salinger.

Digressions of a Naked Party Girl (Toronto: ECW Press, 1998); *Temptations for a Juvenile Delinquent* (Toronto: ECW Press, 2003).

Vaughan, R. M., "Arguments in Motion," *Books in Canada* 23 (April 1994): 16–19.

John Glassco was born in Montreal in 1909. He enrolled in McGill University in 1925, but moved to Paris against his family's wishes in 1928 to lead a bohemian life in the café society of the Lost Generation. Three years later, after contracting tuberculosis, he returned to Montreal and, while recuperating in hospital, ostensively wrote his now infamous autobiography of his Paris years, *Memoirs of Montparnasse*, which he published to acclaim in 1970, after having apparently "suppressed" it for forty years. Later scholarly research has revealed it to be—even by Glassco's admission—a fictionalization distorting actual events that he initially drafted in 1964. Besides also being known as a poet, Glassco was a novelist, pornographer (often publishing under a pseudonym), and translator respected for his deft translations of the poetry of Saint-Denis Garneau and other Québécois poets (collected in *The Poetry of French Canada in Translation* [1970]) as well as three novels by Monique Bosco, Jean-Yves Soucy, and Jean-Charles Harvey. He completed Aubrey Beardsley's unfinished novel, *Under the Hill*, in 1959. In 1971, he won a Governor General's Award for *Selected Poems*. He spent most of his adult life residing in the countryside of Quebec's Eastern Townships. He died in Montreal in 1981. In 1982, the Literary Translators' Association of Canada established a translation prize in his name.

The Deficit Made Flesh (Toronto: McClelland & Stewart, 1958); *A Point of Sky* (Toronto: Oxford University Press, 1964); *Squire Hardman* (George Colman, pseudonym; Foster: Pastime, 1966); *Selected Poems* (Toronto: Oxford, 1971); *Montreal* (Montreal: DC Books, 1973); *John Glassco: Selected Poems with Three Notes on the Poetic Process*, Michael Gnarowski, ed. (Ottawa: Golden Dog, 1997).

Bennett, John, "John Glassco: the Canadian Wordsworth," *Canadian Poetry* 13 (1983): 1–11.

Dellamora, Richard, "Queering Modernism: a Canadian in Paris," *Essays on Canadian Writing* 60 (1996): 256–273.

Jewinski, Ed, "Troubled Joy: Style and Syntax in Glassco's Poetry," *Canadian Poetry* 13 (1983): 12–20.

Lesk, Andrew, "Having a Gay Old Time in Paris: John Glassco's Not-So-Queer Advantures," *In a Queer Country*, Terry Goldie, ed. (Vancouver: Arsenal Pulp Press, 2001): 175–187.

R. W. Gray's short prose and poetry have appeared in *Arc, Absinthe, The Blithe House Quarterly, Dandelion, Event, Grain, The James White Review, The Malahat Review,* and *The Windsor Review,* as well as the anthologies *Quickies 2* and *3* and *Carnal Nation*. He has published two serialized novels, *Tide Pool Sketches* and *Waterboys* (*www.tidelines.ca*), in *Xtra! West,* has written for film and television, and has had six short films of his scripts produced. His interviews with Canadian gay poets have appeared in *Arc* and *Open Letter.* Born in Nanaimo in 1969, he spent most of his childhood on the Northwest mainland coast. He trained at Banff and Sage Hill Writers' Retreat and has a PhD in literature and psychoanalysis from the University of Alberta.

John Grube was born in Toronto in 1930. He graduated from the University of Toronto and the Ontario College of Art and Design, where he taught English and Creative Writing for many years. He is the author of two books on Quebec, *Bâtisseur de pays, la pensée de François-Albert Angers* (Action Nationale, 1981) and *Une Amitié bien particulière, les lettres de Jacques Ferron à John Grube* (Éditions du Boréal, 1990), and a book of fiction, *I'm Supposed to be Crazy and Other Stories* (Darlington Press, 1997).

Sunday Afternoon at the Toronto Art Gallery (Fredericton: Fiddlehead Books, 1966); *Voodoo* (Toronto: Ontario College of Art, 1982); *God, Sex, and Poetry* (Toronto: Darlington Press, 2002).

Brion Gysin was born in England in 1916 to a Canadian mother and an Anglo–Swiss father, who, soon after his son's birth, was killed in the Battle of the Somme. Gysin moved with his mother to Edmonton in 1921, where he lived until he was sixteen. After finishing his schooling at a British public school, he moved to Paris and travelled around Europe. He returned to North America in 1940, living in New York where he worked on Broadway before enlisting in the U.S. Army. Soon after, he transferred to the Royal Canadian Army during the Second World War and was stationed on the home front. During that time he published his first book, *To Master—a Long Goodnight* (1946), a narrative history of Josiah Henson, the real-life model for Uncle Tom. On the basis of that work he was awarded one of the first Fulbright Scholarships and returned to Europe, but soon settled in Tangiers, where he moved easily among local and expatriate residents alike, associated with the writers around Paul Bowles, and ran the famous 1001 Nights restaurant, the venue that introduced the Master Musicians of Jajouka to the world. In 1958, he returned to Paris, where he lived at the Beat Hotel; it was then that he developed his influential cut-up and permutation-poem writing techniques, applying them to both text and tape in collaboration with William Burroughs. He also patented the Dreamachine with British mathematician Ian Sommerville. Gysin by this time was also an artist of note. In his last decades, he moved between Paris, London, New York, and Tangiers, and continued his literary and artistic experimentations. He completed two novels, *The Process* (1969) and *The Last Museum*, published posthumously in 1986, the year he died in Paris, his home since 1973. Months before his death, the French government made him a Chevalier de l'Ordre des Arts et de Lettres. In 2001, when most of his literary work had gone out of print, an extensive anthology of his writings appeared, *Back in No Time: The Brion Gysin Reader*, edited by Jason Weiss.

Minutes to Go, with William S. Burroughs, Gregory Curso, and Sinclair Beiles (Paris: Two Cities, 1960; San Francisco: Beach

Books, 1968); *The Exterminator*, with William S. Burroughs (San Francisco: The Auerhahn Press, 1960); *Brion Gysin Let the Mice In* (West Glover, Vt: Something Else Press, 1973); *The Third Mind*, with William S. Burroughs (New York: Viking, 1978).

Geiger, John, *Nothing is True, Everything is Permitted: The Life of Brion Gysin* (New York: Disinformation, 2005).
Gysin, Brion, *Here to Go: Planet R–100*, interviews with Terry Wilson (San Francisco: Re/Search, 1982).
Kuri, José Férez, ed. *Brion Gysin: Tuning in to the Multimedia Age*. (London: Thames & Hudson / Edmonton: Edmonton Art Gallery, 2003).
Weiss, Jason, ed., "Brion Gysin," *Writing at Risk: Interviews in Paris with Uncommon Writers* (Iowa City: University of Iowa Press, 1991): 57–84.

Daryl Hine was born in Vancouver in 1936. He studied Classics and Philosophy at McGill and obtained a PhD in Comparative Literature at the University of Chicago in 1967. From 1968 to 1978 he edited *Poetry* (Chicago) and also taught at the University of Chicago, the University of Illinois, and Northwestern. He is the recipient of a Guggenheim Fellowship, a MacArthur Fellowship, and a medal from the American Academy of Arts and Letters. He is well known internationally as a poet, editor, novelist, and translator of Greek and Roman texts. He lives in Evanston, Illinois.

Five Poems (Toronto: Emblem, 1954); *The Carnal and the Crane* (Montreal: Contact, 1957); *The Devil's Picture Book* (London: Abelard-Schumann, 1962); *The Wooden Horse* (New York: Atheneum, 1965); *Minutes* (New York: Atheneum, 1968); *In & Out* (1975, republished by Atheneum, 1989); *Resident Alien* (New York: Atheneum, 1975); *Daylight Saving* (New York: Atheneum, 1978); *Selected Poems* (New York: Atheneum / Toronto: Oxford University Press, 1980); *Academic Festival Overtures* (New York: Atheneum, 1985); *Postscripts* (New York: Knopf, 1991); *Recollected Poems* (Toronto: Fitzhenry & Whiteside, 2007).

Guy-Bray, Stephen, "Daryl Hine at the Beach," *Canadian Literature* 159 (1998): 74–88.

Sean Horlor was born in Edmonton in 1981 and raised in Victoria, where he graduated from the University of Victoria in 2004. He now lives in Vancouver. His influences include Louise Glück, Margaret Atwood, Robert Bringhurst, Patrick Lane, Roo Borson, Mark Doty, Karen Solie, and Lorna Crozier. "In Praise of Beauty," won

First Prize in the poetry category of *This Magazine*'s 2006 Great Canadian Literary Hunt.

Our Mission, Our Moment (Vancouver: Mosquito Press, 2003); *Made Beautiful By Use* (Winnipeg: Signature Editions, 2007).

Michael Knox was born in Hamilton in 1978 and educated at Queen's University, the University of Toronto, Memorial University of Newfoundland, and the University of Konstanz (Germany). His poems have appeared in literary journals across North America and in Britain. He lives in Toronto.

Play Out the Match (Toronto: ECW Press, 2006).

Edward A. Lacey was born in 1937 in Lindsay, a farming community in eastern Ontario. In 1955, he entered University College, University of Toronto, where he studied modern languages and literatures with Robert Finch, among others. After graduating in 1959, he began an advanced degree in linguistics at the University of Texas in Austin. In 1960, he was given a suspended sentence (after being stopped at the border from Mexico in possession of marijuana) and was barred permanent entry to the United States. He began teaching English in northern Mexico and, except for a seasonal appointment at the University of Alberta and occasional visits to his family, he spent most of his adult life away from Canada, which he claimed vehemently to abhor. Instead, he worked as an English tutor and translator while travelling in the Caribbean, South America, southern Europe, north Africa, India, Thailand, and Indonesia. Throughout this very itinerant life, during which he smoked, drank, and pursued sex prodigiously, he wrote a remarkable body of work. In 1965, he published *The Forms of Loss*, a privately printed collection that is considered to be the first openly gay poetry to have been published in book form in English Canada. He followed this book with three more volumes of poetry that were either printed privately or by very small presses, including Ian Young's Catalyst. The poetry and fiction he translated from Spanish, French, Arabic, and other languages were sometimes published in book form by San Francisco-based Gay Sunshine Press; the best known among several titles is *My Deep Dark Pain is Love* (1983), an anthology of Latin American gay fiction. In 1983, a staged dramatization of his poetry, *Lacey or Tropic Snows: Theatrical Tales of a Canadian Exile in Brazil*, was produced by Sky Gilbert at Toronto's Buddies in Bad Times Theatre. In 1991, while drunk and passed out, he was run over in Bangkok, sustaining severe injuries and brain damage. After being repatriated to

Canada, he lived under the watchful eyes of friends in care facilities in Nova Scotia and Ontario. He died of a heart attack in a rooming house in Toronto in 1995, the same year that *A Magic Prison*, a selection of his letters, was published. In 2000, John Robert Colombo privately published *The Collected Poems and Translations of Edward A. Lacey*, a massive volume edited by Fraser Sutherland that includes almost 250 pages of previously unpublished poems and translations. A *Collected Letters* is in progress.

The Forms of Loss (University of Toronto Press, 1965); *Path of Snow* (Montreal: Ahasuerus, 1974); *Later* (Scarborough: Catalyst Press, 1978); *Third World* (Jakarta: Blacky's Lounge, 1994); *The Collected Poems and Translations of Edward A. Lacey* (Toronto: Colombo & Company, 2000).

Helwig, David, "Robert and Edward: An Uncommon Obituary," *Canadian Notes & Queries* 50 (1996): 4–6.
Sutherland, Fraser, "Documents: Edward Lacey," *Canadian Poetry* 57 (2005): 122–137.

Bertrand Lachance was born in Amos, northern Quebec, in 1948. He moved to Vancouver in 1967, where he published five books of poetry, and worked in collaboration with bill bissett at blueointmentpress and later founded Air Press in 1972. He relocated to Toronto in 1977, where he worked on the production of fashion shows while obtaining a degree in journalism at Ryerson. Later, in Montreal, after the success of their first short film, *Ma Vie*, he cofounded the film-production company, Castor & Pollux, Inc., with filmmaker Daniel Langlois in 1992. Their subsequent feature films include *L'Escorte* (1996), *Danny in the Sky* (2001), and *Amnesia: the James Brighton Enigma* (2005), which won the 2006 Entertainment Partners Canada Award for Best Canadian feature-length film at Toronto's Inside Out Film Festival. Three films are currently in development: *The Incredible Destiny of Matthew-the-Drummer* (the 1648 story of New France's first executioner), *Rainbow Music* (a fictional story based on the author's relationship with bill bissett from 1969 to 1972), and *My First Film* (the story of a young actor turned violently homophobic on the set of a gay film in the 1990s). *www.prod-castorpollux.com*

Eyes Open (Vancouver: blewointmentpress, 1970); *Tes rivières t'attendant* (Vancouver: blewointmentpress, 1971); *Street Flesh* (Vancouver: blewointmentpress, 1972); *Bertrand Lachance: Poems* (Vancouver: Air, 1973); *Cock Tales* (Vancouver: Talonbooks, 1973).

Douglas LePan was born in Toronto in 1914. He studied at the University of Toronto, Harvard, and Oxford before serving with the Canadian Army in Italy. After the Second World War, he joined the Foreign Service, leaving to teach at Queen's University before becoming Principal of University College, University of Toronto. Among other awards, his books have won the Governor General's Award for Poetry (*The Net and The Sword*, 1953) and for Fiction (*The Deserter*, McClelland & Stewart, 1964). He published a memoir, *Bright Glass of Memory* (McGraw-Hill Ryerson, 1979) and in 1990, he published *Far Voyages*, a book of poems that broke personal ground in its open explorations of a relationship with a younger man. LePan died in 1998.

The Wounded Prince (London: Chatto & Windus, 1948); *The Net and The Sword* (Toronto: Clark, Irwin, 1953); *Something Still to Find* (Toronto: McClelland & Stewart, 1982); *Weathering It: Collected Poems, 1948-1987* (Toronto: McClelland & Stewart, 1987); *Far Voyages* (Toronto: McClelland & Stewart, 1990); *Macalister or Dying in the Dark* (Kingston: Quarry Press, 1995).

Barton, John, "Men of Honour: Prototypes of the Heroic in the Poetry of Douglas LePan," *Arc* 58 (2007).

Michael Lynch was born in North Carolina in 1944 and taught English at the University of Toronto from 1971 until his death in 1991 from AIDS complications. An early activist in Toronto's lesbian and gay community, he participated in the Gay Alliance toward Equality and Gay Academic Union, founded Gay Fathers of Toronto, and wrote for *The Body Politic*. He was a pioneer in lesbian and gay academic studies, editing the *Lesbian & Gay Studies Newsletter* for the queer caucus of the Modern Languages Association for many years, and founding the Toronto Centre for Lesbian and Gay Studies in 1990. He made notable and articulate contributions to the growth of an AIDS movement in Canada, was a founder and early chair of a number of key organizations, in particular The AIDS Committee of Toronto and AIDS Action Now. His poem "Cry" is etched on the lead panel of The AIDS Memorial in Toronto, which he also founded.

These Waves of Dying Friends (New York: Contact II, 1989).

Silversides, Ann, *AIDS Activist, Michael Lynch and the Politics of Community* (Toronto: Between the Lines, 2003).

Blaine Marchand was born in Ottawa in 1949, where he was involved in the founding of three literary magazines, *The Canadian*

Review, *Sparks*, and *Anthos*, the Ottawa Valley Book Festival, and Ottawa Independent Writers. He also writes fiction, has published a young adult novel, and was a columnist for *Capital Xtra!* from 1997 to 2005. While he was president of the League of Canadian Poets from 1992 to 1993, his third book of poetry won the 1992 Archibald Lampman Award. He placed second in the 1990 National Poetry Contest. He has recently completed a new manuscript of poems, "The Craving of Knives."

After the Fact (Ottawa: Borealis, 1979); *Open Fires* (Perth: Anthos, 1987); *A Garden Enclosed* (Dunvegan: Cormorant Press, 1991); *Bodily Presence* (Kingston: Quarry Press, 1995); *Equilibrium* (London: Pendas, 2007).

Daniel David Moses is a Delaware, born at Ohsweken in 1952 on the Six Nations lands in southern Ontario. A poet and playwright, he was educated at York and the University of British Columbia. His plays include *Coyote City* (a nominee for the 1991 Governor General's Award for Drama), *Big Buck City, The Indian Medicine Shows* (winner of the 1996 James Buller Memorial Award for Excellence in Aboriginal Theatre), *Almighty Voice and His Wife, Brébeuf's Ghost,* and *City of Shadows*. Co-editor of *An Anthology of Canadian Native Literature in English* (Oxford University Press, 3rd edition, 2005), he published a book of essays, *Pursued by a Bear* (Exile Editions) in 2005. He lives in Toronto where he writes and in Kingston where he teaches at Queen's University. *www.danieldavidmoses.com*

The White Line (Saskatoon: Fifth House Publishers, 1990); *Delicate Bodies* (Sechelt: Nightwood Editions, 1992); *Sixteen Jesuses* (Toronto: Exile Editions, 2000).

Gray, R. W., "'The nice thing about being two-spirited is it exists despite the patriarchy': An Interview with Daniel David Moses," *Arc* 42 (1999): 29–39.

Lindberg, Tracey and David Brundage, eds., *Daniel David Moses: Written and Spoken Exploration of His Works* (Toronto: Guernica Editions, 2007).

Jim Nason, born in Montreal in 1957, was educated at York, McGill, and Ryerson universities. He lives in Toronto where he works as a social worker with marginalized groups, including women and men diagnosed with HIV/AIDS. He has also worked as a flight attendant and a bookseller, has taught writing at Ryerson University, and was book review editor for *Lexicon Magazine*. His poetry has appeared across North America and he published a novel, *The Housekeeping Journals*, with Turnstone Press in 2006.

If Lips Were as Red (Toronto: Palmerston Press, 1991); *The Fist of Remembering* (Toronto: Wolsak and Wynn, 2006).

Émile Nelligan was born in Montreal on Christmas Eve in 1879 to an Irish father and a Québécois mother. Never an accomplished student, he left school against his parents' wishes at seventeen to write. His active career as a poet was short but colourful. A disciple of Symbolists Charles Baudelaire and Paul Verlaine, he published his first poem under a pseudonym in *Le Samedi*, a weekly newspaper, in 1896. He joined the École littéraire de Montréal, an important intellectual movement composed of a diverse group of poets who eschewed the controlling influences of religion and politics on poetics, and participated in its regular public readings. In May 1899, at what would be his last public appearance, he triumphantly recited "Song of Wine," a poem construed as a defense of poetry. Later that year, his fragile mental stability deteriorated, and his family admitted him to the Saint Benoît asylum, where he remained for over two decades. Up until this time, he had only published twenty-three poems; under the auspices of Louis Danton, 107 of his poems were collected into *Émile Nelligan et son oeuvre* (1904), which would be progressively expanded over a series of editions that established his reputation. He remained in permanent care, transferring to St-Jean-de-Dieu hospital in 1924. Throughout his long confinement, he attempted to write new or revise existing poems, often recalled from memory. He died in Montreal in 1941.

Oeuvres complètes (Montreal: Éditions Fides, 1991).

English translations: *The Complete Poems of Émile Nelligan*, Fred Cogswell, tr. (Montreal: Harvest House, 1983); *Selected Poems*, P. F. Widdows, tr. (Toronto: Guernica Editions, 1995).

Wyczynski, Paul, *Bibliographie descriptive et critique d' Émile Nelligan* (Ottawa: Éditions de l'Université d'Ottawa, 1973).
Wyczynski, Paul, *Émile Nelligan* (Montreal: Éditions Fides, 1967).

Billeh Nickerson was born on Valentine's Day, 1972, in Halifax. He was raised in Langley, BC, was educated at the Universities of Victoria (1998) and British Columbia (2003), and teaches at Kwantlen University College in Richmond, BC. He is a contributing editor at *Geist* and was the editor of *Event* from 2004 to 2006. He is a founding member of the performance troupe, Haiku Night in Canada, a contributor to CBC Radio 3, and an event programmer at the Vancouver International Writers Festival. He has published *Let Me Kiss It Better* (2002), a book of essays drawn from his *Xtra! West* column, "Hardcore Homo." *The Asthmatic Glassblower and Other Poems* was nominated for the 2002 Publishing Triangle Gay Men's Poetry Award. *www.billehnickerson.com*

The Asthmatic Glassblower and Other Poems (Vancouver: Arsenal Pulp Press, 2000).

Stan Persky was born in Chicago in 1941, served in the U.S. Navy from 1958 to 1962, and lived in San Francisco from 1959 to 1966, when he immigrated to Canada. He was educated at the University of British Columbia and has taught philosophy at Capilano College since 1983. His peers and influences include Jack Spicer, Allen Ginsberg, Robin Blaser, and Robert Duncan. He has written for numerous national and international magazines and newspapers, including *The Globe and Mail* and *The Body Politic*. He is best known for several groundbreaking non-fiction works, including *Buddy's: Meditations on Desire* (1991) and *The Short Version: an ABC Book*, which won the 2006 BC Book Prize for Non-Fiction.

Wrestling the Angel (Vancouver: Talonbooks, 1977).

Craig Poile was born in Ontario in 1967 and grew up in New Brunswick. He attended Carleton University, where he earned degrees in Journalism and English Literature. The topic of his Master's thesis was the nature of Eros in James Merrill's *The Changing Light at Sandover*. He lives in Ottawa, where he works as a technical writer, is a playwright and producer, and co-owns Collected Works Bookstore. His first book of poetry, *First Crack*, was shortlisted for the 1999 Gerald Lampert Memorial Award.

First Crack (Ottawa: Carleton University Press, 1998).

Lundberg, Norma, "The Life of Our Making: McInnis, Taylor and Poile," *Arc* 43 (1999): 66–70.

Andy Quan was born in Vancouver in 1969, a third-generation Chinese-Canadian and fifth-generation Chinese-American, with roots in the villages of Canton. He earned Bachelor and Master degrees at Trent and York universities and now lives in Sydney, Australia, where he works for a national, community-based HIV/

AIDS organization. His first book of short stories, *Calendar Boy* (New Star, 2001), was nominated for a Lambda Literary Award. He co-edited *Swallowing Clouds: an Anthology of Chinese-Canadian Poetry* (Arsenal Pulp Press, 1999) and has published a book of gay erotica, *Six Positions* (Green Candy Press, 2005). *www.andyquan.com*

Slant (Madeira Park: Nightwood Editions, 2001).

Ian Iqbal Rashid is a writer and filmmaker. He was born in Dar es Salaam in 1964, grew up in Toronto, and now lives in Toronto and London. His film and TV credits include writing for the BBC TV series, *This Life* (recipient of the Writers Guild of England Award, and the Royal Television Society Prize), writing and directing the feature film, *Touch of Pink* (recipient of festival prizes in Toronto and Long Island), and the forthcoming feature, *Step* (working title). In 1992, his first book of poems received a Gerald Lampert Memorial Award nomination; in 1999, he received the Aga Khan Award of Excellence in the Arts.

Black Markets, White Boyfriends and Other Acts of Elision (Toronto: TSAR Publications, 1992); *The Heat Yesterday* (Toronto: Coach House Press, 1996).

Shane Rhodes was born in 1973, grew up in a small Alberta farming town, and currently lives in Ottawa. He received his BA in English from the University of Calgary and his MA in English from the University of New Brunswick. He has published poetry, articles, and reviews in newspapers and magazines across Canada. His first book of poetry won the 2001 Alberta Book Award; his second won the 2003 Archibald Lampman Award.

The Wireless Room (Edmonton: NeWest Press, 2000); *Holding Pattern* (Edmonton: NeWest Press, 2002); *The Bindery* (Edmonton: NeWest Press, 2007).

Bill Richardson was born in Winnipeg in 1955. He was educated at the Universities of Winnipeg (BA, 1976) and British Columbia, where he obtained a Master of Library Science. He has been a broadcaster on CBC Radio since 1992, hosted *Richardson's Roundup* (1997–2003,) and has moderated *Canada Reads* since 2003. As a writer, he is best known for the *Bachelor Brothers* series of books, the first of which, *Bachelor Brothers' Bed and Breakfast* (1993) won the Stephen Leacock Medal for Humour in 1994. His other publications include several books for children and *Guy to Goddess: An Intimate Look at Drag Queens* (1994, with Rosamond Norbury).

Queen of All the Dustballs and Other Epics of Everyday Life (Vancouver: Polestar, 1992); *Come Into My Parlour: Cautionary Verses and Instructive Tales for the New Millennium* (Vancouver: Polestar, 1994).

Brian Rigg was born in Jamaica in 1971. He has been living in Toronto for over two decades. His writing has appeared in numerous magazines and anthologies.

A False Paradise (Toronto: ECW Press, 2001).

André Roy was born in Montreal in 1944. He obtained a PhD from the University of Sherbrooke. He is known as an essayist, film and literary critic, and a video artist, has worked as an editor, reviews editor, and publisher, and has published thirty-three books. He won the 1986 Governor General's Award for Poetry, the 1987 Grand prix de la poésie, Festival international de poésie de Trois-Rivières, and the 1999 Prix Terrasses Saint-Sulpice/revue *Estuaire*. He lives in Montreal.

Selected titles: *Les passions du samedi* (Montreal: Les Herbes Rouges, 1979); *Nuits* (Montreal: Les Herbes Rouges, 1984); *C'est encore le solitaire qui parle* (Montreal: Les Herbes Rouges, 1986); *Action Writing* (Montreal: Les Herbes Rouges, 1986); *L'accélérateur d'intensité* (Trois-Rivières / Pantin: Écrits des Forges / Le Castor Astral, 1987); *On sait que cela a été écrit avant et après la grande maladie* (Montreal: Les Herbes Rouges, 1992); *Vies (*Montreal: Les Herbes Rouges, 1998); *Professeur de poésie* (Montreal: Les Herbes Rouges, 2004); *Traité du paysage (*Montreal: Les Petits Villages, 2005).

English translation: *The Passions of Mr. Desire*, Daniel Sloate, tr. (Montreal: Guernica Editions, 1986).

Norm Sacuta, born in Montreal in 1962, moved to Edmonton in 1968, where he still lives. He has graduate degrees in English and Creative Writing from the Universities of Alberta and British Columbia, and started a doctorate at the University of Sussex. His poetry is influenced by Djuna Barnes, Mina Loy, Hart Crane, Gerard Manley Hopkins, and Walter Benjamin. He earned a nomination for Alberta's 2001 Henry Kriesel Award for the Best First Book. He also won the Robin E. Lee Award for Poetry (University of Sussex) in 1994 and 1996 and the 1990 Alberta Culture Playwriting Competition. *www.normsacuta.com*

Garments of the Known (Madiera Park: Nightwood Editions, 2001).

Alexander, Jonathan, "Making Strange," *Lambda Book Report* (April 2002): 20–22.
Moore, Robert, "Truths Told Slant," *Books in Canada* 32:2 (2003): 33–34.

Stephen Schecter was born in 1946. He has a PhD in political sociology from the London School of Economics and is a full professor of sociology at the University of Quebec in Montreal. In addition to writing poetry and fiction, he is a performance artist, specializing in the telling of stories from the Hebrew Bible. He was nominated for the 1997 A. M. Klein/QSPELL Award for Poetry and won the Montreal Jewish Public Library's J. I. Segal Award for English literature on a Jewish theme in 1998. He splits his time between Montreal and Vancouver.

David and Jonathan (Montreal: Robert Davies Publishing, 1996).

Gregory Scofield, a Métis poet and memoirist, was born in Maple Ridge, B.C., in 1966 and spent his early childhood in northern Saskatchewan, Manitoba, the Yukon, and the B.C. Lower Mainland. He has won the Dorothy Livesay Award, CAA Award for Most Promising Writer, and *Arc*'s Confederation Poets Prize. In addition to five books of poetry, he published *Thunder Through My Veins: Memories of a Métis Childhood* in 1999 and has taught creative writing and First Nations and Métis literature at the Emily Carr Institute of Art + Design, the First Nations University of Canada, and Brandon University. He was writer in residence at Memorial University and currently teaches at the Alberta College of Art and Design. He lives in Calgary.

The Gathering: Stones for the Medicine Wheel (Vancouver: Polestar, 1993); *Native Canadiana* (Vancouver: Polestar, 1996); *Love Medicine and One Song* (Vancouver: Polestar, 1997); *I Knew Two Métis* Women (Vancouver: Polestar, 1999), *Singing Home the Bones* (Vancouver: Polestar, 2005).

Andrews, Jennifer, "Irony, Métis Style: Reading the Poetry of Marilyn Dumont and Gregory Scofield," *Canadian Poetry* 50 (2002): 6–31.

Gray, R. W., "...in my writing I see myself as a community worker...": an interview with Gregory Scofield, *Arc* 43 (Autumn 1999): 21–29.

Jamieson, Sara, "*Âyahkwêw* Songs: AIDS and Mourning in Gregory Scofield's 'Urban Rez' Poems," *Canadian Poetry* 57 (2005): 52–64.

Michael V. Smith was born in 1971 in Winchester, Ontario, and grew up in Cornwall. He earned degrees in English, creative writing, and drama at York University and the University of British Columbia. His novel, *Cumberland* (Cormorant Books, 2002), was nominated for the 2003 Amazon/Books in Canada First Novel Award. He was nominated for the Journey Prize and won a Western Magazine Award for Fiction in 2004. As a filmmaker, he won awards at Toronto's Inside Out Lesbian & Gay Film & Video Festival in 2005 and is a two-time recipient of the Community Hero Award for Achievement in the Arts (Vancouver) in 2003 and 2005. *www.michaelvsmith.com*

What You Can't Have (Winnipeg: Signature Editions, 2006).

George Stanley was born in San Francisco in 1934. In the 1960s, he was part of the San Francisco Renaissance that included Jack Spicer, Robert Duncan, and Robin Blaser. He moved to Canada in 1971 and taught for fifteen years at Northwest College, Terrace, BC, before moving to Vancouver, where he taught in the English Department, Capilano College. Since 1958, he has published over a dozen collections of poetry, chapbooks, and broadsides in Canada and the United States. In 2006, he won the Shelley Memorial Award from the Poetry Society of America.

Tete Rouge / Pony Express Riders (San Francisco: White Rabbit, 1963); *Flowers* (San Francisco: White Rabbit, 1965); *Beyond Love* (San Francisco: Open Space / Dariel Press, 1968); *You: Poems, 1957–1967* (Vancouver: New Star Books, 1974); *The Stick: Poems, 1969–73* (Vancouver: Talonbooks, 1974); *Opening Day: New and Selected Poems* (Lantzville: Oolichan Books, 1983); *Gentle Northern Summer* (Vancouver: New Star Books, 1995); *At Andy's* (Vancouver: New Star Books, 2000); *A Tall, Serious Girl: Selected Poems, 1957–2000* (Jamestown, RI: Qua, 2003); *Seniors* (Vancouver: Nomados Press, 2006).

Thesen, Sharon, "Chains of Grace: The Poetry of George Stanley," *Essays on Canadian Writing* 32 (1986), 106–113.

Ian Stephens was born in 1954. As well as being a poet, he was a singer in a number of Montreal underground bands, including DAF, RedShift, and Wining Dining Drilling. At different times in his life, he worked as a journalist, a model, and a bodyguard. Author of numerous chapbooks, he published one book of poetry before his death in 1996.

Diary of a Trademark (Montreal: Muses' Company, 1994).

Richard Teleky was born in Cleveland, Ohio, in 1946. He graduated from Case-Western University in 1968 and pursued graduate studies at the University of Toronto, where he earned an MA in 1969 and a PhD in 1973. He has published one critical study and four works of fiction, including *The Paris Years of Rosie Kam* (Steerfield, 1998), which won the 1998 Vermont Professional Association Award and 1999 Harold Ribalow Award, and *Pack Up the Moon* (Thomas Allen, 2001), which was nominated for the 2001 ReLit Award for Fiction. He lives in Toronto, where he is a professor of humanities at York University.

The Hermit's Kiss (Toronto: Fitzhenry & Whiteside, 2006).

Toye, William, ed., *The Concise Oxford Companion to Canadian Literature* (Toronto: Oxford University Press, 2001): 471–472.

H. Nigel Thomas was born in St. Vincent and the Grenadines in 1947. He has lived in Canada since 1968. He holds BA and MA degrees from Concordia University, a diploma in secondary education from McGill, and a PhD from Université de Montréal. In 1994 his novel, *Spirits in the Dark*, was shortlisted for the Hugh MacClennan Fiction Award (House of Anansi, 1993). His other books include *How Loud Can the Village Cock Crow? and Other Stories*, *Behind the Face of Winter*, and *Moving through Darkness*; he also edited the anthology Why We Wrtie (TSAR Publications) in 2006. In 2000, he received the Jackie Robinson Professional of the Year Award from the Montreal Association of Black Business Persons and Professionals. He taught at Laval University in Quebec City from 1988 to 2005 and now lives in Greenfield Park, Quebec.

Moving Through Darkness (Saint-Laurent: AFO Enterprises, 2000).

Umoja, Nailah Folami, "Thomas Throws the Light Switch," *The Nation* (Barbados) (May 12, 1996): Arts 11.

Chin, Timothy S., "'Bullers' and 'Battymen': Contesting

Homophobia in Black Popular Culture and Contemporary Caribbean Literature," *Callaloo* 20 (1997): 127–141.

Marsh-Lockett, Carol P., "The Colonial State as Supreme Being: Visions and Revisions in H. Nigel Thomas' *Spirits in the Dark*," *South Atlantic Review* 62.4 (1997): 18–31.

Nurse, Donna Bailey, "Not quite the Island of Pedro's Dreams," *Montreal Gazette* (January 19, 2002): H2.

R. M. Vaughan was born in Saint John, NB, in 1965. He holds an MA in creative writing from the University of New Brunswick and is the author of seven books, including two novels, *A Quilted Heart* (Insomniac Press, 1998) and *Spells* (ECW Press, 2003), eleven staged plays, and hundreds of articles on culture and the visual arts. His short films and experimental videos play in festivals and galleries around the world. He lives in Toronto.

A Selection of Dazzling Scarves (Toronto: ECW Press, 1996); *Invisible To Predators* (Toronto: ECW Press, 1999); *Ruined Stars* (Toronto: ECW Press, 2006), *Troubled: A Memoir in Poems and Documents* (Toronto: Coach House Press, 2008).

Brophy, Sarah, "'In Sotto Howl': Sexuality and Politics in the Poetry of R. M. Vaughan," *Essays on Canadian Writing* 63 (1997): 172–196.

David Watmough was born in London, England, in 1926. He was raised in Cornwall and studied theology at King's College, London University; his first book was a study of left-wing French Catholicism, *A Church Renascent* (1951). He came to Canada via the United States, settling permanently in Vancouver in 1962. Best known for novels and short stories, his self-described literary project is a "fictional autobiography of Davey Bryant, a mid-century man, who happens to be an author, an immigrant, and a homosexual," a linked body of work that has been elaborated over eleven books to date, including *Ashes For Easter and Other Monodramas* (1972), *The Connecticut Countess* (1984), *The Book of Fears* (1987), *Thy Mother's Glass* (1993), and *The Time of the Kingfishers* (1994). His most recent work of fiction is *Vancouver Voices* (2005).

Watmough, David, "On Coming to British Columbia: Some Personal & Literary Reflections," *Canadian Literature* 100 (1984): 339–345.

Doug Wilson was born in Meadow Lake, Saskatchewan, in 1950. He first gained prominence in 1975 in a fight for gay rights at the University of Saskatchewan. The dean of the College of Education had refused to allow Wilson, a postgraduate student in the Department of Educational Foundations, to supervise practice teachers because of his public involvement with the gay liberation movement. The University's president, despite organized national opposition, upheld this decision, and Wilson's complaint to the Saskatchewan Human Rights Commission was ultimately unsuccessful. Wilson's achievements include founding Stubblejumper Press in 1977, a small press dedicated to publishing works by Canadian lesbians and gay men; serving from 1978 to 1983 as the executive director of the Saskatchewan Association on Human Rights; acting as an advisor in the Toronto Board of Education's Race Relations and Equal Opportunity Office; cofounding the Rites Collective, publishers of *Rites: For Lesbian and Gay Liberation*, a newsmagazine, in 1984; and standing for Parliament as a New Democratic Party candidate in Toronto. He was the first openly gay person to be so nominated by a major political party in Canada, but fell ill during the campaign. He spent the balance of his life as an AIDS activist, cofounding AIDS Action Now! in 1988, and serving as the founding chair of the Canadian Network of Organizations for People Living With AIDS. Wilson was involved for more than twelve years in a relationship with Peter McGehee. The author of *Boys Like Us*, a tragicomic novel about a group of gay male Toronto friends during the AIDS crisis, McGehee succumbed to the disease in 1991. During his illness Wilson edited McGehee's posthumous novel, *Sweetheart* (1992), and one month before his own death completed his first novel (based on McGehee's notes), *Labour of Love* (1993), the third volume of the *Boys Like Us* trilogy. Wilson died in Toronto in 1992. *www.glbtq.com/social-sciences/wilson_douglas.html*

The Myth of the Boy (Saskatoon: Stubblejumper Press, 1977).

Ian Young was born in London, England, in 1945. He founded Catalyst, the first gay literary press in the world, and co-founded the University of Toronto Homophile Association, Canada's first gay liberation group. He edited *The Male Muse* (Crossing Press, 1973), a landmark international anthology of gay men's poetry, wrote columns for *The Body Politic* and *Torso*, and has published several anthologies, non-fiction studies and reference works, including *The Stonewall Experiment: A Gay Psychohistory* (Cassell, 1995). He lives in Toronto, where he operates a bookstore specializing in out-of-print gay and lesbian titles.

Year of the Quiet Sun (Toronto: House of Anansi, 1969); *Some Green Moths* (Scarborough, ON: Catalyst Press, 1972); *Double Exposure* (Trumansburg, NY: New Books, rev. ed., 1974); *Common-or-Garden Gods* (Scarborough, ON: Catalyst Press, 1976); *Schwule Poesie* (Lollar: Verlag Andreas Achenbach, 1978); *Sex Magick* (Toronto: Stubblejumper Press, 1986).

"Ian Young" in *Who's Who in Contemporary Gay & Lesbian History from World War II to the Present Day* (London: Routledge, 2001).
Young, Ian, *Autobibliography, 1962–2000* (Toronto: TMW, 2001).

Artist and Translators

Attila Richard Lukacs was born in Edmonton in 1962 and raised in Calgary. He graduated from the Emily Carr Institute of Art + Design in 1985 and has lived in Berlin, New York, Hawai'i, and is now based in Vancouver. He has exhibited around the world, including at the Diane Ferris Gallery (Vancouver), Musée de l'art contemporain (Montreal), The Power Plant (Toronto), 49th Parallel (New York), Kunstlerhaus Bethanien (Berlin), Documenta IX (Kassel, Germany), and Galerie Schedler (Zurich). His work is held in private and public collections in Belgium, Canada, Germany, the United Kingdom, and the United States.

Fred Cogswell was born in Eastern Centreville, NB, in 1917. He completed undergraduate and postgraduate degrees at the University of New Brunswick before obtaining a doctorate from Edinburgh University in 1952. Upon returning to Canada, he taught at the University of New Brunswick, until he retired in 1981. He served as the editor of *The Fiddlehead* from 1952 to 1966 and established Fiddlehead Poetry Books, the predecessor of Goose Lane Editions. He published more than twenty-four volumes of his own poetry, six books of translation, and books on Charles G. D. Roberts and Charles Mair. He died in Fredericton in 2004.

Jonathan Kaplansky was born in Saint John, NB, in 1960 and was educated at Tufts University, McGill University, and the University of Ottawa. He has translated novels by former poet laureate Pauline Michel, Hélène Dorion, and Hélène Rioux, a book of poetry by Serge Patrice Thibodeau, and biographies of Samuel de Champlain, René Lévesque, and Louis J. Robichaud. His translation of *Frank Borzage: The Life and Films of a Hollywood Romantic* by Hervé Dumont was published in 2006. He has sat on the jury for the English-translation category of the Governor General's Literary Awards and has participated in various literary festivals.

Daniel Sloate was born in Windsor, Ontario. He majored in French at the University of Western Ontario and then spent fifteen years in France where he obtained a doctorate in French literature and began to publish his first books of poetry. While in France, he began his translation career, which he continued on his return to Canada. He has translated Rimbaud's *Illuminations* as well as the work of several Québecois poets, Jean-Paul Daoust, André Roy, Hélène Dorion, Claude Beausoleil, and Denise Desautels, among others. He taught translation at the Université de Montréal and McGill University. He is now retired.

Credits

PATRICK ANDERSON "Edward Drew" from *First Statement*, Vol I (5). "Rink" and "Drinker" from *A Tent For April* (*First Statement*, 1945). "Armament Worker" and "Boy in a Russian Blouse" from *The White Centre* (Ryerson Press, 1946). "The Candles: Dorcheser Street" and "Spiv Song" from *The Colour As Naked* (McClelland & Stewart, 1953). "Y.M.C.A. Montreal" from *A Visiting Distance* (Borealis Press, 1976). "Advice to Visitors" from *Return to Canada* (McClelland and Stewart, 1977).

JOHN BARTON Reprinted with permission of author: "Him" copyright © John Barton, "My Cellophane Suit" from *Great Men* (Quarry Press, 1990), "Vancouver Gothic" from *Notes Toward a Family Tree* (Quarry Press, 1993); reprinted with permission of House of Anansi Press: "Parallel Lanes" from *Designs from the Interior* (House of Anansi Press, 1994); "Hybrid" from *Hypothesis* (House of Anansi Press, 2001); reprinted with permission of ECW Press: "Saranac Lake Variations" from *Sweet Ellipsis* (ECW Press, 1998).

JEAN BASILE Translated by Jonathan Kaplansky with permission of the estate of Jean Basile: "Give Only What We Can" and "A Rather Sentimental Excursion" from the French originals published in *Journal Poetique: 1964–65* (Les Editions du Jour, 1965).

DAVID BATEMAN "Stark insane voice on some liminal horizon" from *Invisible Foreground* (Frontenac House, 2005); copyright © David Bateman, reprinted with permission of Frontenac House.

BILL BISSETT "a warm place to shit" from *pass th food release th spirit book* (Talonbooks, 1973), "eet me alive" from *beyond even faithful legends* (Talonbooks, 1980), "i was on beech avenue in vancouvr" from *Canada Gees Mate For Life* (Talonbooks, 1985), "i can remembr a corvet" and "my first job" from *what we have* (Talonbooks, 1988), "inkorrect thots" from *inkorrect thots* (Talonbooks, 1992), "my fathr in his bed room th morning i left" and "swallow me" from *scars on th seehors* (Talonbooks, 1999), "i dreemd i livd with keanu reeves" from *narrativ enigma/rumours of hurricane* (Talonbooks, 2004); copyright © bill bissett, all poems used with permission of Talon Books Ltd.

ROBIN BLASER Reprinted with permission of author: "In Remembrance of Matthew Shepard" from *Blood and Tears: Poems for Matthew Shepard* (Painted Leaf Press, 1999); reprinted with permission of UC Press: "The Borrower," "Image Nation 3," "The

City of Merlin," "Image Nation 9," "Image Nation 14," "The Pause," and "Romance" from *The Holy Forest* (New edition: UC Press, 2007); copyright © Robin Blaser.

TODD BRUCE Reprinted with permission of author: "Frieze (Electric Mummy" copyright © Todd Bruce; reprinted with permission of Turnstone Press: "Still Life with Turkey Pie" from *Jiggers* (Turnstone Press, 1993) and "The Charm" from *Rhapsody in D.* (Turnstone Press, 1997).

CLINT BURNHAM Reprinted with permission of author: "Rent-A-Marxist" and "An Evening at Home" from *Be Labour Reading* (ECW Press, 1997); copyright © Clint Burnham.

WALTER BORDEN "Ethiopia the Drag Queen" excerpted from *Tightrope Time: Ain't Nuthin' More Than Some Itty Bitty Madness Between Twilight and Dawn* (Playwrights Canada Press, 2005); copyright © Walter Borden, reprinted with permission of Playwrights Canada.

FRANK OLIVER CALL "To a Greek Statue" from *Acanthus and Wild Grape* (McClelland & Stewart, 1920), "The Hilltop" from *Blue Homespun* (Ryerson Press, 1924), "White Hyacinths" from *Sonnets for Youth* (Ryerson Press, 1924); all poems are from the public domain.

JEAN-PAUL DAOUST "Egyptian Poem," excerpt from "The Magic Boys," excerpt from "Blue Ashes," "Enjoy," "The Air in Your Mouth," "Live Epitaph," and "Song of the Serpent" from *Blue Ashes* (Guernica Editions, 1999).

BRIAN DAY Reprinted by permission of author: "Better Not to Marry" copyright © Brian Day; reprinted with permission of Guernica Editions: "Sleeping Vishnu," "Narcissus at the Pool," and "Faithful to Him" from *Love Is Not Native to My Blood* (Guernica Editions, 2000), "The Love Between Krishna and Jesus" from *Azure* (Guernica Editions, 2004).

DENNIS DENISOFF "Mid Post" from *Tender Agencies* (Arsenal Pulp Press, 1994); reprinted with permission of Arsenal Pulp Press.

GILLES DEVAULT Translated by Jonathan Kaplansky with permission of Écrits des Forges: excerpts from "Ferns of Ash" originally published in French in *Fougères cendrées* (Ecrit des Forges, 1993), excerpts from "White Eye of Sheep" originally published in French in *L'oeil blanc du sommeil* (Ecrits des Forges, 1995).

ORVILLE LLOYD DOUGLAS "Dear Langston Hughes" from *You Don't Know Me* (TSAR Publications, 2005).

MICHAEL ESTOK "as the crisis deepened" and "hydrangeas" from *A Plague Year Journal* (Arsenal Pulp Press, 1990), "Ordination" from *Paradise Garage* (Goose Lane Editions, 1987); all poems reprinted with permission of the Estate of Michael Estok.

ROBERT FINCH "Egg-and-Dart," "The Livery," "Scroll-section," and "The Painters" from *Poems* (Oxford University Press, 1946), "From a Hammock" from *The Strength of the Hills* (McClelland and Stewart, 1948), "The Moth" and "Real and Remembered" from *Acis in Oxford* (University of Toronto Press, 1959), "Midsummer" from *Silverthorn Bush and Other Poems* (Macmillan, 1966), "Summation" and "Gone" from *Has and Is* (Porcupine's Quill, 1981), "Rue de Richelieu, Rue des Petits-Champs" from *Double Tuning* (Porcupine's Quill, 1985).

JEAN CHAPDELAINE GAGNON Translated by Jonathan Kaplansky with permission of Éditions du Noroît: "Do Not Reveal this Word" from the French original published in *Le tant-a-coeur* (Noroît, 1986), "Your Name of Love" from the French original published in *Malamour* (Noroît, 1988), excerpts from *Ile de mémoire* originally published in French in *Ile de mémoire* (Noroît, 1997), excerpt from *Tu* originally published in French in *Tu* (Noroît, 2000).

KEITH GAREBIAN "Sapphic Interlude," "The Life of Art in Thievery," and "Untitled Sound Poem" copyright © Keith Garebian, reprinted with permission of author.

JOEL GIBB "He is the Boss of Me" and "A Miracle" copyright © Joel Gibb, reprinted with permission of author.

SKY GILBERT Reprinted with permission of author: "Assfucking and June Allyson" from *Plush* (Coach House Press, 1995); reprinted by permission of ECW Press: "Winnipeg Farts" and "Something Else" from *Temptations for a Juvenile Delinquent* (ECW Press, 2003).

JOHN GLASSCO "Noyade 1942," "Stud Groom," and "Villainelle" from *The Deficit Made Flesh* (McClelland and Stewart, 1958), "Fly in Autumn" and "Brummell at Calais" from *A Point of Sky* (Oxford University Press, 1964); reprinted with permission of the estate of John Glasco.

R. W. GRAY "How this begins," "Flutter," "Bite," and "Outside the Café" copyright © R. W. Gray, reprinted with permission of author.

JOHN GRUBE "Forgiveness: A Meditation" from *God, Sex & Poetry* (Dartington Press, 2002), reprinted by permission of the author.

BRION GYSIN "Minutes to Go," excerpt from "I Am that I Am," and excerpt from "Poem of Poems" from *Back in No Time: The Brion Gysin Reader* (Wesleyan University Press, 2002).

DARRYL HINE "Lines on a Platonic Friendship," "The Wound," "Sestina Contra Naturam," "Summer Afternoon," "A Visit," "Point Grey," "Commonplaces," and "What's His Face" from *Selected Poems* (Scribner, 1981), "Editio Princeps" from *Postscripts* (Knopf, 1992); copyright © Darryl Hine, reprinted with permission of the author.

SEAN HORLOR "In Praise of Beauty," "For St. Jude, or What Gets Him Where He is," and "For St. Fiacre" from *Made Beautiful by Use* (Signature Editions, 2007); reprinted with permission of Signature Editions.

MICHAEL KNOX "Notes to a Father" and "Swimming in the Bodensee" from *Play Out the Match* (ECW Press, 2006); reprinted with permission of ECW Press.

BERTRAND LACHANCE "send me those eyes again" from *Street Flesh* (blewointmentpress, 1972); reprinted with permission of the author.

EDWARD A. LACEY "Delicate Equilibrium," "Quintallas," "Anacreon," "Canadian Sonnet," "Eggplant," "Rejean," "Desencuentro," and "Abdelfatteh" from *The Collected Poems and Translations of Edward A. Lacey* edited by Fraser Sutherland (Colombo & Co., 2000) reprinted with permission of the estate of Edward A. Lacey.

DOUGLAS LEPAN "Coureurs de bois" from *The Wounded Prince* (Chatto & Windus, 1948), "The Green Man" from *Something Still to Find* (McClelland Stewart, 1982), "A Man of Honour" from *The Net and the Sword* (Clark, Irwin, 1953), "A Head Found at Benevetum" and "A Nightpiece, of London in the Blackout" from *Weathering It* (McClelland and Stewart, 1987), "Walking a Tightrope" from *Far Voyages* (McClelland & Stewart, 1990), "On a Path Behind the Hotel" and "Willow Trees, By Killarney Channel" from *The Malahat Review* 146 (Spring 2004).

MICHAEL LYNCH "Cry" and "Survivors" from *These Waves of Dying Friends* (Contact II Publications, 1989).

BLAINE MARCHAND "The Carver" copyright © Blaine Marchand, "Travelling Alone" and "Subversion" from *Bodily Presence* (Quarry Press, 1995); all poems reprinted with permission of author.

DANIEL DAVID MOSES "A Bone in the Balance of Moonlight," "Offhand Song," and "Cowboy Pictures" from *Sixteen Jesuses* (Exile Editions, 2000).

JIM NASON Reprinted with permission of author: "Shroud" copyright © Jim Nason, "The Water Trough" from *If Lips Were as Red* (Palmerston Press, 1991); reprinted with permission of Wolsak and Wynn: "Andrew" from *The Fist of Remembering* (Wolsak and Wynn, 2006).

EMILE NELLIGAN "Almost a Shepherd," "Song of Wine," and "The Spectre" from *The Complete Poems of Emile Nelligan* ed. Fred Cogswell (Harvest House, 1983).

BILLEH NICKERSON "Why I Love Wayne Gretzky: An Erotic Fantasy," "Gonorrhea," "If You Fit All Your Lovers in an Airplane What Kind of Airplane Would it Be?" and "The Ultra Centrifuge" from *The Asthmatic Glassblower and Other Poems* (Arsenal Pulp Press, 2000); reprinted with permission of Arsenal Pulp Press.

CRAIG POILE Reprinted with permission of author: "Place Royale" copyright © Craig Poile; reprinted with permission of McGill-Queen's University Press: "Lather" and "Accommodations" from *First Crack* (McGill-Queen's University Press, 2003).

STAN PERSKY "The Red-Headed Boy," "Slaves," and "Hockey Night in Canada" from *Wrestling The Angel* (Talonbooks, 1977); reprinted with permission of the author.

ANDY QUAN Reprinted with permission of author: "The Gentle Man" and "Crystal" copyright © Andy Quan; reprinted with permission of Nightwood Editions: "Condensation" from *Slant* (Nightwood Editions, 2001).

IAN IQBAL RASHID "Hot Property" and "Could Have Danced All Night" from *Black Markets, White Boyfriends* (TSAR Publications, 1991), "Another Country" and "Early Dinner, Weekend Away" from *The Heat Yesterday* (Coach House Press, 1995); reprinted with permission of author.

SHANE RHODES "Gravitas" from *The Wireless Room* (NeWest Press, 2000). "Fucking," "His Hands Were Hounds Over Me," and "There Is An Obvious Solution to Your Problem" from *Holding*

Pattern (NeWest Press, 2002); all poems reprinted with permission of NeWest Press.

BILL RICHARDSON "Nothing Like a Dame" from *Come Into My Parlour* (Polestar Book Publishers, 1994); reprinted with permission of author.

BRIAN RIGG "House of Flies" and "Tiger Lily" from *A False Paradise* (ECW Press, 2001); reprinted with permission of ECW Press.

ANDRÉ ROY Translated by Jonathan Kaplansky with permission of Éditions Les Herbes Rouges: "The Surrealistic Sex Hunter" and "The Future" from the French original published in *On sait que cela a été fait avant et après la grande maladie* (Éditions Les Herbes Rouge, 1992), "The Sexuality Professional" from the French originally published in *Vies* (Editions Les Herbes Rouges, 1995); Reprinted with permission of Guernica Editions: "Saturdays and Saturday," "Like in the Movies, Like Making a Scene," and "Far from Montreal, far from" from *The Passions of Mister Desire* (Guernica Editions, 1986).

NORM SACUTA "The Hills Are a Lie," "What I Wanted To Say," and "Alberta Pick-Ups" from *Garments of the Known* (Nightwood Editions, 2001); reprinted with permission of Nightwood Editions.

STEPHEN SCHECTER "Intimacy" and "Waiting for a Boyfriend" copyright © Stephen Schecter, excerpt from "David and Jonathan" from *David and Jonathan* (Robert Davies Multimedia Publishing, 1997); all poems reprinted with permission of author.

GREGORY SCOFIELD Reprinted with permission of author: "My Lover's Mother Laments Her Dancing Shoes" from *Singing Home the Bones* (Polestar Book Publishers, 2005); reprinted with permission of Polestar Book Publishers: "I Used To Be Sacred (On Turtle Island)" and "Queenie" from *Native Canadiana* (Polestar Book Publishers, 1996), "He Is," "My Drum, His Hands," and "I've Looked for You" *from Love Medicine and One Song* (Polestar Book Publishers, 2000).

MICHAEL V. SMITH "The Sad Truth" and "Salvation" from *What You Can't Have* (Signature Editions, 2006), reprinted with permission of Signature Editions.

GEORGE STANLEY "The Achilles Poem" from *You* (New Star Books, 1974), "The Stick" and "After Verlaine" from *The Stick: poems, 1969–1973* (Talonbooks, 1974), "Prince Rupert Blues" from

Opening Day (Oolichan Books, 1983), "Naked in New York," "Sex at 62," and "Veracruz" from *At Andy's* (New Star Books, 2000); copyright © George Stanley, all poems reprinted with permission of the author.

IAN STEPHENS "Wounds: Valentine's Day" from *Diary of a Trademark* (Muses' Company, 1994); reprinted with permission of J. Gordon Shillingford Publishing.

RICHARD TELECKY "The Hermit's Kiss" from *The Hermit's Kiss* (Fitzhenry & Whiteside, 2006); reprinted with permission of Fitzhenry & Whiteside.

N. NIGEL THOMAS "Boy-Child," "Nigger-Kike-Wop," and "Unfulfilled Desire" from *Moving Through Darkness* (AFO Enterprises, 1999); reprinted with permission of author.

R. M. VAUGHAN "Christian Bok's Max Factor Factotum" from *A Selection of Dazzling Scarves* (ECW Press, 1996), "Lost Weekend" and "14 Reasons to Eat Potato Chips on Church Street" from *Immune to Predators* (ECW Press, 1999), "Feverfew" from *Ruined Stars* (ECW Press, 2004); reprinted with permission of ECW Press.

DAVID WATMOUGH "Berlin in 1982" copyright © David Watmough; reprinted with permission of author.

DOUG WILSON "There is a thin gold...," "there is poetry...," and "I dream often..." from *The Myth of the Boy* (Stubblejumper Press, 1977).

IAN YOUNG "The Mutes," "Poem," and "In My Café" from *Year of the Quiet Sun* (House of Anansi, 1969), "Rob , Polishing His Motorbike" from *Common or Garden Gods* (Catalyst Press, 1975), "Sex Magick" and "Photography" from *Sex Magick* (Stubblejumper Press, 1986); all poems reprinted by permission of author.

INDEX